111783

BCFTC

D0298363

UNIVERSITY C… EGE BIRMINGHAM
…SUMMER ROW
…3 1JB
…55

21 NOV 2008

30 JAN 2009
10 FEB 2009

VOLUNTEER TOURISM
Experiences that Make a Difference

Volunteer Tourism
Experiences that Make a Difference

STEPHEN WEARING

School of Leisure, Sport and Tourism,
Faculty of Business,
University of Technology, Sydney
PO Box 222, Lindfield,
NSW 2070, Australia

CABI *Publishing*

B.C.F.T.C.S.
111783

CABI *Publishing* is a division of CAB *International*

CABI Publishing
CAB International
Wallingford
Oxon OX10 8DE
UK

Tel: +44 (0)1491 832111
Fax: +44 (0)1491 833508
Email: cabi@cabi.org
Web site: www.cabi.org

CABI Publishing
10 E 40th Street
Suite 3203
New York, NY 10016
USA

Tel: +1 212 481 7018
Fax: +1 212 686 7993
Email: cabi-nao@cabi.org

©CAB *International* 2001. All rights reserved. No part of this publication may be reproduced in any form or by any means, electronically, mechanically, by photocopying, recording or otherwise, without the prior permission of the copyright owners.

A catalogue record for this book is available from the British Library, London, UK.

Library of Congress Cataloging-in-Publication Data
Wearing, Stephen.
Volunteer tourism : experiences that make a difference / Stephen Wearing.
p. cm.
Includes bibliographical references (p.).
ISBN 0-85199-533-0 (Hardback : alk. paper)
1. Volunteer workers in tourism. I. Title.

G156.5.V64 W43 2001
338.4′791--dc21

2001025771

ISBN 0 85199 533 0

Typeset by AMA DataSet Ltd, UK
Printed and bound in the UK by Cromwell Press, Trowbridge

Contents

List of Figures and Tables

Preface

This book represents an attempt to encapsulate the enthusiasm and positive attempts to use tourism as a means of support for both youth and communities. In a global society that increasingly finds dogma and marketing used to instil values and exploit social relations, volunteer tourism represents both an opportunity and a means of value-adding in an industry that seems to represent consumer capitalism at its worst.

With transnationals everywhere attempting to recast themselves as people-friendly it is time to recognize that they are not the ones who are contributing to any real form of growth for developing countries and local communities. The transnational tourism organizations have pursued the colonialization cum globalization agenda on a 'free and fair trade agenda' for decades, suggesting that a free market economy espouses those principles theorized by Adam Smith in defiance of the system of mercantilism. These are the ideals of a laissez-faire system of government and regulation, free competition, and supply and demand. Mass tourism operates efficiently in this market system, as there are no or few regulations to infringe on operations. Tourism in the free market economy uses and exploits natural resources as a means of profit accumulation and has been described as the commercialization of the human need to travel. This profits the tourism industry promoters and has led to the exploitation of host communities, their culture and environment. This book presents volunteer tourism as an alternative approach. Tourism perpetuates inequality, with the multi-national companies of the advanced capitalist countries retaining the economic power and resources to invest in and control the tourism industries of developing nations. In many cases, a developing country's engagement with tourism serves to simply confirm its dependent, subordinate position in relation to advanced capitalist societies – this can be expressed as a form of neo-colonialism. Developed nations' economic patterns of consumption have enabled transnational tourism organizations to use modern tourism as a vehicle for packaging developing nations cultures as 'commodities of difference', filling a commercially created need in the mass consciousness. The ability of the developed nations to dominate market forces through the tourism industry is changing the shape of developing nations' communities. We find that indigenous cultures that have changed little for centuries are threatened by the powerful influences of Western culture that often accompany the arrival of mass tourism in the developing world.

Volunteer tourism offers an alternative which, in a way, looks forward to the future. However, can volunteer tourism provide a different experience? The experiences presented in this book are offered as a means of best practice in tourism. The focus is around the idea that the volunteer tourism experience is a direct interactive experience that causes value change and changed consciousness in the individual which will subsequently influence their lifestyle, while providing forms of community development that are required by local communities.

Stephen Wearing
University of Technology, Sydney
2001

Acknowledgements

I am indebted to many people for the help I have received in the preparation and research presented in this book.

Thanks firstly to Elery Hamilton-Smith for providing inspiration over many years and acting as a mentor.

The people of Santa Elena for allowing myself and Youth Challenge International to become a part of their community and work with them in developing the Santa Elena Rainforest Reserve.

The participants – 'Challengers' – involved in the Santa Elena Rainforest Reserve and particularly the Australians who participated in the research, with special thanks to Libby Larson. The Youth Challenge staff – Mark Ely, Mark Darby, Chris Klar particularly for their inspired efforts over the years and to all those involved in Youth Challenge Australia and International for your energy and enthusiasm (you know who you are).

A special thanks to John Neil and Mark Jackson who has been involved in proofing, editing and critiquing. The faults in the final presentation are mine. Also to my mother, Betsy, co-author of so many papers who has developed my thinking and spirit to allow me to undertake this type of work.

Lastly, my wife, Julie, son Jamie and daughter Melanie for allowing me the time to volunteer. My family, parents Betsy and Les, sisters Jenny, Sue, Christine and brother Michael: you are all inspirations to me in so many ways, and thanks also to Megan and Gareth for putting up with our family.

Stephen Wearing

Chapter 1

Introduction

Experiences that Make a Difference

Contemporary volunteer tourism has tended to suffer from a lack of differentiation from other forms of tourism or volunteering. Instead it has been the subject of selective pragmatism rather than a specific definition or method, falling into areas such as alternative tourism, international volunteering, social work and conservation corps work. Its treatment in this book desires to provide it with a more substantive boundary and recognition of its more specific identity. So what is volunteer tourism? The generic term 'volunteer tourism' applies to those tourists who, for various reasons, volunteer in an organized way to undertake holidays that might involve aiding or alleviating the material poverty of some groups in society, the restoration of certain environments or research into aspects of society or environment.

Some empirical examples of volunteer tourist operations are those offered by organizations such as Youth Challenge International, World Wide Fund for Nature (WWF) and Earthwatch, to name a few. These operations and their projects obviously vary in location, size, participant characteristics and organizational purpose. The common element in these operations, however, is that the participants can be viewed largely as volunteer tourists. That is, they are seeking a tourist experience that is mutually beneficial, that will contribute not only to their personal development but also positively and directly to the social, natural and/or economic environments in which they participate. The philosophy of Explorations in Travel, a US-based volunteer work-placement firm provides a good insight:

> Travelling is a way to discover new things about ourselves and learn to see ourselves more clearly. Volunteering abroad is a way to spend time within another culture, to become part of new community, to experience

> life from a different perspective . . . Every community needs people willing to volunteer their time, energy and money to projects that will improve the living conditions for its inhabitants. No one needs to travel around the world to find a good and worthy cause to dedicate their efforts to. Volunteering should be something we do as a regular part of our lives, not just when we can take a month or two off, or when we have extra money to spend on travel. Your actions are your voice in the world, saying loudly and clearly what you think is important, what you believe to be right, what you support.

Furthermore, the position of the British Trust for Conservation Volunteers (BTCV) also emphasizes this point in an environmental conservation context:

> Voluntary and community action can support site and species surveys, practical conservation projects, and longer term care and management. In the course of giving their time, energy, and experience to improving biodiversity, people can gain social and economic benefits including understanding, knowledge and skills. All of this can then further enhance their voluntary commitment.
>
> (BTCV, 2000, p. 1)

Volunteer tourism can take place in varied locations such as rainforests and cloudforests, biological reserves and conservation areas. Popular locations include countries in Africa, Central and South America. Activities can vary across many areas, such as scientific research (wildlife, land and water), conservation projects, medical assistance, economic and social development (including agriculture, construction and education) and cultural restoration. Indeed, volunteers can find themselves anywhere between assisting with mass eye surgery operations to constructing a rainforest reserve. There is usually, however, the opportunity for volunteers to take part in local activities and interact further with the community. Hence the volunteer tourist contribution is bilateral, in that the most important development that may occur in the volunteer tourist experience is that of a personal nature, that of a greater awareness of self: 'When volunteers come back, they feel empowered, knowing they have been able to make a difference . . . You come home feeling you don't have limits. You feel a lot more confident in your ideas and beliefs and that you can contribute to society' (Hill, 2001, p. 28).

Of interest, however, is that volunteer tourists will almost always pay in some way to participate in these activities. Furthermore, the amount is usually more than an average tourist would expect to pay on a 'normal' holiday to a similar location. While there are some sponsorship programmes and alternative contribution arrangements provided by some organizations, the financial contribution required of the volunteer tourist is illustrative of the wider nature of the experience; of greater benefits for host and tourist alike. It is this, and

other key aspects of volunteer tourism that will be explored in this book.

While multidisciplinary in approach, and drawing heavily on broader tourism literature, a largely sociological perspective has been taken in this book. In doing so, it is sought to demonstrate that in the case of volunteer tourism each individual will construct the meaning of their experience according to their own cultural and social background, the purpose of the visit, their companions, preconceived and observed values of the host culture, the marketing images of the destination and, above all, the relationships of power between visitor and host cultures, as well as within the host culture.

As part of the volunteer tourism experience, interactions occur and the self is enlarged or expanded, challenged, renewed or reinforced. As such, the experience becomes an ongoing process which extends far beyond the actual tourist visit. Rojek (1993, p. 114) claims 'travel, it was thought, led to the accumulation of experience and wisdom. One began with nothing, but through guidance, diligence and commonsense one gained knowledge and achieved self-realisation.' Furthering this, volunteer tourism provides an opportunity for an individual to engage in an altruistic attempt to explore 'self'. It has been built around the belief that by living in and learning about other people and cultures, in an environment of mutual benefit and cooperation, one is able to engage in a transformation and the development of self.

Still, the broader tourism literature suggests that holidays do not usually have a tremendous impact on the way in which an individual sees him/herself (Kottler, 1997, p. 103). It has been contended that holidays serve as an escape from the constraints and stresses of everyday life (Burkart and Medlik, 1974, p. 56; Cohen and Taylor, 1976; Rojek, 1995), or perhaps as a reward for hard work, but do not ultimately alter a person's everyday life in terms of the way they think, feel or act. The traditional tourism literature suggests that while the individuals may have enjoyed themselves, it is not long before that holiday is a memory in the day-to-day life that they return to. This book seeks to explore a different approach: taking volunteer tourism and investigating the more significant impacts it can have on the individual and on their lifestyle.

While much has been written in relation to the motivations of tourists when engaging in tourism,[1] little research has been presented concerning the impact that leisure experiences such as volunteer tourism may have on the development of self through travel. As such,

---

[1] See for example Gray's wanderlust/sunlust theory (Mathieson and Wall, 1982), Ross' consideration of pull/push determinants (1994, p. 21) or even Plog's (1991) analysis of allocentric and psychocentric personalities in dictating travel behaviour.

this book uses vocabularies of motive through the personal accounts of volunteer tourists to examine this complex notion of volunteer tourism.

In examining volunteer tourists, we will see how they make a difference not only in the places they interact with, but also within themselves.

Historical Context of Alternative Tourism

Historically, the prohibitive costs, transport difficulties and perceived dangers prevented many from experiencing other countries and cultures outside their own. From the early stages of history, as far back as 1244 BC, to arguably the 18th century, leisure travel has largely been the province of the privileged. In the Middle Ages for example, a time of mass Christian pilgrimages, 'travel was still generally considered to be a dangerous and uncomfortable experience that was best avoided if at all possible' (Weaver and Opperman, 2000, p. 61).

It was the phenomenon of the 'Grand Tour', which become popular in the 16th century, that best represents the initial developments of international tourism. Aristocratic young men from 'the United Kingdom and other parts of Europe undertook extended trips to continental Europe for educational and cultural purposes' (Weaver and Opperman, 2000, p. 61). High social value was placed on these expeditions; however, it was here that travel motives began to shift. Travelling for education and social status slowly gave way to travelling for pleasure and sightseeing. The industrial revolution, beginning in the 1700s, saw a growing need for recreation opportunities and, subsequently, transport systems to allow them to occur. Following the introduction of improvements in transport such as railroads, sealed roads and even ocean liners, the nature of travel began to change rapidly. Notably, the widespread application of air travel for leisure purposes and the growing economies of scale meant that travel soon became a commodity to be sold to a growing number of potential tourists. As Hall (1995, p. 38) observes:

> Mass tourism is generally acknowledged to have commenced on the 5 July 1841, when the first conducted excursion train of Thomas Cook left Leicester station in northern Britain. Since that time tourism has developed from the almost exclusive domain of the aristocracy to an experience that is enjoyed by tens of millions worldwide.

As tourism advanced into the 19th century, it became more and more insulated from the real world. In opposition to its origins where travellers sought the unknown, tourism was fast becoming a home away from home where participants no longer had to expose themselves to the dangers of having to meet and associate with the host

community as they were now able to 'gaze' (Urry, 1990, p. 135) from the safety and comfort of coaches, trains and hotel rooms without actually involving themselves in any way. Group sizes and frequency of excursions increased, thus giving way to the term 'mass tourism'.

The massive growth of international tourism is evident in figures such as worldwide international arrivals, which have increased from 25,282,000 in 1950 to 625 million in 1998 (WTO, 1999). Tourism is said to be the world's largest group of industries (Boer, 1993), with international tourism receipts rising 2% in 1998 to reach a level of US $445 billion (WTO, 1999). The tourism industry employs around 200 million people worldwide, accounting in 1999 for over 11% of the world's gross domestic product (GDP) (WTTC, 1999). It has been argued that this recent proliferation is a result of increases in leisure time, disposable income, mobility, demographic changes and technological improvements in communication technologies (Young, 1992).

In accounting for tourism as a global phenomenon, much of the initial sociological work was concerned with the individual tourist and the part that holidays play in establishing identity and a sense of self. This self was posited predominantly as universal, and tourism, like leisure, was seen in an opposing relationship with the 'workaday world'. Cohen and Taylor (1976), for example, drew on Goffman's (1974) concern with the presentation of self in everyday life, to argue that holidays are culturally sanctioned escape routes for western travellers. One of the problems for the modern traveller, in this view, is to establish identity and a sense of personal individuality in the face of the morally void forces of a technological world. Holidays provide a free area, a mental and physical escape from the immediacy of the multiplicity of impinging pressures in technological society. Thus, holidays provide scope for the nurture and cultivation of human identity; as Cohen and Taylor argue, overseas holidays are structurally similar to leisure because one of their chief purposes is identity establishment and the cultivation of one's self-consciousness. The tourist, they claim, uses all aspects of the holiday for the manipulation of well-being.

However, in the tourist literature, these arguments became diverted into a debate about the authenticity or otherwise of this experience (see MacCannell, 1976; Cohen, 1988), serving to focus attention on the attractions of the tourist destination. Such a shift objectified the destination as place – a specific geographical site was presented to the tourist for their gaze (Urry, 1990). Thus the manner of presentation became all important and its authenticity or otherwise the focus of analysis: 'I categorised objects of the gaze in terms of romantic/collective, historical/modern, and authentic/unauthentic', says Urry (1990, p. 135). The tourist themselves became synonymous with the Baudelarian *flaneur* (French for 'gazer': 'the strolling *flaneur* was a forerunner of the 20th century tourist'; Urry, 1990, p. 138). This *flaneur* was generally perceived as escaping from the workaday world for an 'ephemeral', 'fugitive' and 'contingent' leisure experience (see Rojek, 1993, p. 216).

Similar to the way in which this type of 'flaneurism' (Urry, 1990, p. 138) characterized tourism of the late 19th and early 20th centuries, alternative tourism has characterized the latter part of the 20th century. Tourists began searching for new and exciting forms of travel in defiance of the mass-produced tourism product born out of the industrial revolution and, prior to that, the need for social standing (Hall, 1995; Weaver and Opperman, 2000). Backpacking, adventure tourism and ecotourism are some of the types of alternative tourism that emerged during this time and have since confirmed, via their popularity, their place as targeted market segments. Niche markets were developed that allowed the tourist to choose the holiday they felt best suited their needs and wants, while, at the same time, maintaining an appropriate level of social status among their peers.

But how significant are these alternative tourist markets? To begin with one of the most popular markets, ecotourism, The International Ecotourism Society admit that while their ecotourism 'definition has been widely accepted . . . [it] does not serve as a functional definition for gathering statistics. No global initiative presently exists for the gathering of ecotourism data. Ecotourism should be considered a specialty segment of the larger nature tourism market' (The International Ecotourism Society, 2001, p. 1). Indeed, other 'alternative' niche markets also suffer from the same data collection shortcomings on an international and national level. While a supply-side attempt to measure the volunteer tourist market could prove useful, it would be likely to face definitional, temporal and geographical limitations.

Still, alternative tourism is now being seriously considered as a significant area of tourism experience (Holden, 1984; Cohen, 1987, 1995; Vir Singh *et al.*, 1989; Pleumarom, 1990; Smith and Eadington, 1992; Weiler and Hall, 1992). However, a number of authors (Butler, 1992; Cohen, 1995) have attempted to incorporate it into the analysis of 'mass tourism', thus subordinating it to mainstream tourism research. Questions thus arise as to the feasibility of alternative tourism being analysed in terms of a separate construct or different paradigm. This has been a problem historically within new and emergent areas of research, as explained in the case of feminist research by Stanley and Wise (1984).

The popularity of specific forms of alternative tourism, such as ecotourism[2] (a relatively new term in the world's vocabulary) and now

[2] Boo (1990, p. 10) provides the most cited definition to date: 'We may define ecological tourism or ecotourism as that tourism that involves travelling to relatively undisturbed or uncontaminated natural areas with the specific object of studying, admiring and enjoying

volunteer tourism (coined 'voluntourism' at a recent conference), has increased significantly. Ecotourism itself has, in recent years, been the subject of a great deal of discussion. This was highlighted by the United Nations Conference on Environment and Development (UNCED) held in Rio de Janeiro, Brazil, in June 1992. The conference brought together heads of state and government representatives from 120 nations and delegates from 178 countries looking for 'win–win' policies in relation to human interaction with the environment (World Bank, 1992, p. 8), and a significant number of papers addressed the issues surrounding ecotourism.

The question of sustainability – and, by implication, sustainable development – in relation to alternative forms of tourism experiences has become central in the analysis and provision of these types of experiences. The *World Conservation Strategy* initially posited sustainability as an underlying premise for a large number of projects based in developing countries, and *Our Common Future* (widely known as the Brundtland Report) attempted to give it an operational context (World Commission on Environment and Development, 1987; de La Court, 1990; Farrell and Runyan, 1991; Hare, 1991) which enabled agencies to engender it into their operating philosophies.

The provision of alternative tourism experiences – such as ecotourism and volunteer tourism – are fundamentally aligned to sustainability in attempting to ensure that the resource and destination impacts are minimized. Environmental factors such as the host community (the community associated with the destination area), biodiversity and avoiding irreversible environmental change are emphasized in the literature on sustainability (e.g. World Commission on Environment and Development, 1987; Cronin, 1990; Ecologically Sustainable Development Working Groups, 1991; Sofield, 1991). As a result of these factors, volunteer tourism recently has arisen as a phenomenon in the realm of alternative tourist experiences. However, as yet, the current body of tourism literature has neglected this growing area of the tourism phenomenon.

The significance of alternative tourism for this book is premised on the idea that an understanding is needed of its role and function in the everyday interactions as they occur in the process of the tourist

---

the scenery and its wild plants and animals, as well as any existing cultural aspects (both past and present) found in these areas. Ecological tourism implies a scientific, aesthetic or philosophical approach, although an ecological tourist is not required to be a professional scientist, artist or philosopher. The main point is that the person that practices ecotourism has the opportunity of immersing him or herself in nature in a way that most people cannot enjoy in their routine, urban existences . . .'. As there is no strict consensus on a specific definition of ecotourism (as will be discussed in Chapter 2), numerous examples abound. The Ecotourism Society (1992) in the USA defines ecotourism as 'responsible travel that conserves natural environments and sustains the well-being of local people'.

experience. Alternative tourism is explored in relation to individual utilization of tourism experiences in the negotiation and definition/ redefinition of a sense of self and identity, contributing to a development of the process whereby specific social meanings are created, communicated and interpreted both spatially and temporally. The in-depth analysis of one particular project enables the ideas inherent in volunteer tourism, and what it might contribute to both tourism theory and practice, to be brought to life. The book contributes to the development of the research area of volunteer tourism by focusing upon the experiences of participants in a community-based project – the Santa Elena Rainforest Reserve (SERR).

The focus of the research on experience is contextualized within a framework stemming from the literature on tourism and leisure experiences. The experiential focus allows for the analysis of the volunteer tourism experience as a participative process involving direct interaction with the natural environment/local community within a specific social situation, contextualized by the differential elements of ecotourism, volunteering and serious leisure. This provides the initial basis for the exploration of alternative tourist experiences.

Selves in the Tourism Experience

To date, sociologies of tourism have developed two major themes concerning the self of the traveller. On the one hand, there has been an emphasis on tourism as a means of escape from the everyday, even if such escape is temporary. On the other, travel has been constructed as a means of self-development, a way to broaden the mind, experience the new and different and to come away in some way enriched. Both involve the self of the tourist. One adopts a pessimistic view, suggesting there is no escape (e.g. Cohen and Taylor, 1976; Rojek, 1993) and the other moves to an optimistic outlook in which everyone will benefit from the tourist experience (e.g. Pearce, 1984; Brown, 1992). Others, such as MacCannell (1992) attempt to balance the two views. MacCannell, for example, sees the touristic movement of peoples both to and from the western world as an opportunity to form hybrid cultures, a pre-condition for inventing and creating subjectivities that resist cultural constraints. He claims that the neo-nomads of tourism in the post-modern era cross cultural boundaries not as invaders, but as imaginative travellers who benefit from displaced self-understanding and the freedom to go beyond the limits that frontiers present. The 'true heroes' of tourism, he claims, are those who know that 'their future will be made of dialogue with their fellow travellers and those they meet along the way' (1992, p. 4). On the other hand, he debunks the traveller who seeks escape through tourism while demanding the comforts of

home, at an exaggerated and luxurious level. 'This', he says, 'is an overturned nomadic consciousness in which the ultimate goal of travel is to set up sedentary housekeeping in the entire world, to displace the local peoples, or at least to subordinate them in the enterprise, to make them the 'household' staff of global capitalists' (MacCannell, 1992, p. 5). This form of ingesting the 'other' into the self – and subsequently eliminating it – is termed contemporary cannibalism: where the tourist consumes and destroys the culture of the host peoples in developing countries. Far from enlarging the self, he sees this form of tourism as supplying the energy for 'autoeroticism, narcissism, economic conservatism, egoism, and absolute group unity or fascism' (1992, p. 66). The tourist self, in this view, remains rigid or static and turned in on her/himself – shrinking, rather than expanding, or, in Craib's terms (1998), closing down psychic space where the self of the host person is devalued and diminished.

This book seeks to pursue another direction. Building on Kelly's (1996, p. 45) work on leisure, where he proclaims that 'this relative freedom makes possible the investment of self that leads to the fullest development of ourselves, the richest expression of who we want to become, and the deepest experience of fulfilment', the volunteer tourist seeks to discover the type of life experiences that best suits their needs. In undertaking this, they launch themselves into a journey of personal discovery. The volunteer tourist experience offers an opportunity to examine the potential of travel to change self, in the belief that these experiences would be of a more permanent nature than the average guided, packaged holiday that lasts 2 or 3 weeks (Kottler, 1997, p. 103). Craik (1986) and Cohen (1987) have given mention to the phrase 'modern day pilgrims' which propounds the idea that during the process of searching for something else, one may be better able to identify with self. The reasons for this could relate to the fact that as a result of travelling for a longer period of time, people come out of holiday mode and begin to accept things as being normal and respond accordingly (Hansel, 1993, p. 97). As the volunteer tourist learns and interacts more with the people and the culture of the place in which they are living, the surrounding environment becomes more familiar, and so they naturally absorb, integrate and adopt elements of that environment. Being able to accept and deal with one's environment is an important element in the development of self and it can be through volunteer tourism experiences that an individual must learn to rely on him or herself.

Seeking out the new and unfamiliar and going beyond our daily concept of self is an essential step in the development of self. Such 'rites of passage' (Withey, 1997, p. 3) see that each individual is tested through arduous and sometimes painful ordeals (Craik, 1986, p. 24). Tourism can be considered an excellent example of such a test, as many situations encountered whilst embarking on touristic activities can be fraught with problems – problems often born out of ignorance for one's surroundings. However, a number of tourists 'actually pay to be put in uncomfortable and dangerous situations' (Craik, 1986, p. 25) so that they can feel a sense of achievement and reward once it is over.

Despite such suggestions, volunteer tourist experiences do not necessarily have to be dangerous in order for an individual to benefit from them. Darby (1994) and Wearing (1998) both suggest that an examination of travel experiences such as volunteer tourism endured by people during the stage of late adolescence can provide a clearer understanding of how an individual goes about developing their sense of self. A common element of late adolescence seems to be that each person needs to feel independent and to be able to handle any difficulties that they encounter without the aid of others. As Darby (1994, p. 131) has suggested in relation to Youth Challenge International volunteer tourist participants: 'breaking away from previous social groups and perceptions . . . gave the participants a chance to review their self; their relation to other people; and their goals and aspirations for the future'. Therefore, it may be argued that separation from 'the familiar' can provide an excellent opportunity for an individual to seek new challenges and expand or reconfirm their identity.

Evidence from international volunteer tourist operations (see Darby, 1994; Wearing, 1998) and other volunteer agencies suggests that a high percentage of participants are between the ages of 18 and 25 years. This experience of being away from their familiar culture is imperative in the sense that they are able to begin focusing on what they, as individuals, desire in their lives independently of their peers and parents or other reference groups (Hattie, 1992, p. 18). Hewitt (1979, p. 74) maintains that each person is assigned a character both by others and by themselves (whereby they are expected to act in a particular way in all circumstances). However, they may feel trapped or stifled by the boundaries of this character and be forced to seek out a new environment. Iso-Ahola (1994, p. 53) makes a valid point:

> Given the essence of perceived freedom to leisure and the positive relationship between perceived freedom and perceived control, much of leisure has to do with exercise of personal control over one's behaviour and environment . . . leisure develops self-determination personality and thereby helps buffer against stressful life events.

This freedom and resulting self-determination (Iso-Ahola, 1994, p. 53) may have the effect of providing an individual with the opportunity to develop their sense of self. Through being largely in control, not feeling pressured to act in any specific manner, taking 'time out' from normal daily life and adopting different roles, volunteer tourists may become more aware of what they are seeking and be better equipped to deal with the challenges faced in their 'real' lives (Kottler, 1997, p. 29).

Examinations of prior practices in the field of tourism reinforce the belief that tourism does, in fact, improve the mind and overall character of its participants. Tourism, as it is known today, has been suggested by Craik (1986, p. 30) to include certain elements of pilgrimage. This statement implies that through the travel experience, a person can hope to discover things about the world around them and their particular place within it. Through the self-testing element of tourism, a person gains knowledge and confidence about themselves, their abilities/limitations (Darby, 1994) and possibly an insight into the direction that they feel their life should take.

Analyses of tourist destinations as image in tourist advertising and tourist research (Dilley, 1986; Telisman-Kosuta, 1989; Echtner and Ritchie, 1991; Gartner, 1993; Cohen, 1995; Bramwell and Rawding, 1996) assumes that each individual's experience of the tourist destination will be similar. There is, however, a significant body of research that indicates that such a conceptualization is, in fact, counterproductive (Rowe and Stevenson, 1994; Dann, 1995). Thus, this book seeks to explore the possibility of a more useful conceptualization of the tourist: that is, as someone who is influenced by the subjective meanings through which they are affected, constructed in interaction with the space and people that form the destination site. It is the experience of the interaction in this specific space that affects the socially constructed self who travels between specifically bounded spatio-temporal coordinates and this is the core of the volunteer tourist's experience. Therefore, the alternative tourist as a wanderer seeking simply to repudiate established tourism experiences (Cohen, 1995, p. 13) is critiqued as still failing to incorporate or recognize elements that may provide for an understanding of the experience.

Operators, Communities and Volunteer Tourism

The ecotourism literature illustrates that there is a particular focus on communities that are living in marginal or environmentally threatened areas. These communities are encouraged to take an economic interest in the preservation of their natural resources through ecotourism development. One of the ways this can be achieved is by finding assistance through organizations that offer volunteer programmes to work on such projects.

Significantly, it has been claimed that ecotourism – and by default volunteer tourism – is mass tourism in its early pre-tourism development stage. However, if the criteria used to describe the various components of ecotourism are applied to each particular tourism situation, it becomes clearer if the type of tourist activity being undertaken conforms to what Wallace (1992, p. 7) describes as 'real' ecotourism.

Essential to this is a two-way interactive process between host and guest and, therefore, 'the culture of the host society is as much at risk from various forms of tourism as physical environments' (Sofield, 1991, p. 56). From definitions of volunteer tourism and ecotourism, we see a major aim of sustaining the well-being of the local community where tourism takes place. Volunteer tourism can be viewed as a development strategy leading to sustainable development and centring the convergence of natural resource qualities, locals and the visitor that all benefit from tourism activity.

One of the key questions this book will address is: can a philosophy and practice of volunteer tourism exist outside the market priorities defined and sustained in the global market place of tourism? The global commodification or commercial globalization of ecotourism, for example, is almost complete in international tourist markets. As Campbell (1983) observes, consumption can become an end in itself. This commodification can be seen in the ambiguity over definition as to what ecotourism is and, as such, the profit objective has perhaps led to ecotourism's misinterpretation by the industry and to the inclusion of a range of unethical products. Butler (1992, p. 1) believes that for this reason a general understanding must be arrived at so that ecotourism is not just defined purely by commercial activity but also by ethics and a coherent philosophy. What volunteer tourism appears able to offer is an alternative direction where profit objects are secondary to a more altruistic desire to travel in order to assist communities.

In examining the role of volunteer tourists, ecotourism operators (giving a context for volunteer tourism operators, i.e. as they have a motive beyond pure profit, sustainability) and local communities, it is hoped that such organizations can become examples for the tourism industry to become more sensitized to the differing needs of local communities, while simultaneously aligning both these groups with national conservation/development strategies. It has been suggested that ecotourism can only operate effectively if it is developed and interlinked with certain concepts, such as national conservation strategies, designed to demonstrate to sectoral interests how they inter-relate to other sectors. This thereby reveals new opportunities for conservation and development to work together (McNeely and Thorsell, 1989). These different sectors include governments, private enterprise, local communities and organizations, conservation non-governmental organizations and international institutions.

If each sector has an understanding of where volunteer tourism fits within the broader framework of the tourism and conservation sectors, then there is a better chance of well-designed volunteer programmes. These could, for example, take protected areas as a focus for fostering host community values while providing education for outsiders (Kutay, 1990, p. 38), which would in a way legitimize volunteer tourism. The ecotourism organizations and their approaches therefore are an essential part of what the volunteer experience is. These organizations need to ensure that their operations have considered the basic principles that underlie ecotourism if they are to fit within the tourism industry.

Generally, ecotour operators need to instil a conservation ethic for environmentally sensitive travel in their clients (Whelan, 1991). By creating appreciation for natural areas and traditional cultures, tour companies can teach their clients to 'tread lightly' when they travel to remote regions. This is also applicable as a guide for volunteer tourism.

By their very nature, ecotourism and volunteer tourism suggest that there is a need for:

- tourism infrastructure that is sensitively developed where the tourism industry accepts integrated planning and regulation;
- supply-led marketing by the tourism industry;
- the establishment of carrying capacities (environmental and cultural) and strict monitoring of these; and
- the environmentally sensitive behaviour and operations of tourists and operators.

It is envisaged that volunteer tourism can operate successfully within this framework.

A wide range of institutions and organizations do, and will continue to, play an important role in providing volunteer tourism experiences. The types of organizations vary considerably and a number provide international support and sponsorship for the implementation of research projects and community development. These organizations facilitate this process through provision of necessary resources that may not otherwise be available. The international scope of these organizations can prove invaluable assistance in terms of their accumulated knowledge and experience. These types of organizations provide a large number of recruits through volunteer tourism with free time and money to spend on sustainable development efforts (Whelan, 1991). As such, they need access to relevant educational information before, during and after their experience. This will ensure maximization of their experience both on site and back in their own community.

Lea (1993, p. 702) suggests that there is clear evidence that highly commodified tourism is leading to unacceptable impacts on social and cultural values in some developing countries. Economics is the focus of the free market economy, whereas communities and the environment are generally the priority of volunteer tourism. The conflict of interests between the two can lead to a mutually exclusive operating environment. Tourism in the free market economy uses and exploits communities and natural resources as a means of profit accumulation and has been described as the commercialization of the human need to travel. This profits the tourism industry promoters and can lead to the exploitation of host communities, their culture and environment (Lea, 1993, p. 714). A further concern over the impact of tourism on local culture is that organizations operating under the banner of ecotourism and volunteer tourism may need to accept regulations to protect natural environments from the exploitative attitudes of the free market society.

It is conceivable that if volunteer tourism became overly dictated by the market economy and the volunteer tourist was unable to form a link to the destination areas, then it would be unidentifiable within the array of commercially created choices – and its purpose or significance becomes benign. This book seeks to address the idea that volunteer tourism enables the individual to have an experience that incorporates social value into identity and hence links host community and/or nature and self. If the key to a volunteer tourist experience is appreciation and awareness of the local environment (cultural and social), then the danger is that the volunteer tourist just becomes another consumer of a market product and thus eliminates or 'filters out' the underlying self–community link in the experience.

Volunteer tourism experiences can be examined differently from other experiences, allowing us to analyse closely the notion of self in tourism. Does it matter if it is just commodified leisure and not differentiated in any way from ordinary tourism? The focus lies in the idea that volunteer experiences cause value and consciousness changes in the individual that subsequently will influence their concept of self. Perhaps the volunteer tourist experience even predicates a change in identity; however, Glasser argues that the pursuit of a desired identity is often channelled into consumerism through the promulgation in modern complex societies of an ideal consumer whose main 'freely chosen' leisure activity is consumption (Glasser, 1976), i.e. consumption, culture and/or nature meet in volunteer tourism. The volunteer tourist can therefore never achieve what they seek. The experience becomes a tranquillizer rather than an awareness-raising attempt to cancel out the stress of life. The individual is left with an unsatisfactory search for some form of identity and an endless need to follow the latest dictates of big business and tourist markets. Local destination communities are consumed under the guise of a legitimate altruistic activity rather than leading to awareness and appreciation of culture, nature and discovery of the travel–self link.

Campbell (1983) argues (following Weber) that the 'spirit' of modern consumerism rests upon an attitude of restless desire and discontent, which produces consumption as an end in itself. Romanticism, he claims, conceived as a 'cultural movement, which introduced the modern doctrines of self-expression and fulfillment', is the most likely source of an ethic, which legitimates such a spirit. Thus the 'romantic ethic' of the enlightenment provides a contradictory and compensatory ethic to the self-disciplinary future orientation of the Protestant work ethic, but one which is necessary for perpetual consumption. He does not acknowledge that the two contradictory ethics have been accommodated in contemporary society by separating out the sphere of leisure – with its emphasis on self-expression and fulfilment – from the sphere of work with its self-denying disciplinary ethic.

Volunteer tourism therefore does not legitimize the rights of host communities and their rights outside of the tourism industry as an entity with its own history and sense of place, but rather provides another source of consumption that will only endanger the very communities and environments that the volunteer tourist seeks to protect. Further, the volunteer tourists themselves are complicit in this consumption and commodifying process and are then the economic 'units' targeted by the industry.

The Santa Elena Experience

The Santa Elena Rainforest Reserve (SERR) project,[3] established in a rural community of 800 people in Costa Rica, Central America, provides the focus for the analysis of volunteer tourism as a subset of alternative tourism experiences.

Tourism is generally recognized as an important contributor to sustainable development for Costa Rica, in offering a much needed alternative source of economic return whilst providing a stimulus for conserving natural resources. Costa Rica's diverse topography and climate support a wide variety of plant and animal life that continue to attract visitors.

The presence of international research organizations (such as Earthwatch and WWF) has played a large role in encouraging scientists and students to study the unique natural heritage offered in the area. Research, the media and publications have promoted widespread interest in Costa Rica as a destination for nature lovers, whether involved in scientific research or not.[4]

---

[3] The tourism experience examined in this book is based on the development of an ecotourism rainforest reserve in Costa Rica. The author initially completed a feasibility study for the project, later becoming a project manager in the facilitation of what is now known as the Santa Elena Rainforest Reserve (SERR). This involvement consisted of obtaining additional land for the reserve, design and construction of an interpretation centre and trails, establishing a tour-guide training course, various aspects of project management and, finally, the facilitation of the community management plan.

[4] Rovinski (1991) highlights the importance that science-based tourism has played in the development of more broad-based ecotourism. Additionally, the Office of National Tourism (1996) highlights the success of encouraging and educating visitors to treat the environment with care and respect and how this can increase visitor experience, satisfaction and interest.

Authors such as Lea (1993, 1995) and Boo (1990, p. 11) identify a number of economic benefits that can accrue from tourism. Tourism can increase a country's foreign exchange earnings and thereby improve the balance of payments, whilst its place as part of the expanding service sector can generate employment. Ecotourism in particular is often promoted for its ability to create investment for infrastructure development, contributing to the diversification of the economy in ameliorating the reliance on a small export base and assisting in stimulating the economic activity and growth in isolated areas. Within rural communities, ecotourism is seen as providing an economic alternative to traditional land uses such as agriculture, and may, in cases such as the SERR, slow down deforestation (see Boo, 1990, p. 17). Valentine (1987, p. 17) indicates that capital investments and operational expenditure can be multiplied throughout the economy because of the 'trickle down effect' or multiplier. In addition to this, the visitor expenditure within rural communities provides valuable direct income. This would indicate that there is significant scope for rural communities such as Santa Elena to benefit from projects like the SERR project that rely on volunteer tourism in their establishment and an ongoing commitment from volunteers to continue running.

Monteverde forest is at the peak of the Tilaran Mountain Range in Costa Rica, which forms the continental divide between the Atlantic and Pacific Ocean. Dairy farming was the foundation of the region's economy and the new settlers arriving from other regions of Costa Rica in search of land (Boo, 1990) founded Santa Elena 6 km north-west of Monteverde. The new settlers produced milk for sale to the 'Friends' cheese factory, and the early cheese production was around 10 kg per day. Today, Monteverde's modern cheese factory produces about 100 kg of cheese daily and it is sold throughout Costa Rica (Rachowiecki, 1991).

The initial land set aside in the area for conservation was formally named the Monteverde Cloud Forest Preserve (MCFP). The Tropical Science Centre of San Jose (a Costa Rican non-profit organization founded in 1962) has owned and managed the reserve since its inception in 1971 and, together with the Monteverde Conservation League (MCL) which was formed in 1989, has successfully brought about the expansion of the preserve to 10,000 ha (Tobias, 1989).

The MCFP is the habitat for more than 2000 species of plants, 106 species of mammals, 336 species of birds (with 40% being rare species) and 123 species of reptiles and amphibians (Boo, 1990). Scientists came in growing numbers to this area, and increasing numbers of visitors, drawn in large part by the accounts of these scientists, were attracted to the reserve (Boo, 1990). Subsequently, tourism to the MCFP has increased from approximately 300 in 1973 to 40,000 in 1992. Unfortunately, the increased tourism to the

Monteverde area has bestowed very few benefits upon the adjacent Santa Elena community.

In 1990, the community and high school saw the potential of tourism and initiated an ecotourism project on the 'high school farm'.[5] This led to a general goal to rebuild the local community's economy and provide employment for local high school students. The SERR is now owned and operated by the high school through its Board of Directors. The school currently is changing its curriculum from an agricultural base to one based on ecology, English language, hospitality, and arts and crafts.

Funds for the SERR were raised from the local community, Canadian high schools, private and public sector sponsors and international development organizations. The Canadian International Development Agency (CIDA) and Youth Challenge International (YCI) initially provided the material, equipment, and staff necessary to develop and construct an interpretation centre and trails. The local and regional government authorities cooperated by directing national government funds into the building of an all-weather road to the reserve (access to which previously was restricted due to high rainfall, clay soils and severe erosion in some sections).

The SERR was opened to visitors after construction of the interpretation centre, and trails were completed in 1992. The SERR project seeks to capitalize on the increase in tourism to protected areas renowned for their outstanding beauty and extraordinary ecological interest. It works on the premise that ecotourism can only survive and prosper if natural areas themselves survive and prosper. The project relied heavily on the interest of developed countries in the natural environment, as these countries provided much needed funds and support, and which may, in the future, provide a significant visitor base for the SERR.

The SERR project was designed and implemented specifically with an adherence to the principles of ecotourism and, as such, ecotourism itself is a fundamental element of the project. Previous studies of recreationalists (and tourists) in protected areas (such as national parks) often acknowledge, or on analysis suggest, that complete theoretical explanations of leisure (and by definition tourist) experiences are lacking (see McCool *et al.*, 1984; Manning, 1986; Colton, 1987;

---

[5] The Santa Elena High School (or Agricultural College) was established in 1977. Architecturally it is a part of the primary school but it added 4 years to the existing schooling in the area, allowing students to go on to study up to 16 years of age. In 1983, the government presented the school with a 10-year lease on a parcel of land on which students could conduct agricultural projects. The project was seen as a sound initiative but, later, due to the difficulties of clearing the forest and because of the severe climate, infertile soils and lack of resources, the project was abandoned.

Lucas and Stankey, 1988; Kelly, 1991). Both the general literature on the sociology of tourism experience (as discussed earlier) and the more specific literature in the social sciences on experience and natural environments suggest a need to re-examine the influences of elements of the natural environment experience.

Fundamental to ecotourism, as an element of alternative tourism experience, is the host community and its relationship with tourists. The host community as defined in this context is the community that has a direct affiliation to the natural environment visited by the tourist. Commonly this community would provide support services for the tourist and have some involvement in the management of these natural environments. However, Butler (1980, 1991) has found that there is generally an inevitable decline of the host community's sustainability and this is directly related to the host community's role as part of the tourism product. According to Murphy (1985, 1988), the success of the tourism industry depends upon the acceptance and support of the host community. Therefore, in the exploration of the differential elements of the tourism experience, it is essential to ensure the inclusion of the natural and cultural environments of the destination area.

Set against this background are the experiences of several volunteer tourists as part of a YCI project in the SERR. Their efforts and experiences are analysed to provide us with an empirical view of what volunteer tourists actually do, experience and come away with.

A New Approach

In placing the concept of alternative tourism in an experiential and historical context, the scene is now set to begin exploring and examining volunteer tourism and the volunteer tourist experience.

Chapter 2 examines alternative tourism experiences and how tourists themselves construct them, then contextualizes the concept of volunteer tourism within those boundaries of alternative tourism and, subsequently, mass tourism. In exploring alternative tourism experiences within the context of wider discussions about culture and society, it is proposed that alternative tourism experiences can best be clarified by the particularity of the specific tourist experience.

The dominant questions that arise with regard to volunteer tourism relate to the relationship between alternative tourism types and the tourism industry as a whole, i.e. the specificity of an experience which relates to the utilization of 'alternative tourism' as a label – such as ecotourism or volunteer tourism – in the marketing of conventional tourism ventures. This debate is explored at this point in an attempt to clarify the position for providers of alternative tourism experiences and their relationship to the tourism industry. Much of the work on touristic experience has been focused on producers (the industry) rather than on consumers (tourists), and little empiric research has considered the tourist with a focus on the symbolic meanings and values they associate with their activities (see Squire, 1994).

YCI is discussed to illustrate volunteer tourism empirically. YCI is examined to move towards a comprehensive theoretical analysis of volunteering as a form of tourism experience. A discussion is presented of the three elements considered important to this type of tourism, that of ecotourism, volunteerism and serious leisure.

Chapter 3 examines one of the 60 environmental projects undertaken by YCI between 1991 and 1995, which provides a microsocial context for the examination of the SERR experience of YCI participants. This chapter contextualizes the SERR project undertaken by YCI in Costa Rica, focusing particularly on the project and its context in Costa Rica and the Santa Elena community, and as a community-based ecotourism project.

The insights from 100 interviews conducted with the actual Santa Elena community are presented in providing for the specific social context for the on-site SERR experience. Given that this book examines the effects that the site (community/natural area/group/project) has on the alternative tourist experience, it is considered important to have an understanding of the community and its general attitudes towards tourism in order to contextualize the comprehensive scope of the analysis.

Chapter 4 presents the data obtained from the in-depth interviews with the participants from Australia, over the 3 years of the Costa Rica project. Each participant was in Costa Rica for 3 months; they spent between 2 and 6 weeks on individual projects such as the SERR project. It provides information from the participants' 'stories' on the SERR experience and analyses the participant's views of their experience by reviewing their recollection of the experience.

Chapter 5 examines the elements of ecotourism, volunteerism and serious leisure in conjunction with the themes that emerged from the participant's definitions of the experience and links them to related information in the interviews and the literature. An overall picture of the experience that participants have had with YCI on the SERR project is presented.

Chapter 6 is focused on the centrality of the natural environment. The site is examined to explore what other elements may have affected the participant's sense of self and identity, ultimately presenting an overall picture of the symbolic influences of elements of the site on their sense of self and identity.

Chapter 7 explores how volunteer tourism experiences actually contribute to the development of self, framing the experience in the very words of the participants. This attempts to satisfy one of the underlying aims of this book: the movement towards social analyses that will provide a better understanding of alternative tourism experiences. The SERR project was able to provide crucial information about the social construction of such experiences in assisting in the development of social theory that will provide an understanding of the key elements of the experience. The development of theory in this area may initiate and enable a sounder basis in establishing tourism in developing and developed countries at both the individual and community level.

Chapter 8 examines the growing convergence of aims between local communities and the tourism sector. If tourism is developed and managed carefully with involvement from the host communities, it can assist in efforts to maintain and enhance environments. This in turn means not only presenting the natural environment and community heritage, but also providing demonstrable support to the maintenance of that heritage.

Chapter 9 argues that the alternative tourism experience should not be reduced, as MacCannell (1992, p. 6) suggests, to a dialogic model of impossible realities related to dialectal materialism. Instead, its understanding should be grounded in human interactions and the concrete social reality in which it takes place. The SERR project site, in this respect, provides a means of representing and examining the 'empty meeting ground' that MacCannell (1992) posits.

The recognition that the alternative tourist experience is fundamentally based on the interactive elements of the space visited provides the possibility for a comprehensive and contextually holistic understanding. Such an approach enables the elaboration of the potentiality inherent in the on-site interactions and their importance to tourism in the development of strategies for the provision, and understanding of, tourism experiences that move beyond discussions of the 'authentic', 'objects of the gaze' or places of escape (see MacCannell, 1976, 1992; Urry, 1990; Rojek, 1993).

The volunteer tourism site is a means of examining the empty meeting ground that MacCannell (1992) presents. He sees that 'the one path that still leads in the direction of scholarly objectivity, detachment, and neutrality is exactly the one originally thought to lead away from these classic virtues. That is, an openly autobiographical style in which the subjective position of the author, especially on political matters is presented in a clear and straightforward fashion. At least this enables the reader to review his or her own position to make adjustments necessary for dialogue' (1992, p. 10). The book process has seen many of those adjustments occur as the author has struggled with providing a picture of the alternative tourism experience that is not obscured by the author's interpretation. The book has proposed that alternative forms of tourism experiences can exist apart from the realm of the mass tourism experiences as proposed by authors on tourism

(MacCannell, 1976, 1992; Urry, 1990; Rojek, 1993). In doing so, it has provided a model of tourist behaviour that gives perspective to the tourist experience. Such a perspective provides a wider view of this experience. In order to capture the individual tourist's construction of her/his experience, the meanings given and the remembrance of the tourist space, qualitative methods would appear to allow for greater variety of response as well as being able to explore the impacts on the self.

If it is recognized that the alternative tourist experience is based on interactions that people have with elements of the space visited, then this can be invaluable for understanding and therefore providing sustainable tourist experiences. Documentation of the real value of the tourist experience to the tourist could suggest that the industry is not compelled to create an environment artificially and to promise this as an image but focus on the on-site interactions and the importance of them to the tourist and develop strategies around these ideas rather than attempting to create authentic objects to gaze at or places to escape to (see MacCannell, 1976, 1992; Urry, 1990; Rojek, 1993). This can enable another look at how the industry structures tourism and may provide directions for policy in the future.

What we are beginning to see is a new form of alternative tourism, that of volunteer tourism, where new business structures, new motivations for travelling, new experiences to be had and indeed a new type of tourist are emerging. There is not only a greater consideration for the contribution the volunteer can make to the community in which they take part, but also a much greater awareness of the impact the experience has on the personal development of the participant. It is through the latter that we will uncover the nature of volunteer tourism.

Chapter 2

Alternative Tourism Experiences

> You don't feel like you're there watching [the community], because you're talking with them and picking up their mannerisms and in a way slipping into their style of living. You're eating their food, you're eating when they do, you're eating their style of food.
>
> (Mic, SERR participant)

Tourism is essentially a modern western phenomenon, the analysis of which has evolved from pre-modernism through to post-modernism. It differs significantly from non-western and historical forms of travel (although having some similarities; see Graburn, 1995), being closely related to the emergence of modernity (see Cohen, 1995). The profusion of the modern western touristic experience during this evolution, particularly over the last 20 years, has spawned a variety of means of researching tourism. Tourism theories and research have ranged from microsocial psychological explanations to macrosocial explorations concerning the globalization of tourist venues.

The diversity of tourism experience, and its subsequent analysis in the tourism literature, has precipitated a profusion of terms designating both a market-differentiated and an ideologically divergent form of tourism that is located under the term of 'alternative tourism'. This includes a diversity of touristic forms, including (and not exclusive to) nature, green, special interest and ecotourism – many of which have caught the imagination of local communities, governments, international organizations and the tourism industry itself, with a variety of such 'alternative' projects being actively promoted, especially in developing countries (see Britton, 1977; Saglio, 1979). These projects have been used in part as definitional examples of 'alternative tourism' in order to clarify the associated issues relating to touristic practices

(Pearce, 1980; Dernoi, 1981, 1988; Holden, 1984; Britten and Clarke, 1987; Cohen, 1987). However, there currently is debate, worldwide, concerning the benefits and costs of this type of tourism.

Given the divergent backgrounds and concerns of these individuals and organizations, it is not surprising that no universally agreed upon, or widely adopted definition of alternative tourism is to be found, nor that few explicit links have been made between its different forms. It is not the purpose of this book to pursue the quest for an all-embracing single definition of alternative tourism. However, a recognition of the diversity of the various forms of tourism in no way devalues the need for a systematic basis for distinguishing between and classifying the elements that make up specific forms of tourism experience (Pearce, 1989), in this case volunteer tourism.

In this book, the context of volunteer tourism is located firmly within the sphere of alternative tourism. It is elaborated theoretically and analysed systematically using the ideas surrounding tourism experiences. This chapter examines the concepts of volunteer and alternative tourism in a wider context, with the body of literature concerning 'alternative tourism' and touristic practices themselves used in the exploration of how tourism experiences may relate to what are considered as mainstream or conventional tourism experiences, mindful of the commodification that currently is occurring. Through the identification of the specific elements of a particular tourism experience, it will be suggested that such a form of tourism practice can be considered, within a framework provisionally moved towards in what follows, as a form of *alternative* tourism experience and, more precisely, a volunteer tourism experience.

A major pitfall in specifying alternative forms of tourism and the experiences that may be aligned to it are, as Smith and Eadington (1992) observe in relation to alternative tourism, surrounded by ambiguity in the perceptions and conceptualization of what defines it. A significant and often raised question in this respect is to what extent has the primacy of commercial considerations led to a misinterpretation by the industry of alternative tourism and the inclusion of a range of experiences that may not relate to the original ideals that underpin it. In response, Butler (1992), also in relation to ecotourism, states that a general understanding must be arrived at, suggesting that ecotourism is not just an activity but a philosophy. Furthermore, this philosophy must be modelled on a sustainable approach to the environment if the unique nature of the experience is also to be sustained.

Situated in this respect, volunteer tourism needs to have developed a more comprehensive theoretical understanding, and hence enable the tourism industry to examine the provision of these types of experiences. It is suggested that a volunteer tourism experience falls under the auspices of an alternative tourism experience and is constructed from a number of varying and interdependent elements each of which overlap significantly. For conceptual clarity, these elements are explored as ecotourism, international volunteering and 'serious leisure'. It is hoped that this initial structure will provide the basis from which others can explore this area.

Ecotourism is essential in the understanding of not only volunteer tourism, but of alternative tourism. Ecotourism is one specific element that influences the form of the volunteer experience, particularly in relation to international tourists from developed countries that are visiting developing countries. It is not suggested, however, that all experiences of volunteer tourists fall within what may be considered ecotourism, particularly as the definitions of ecotourism are far from conclusive. However, the form of ecotourism experience examined here in part makes up the volunteer tourism experience, since an element of that experience will lead to both an understanding of ecotourism itself and the conceptualization of the more general form of alternative tourism experiences.

> Mindful that the arguments over a definition of ecotourism have raged for well over the last decade, ecotourism is taken here to refer to tourist experiences that are environmentally sustainable, occur in natural areas, involve an interpretive element, contribute to the local community and involve local or indigenous peoples.

If it is possible to identify how alternative tourism organizations relate to the tourism industry itself and, specifically here, how analysis of enterprises such as volunteer tourism can provide an understanding of the components that make up an alternative tourism experience, then there exists the potential to provide experiences that go beyond the defined boundaries of mass tourism – as suggested by MacCannell (1976, 1992), Urry (1990) and Rojek (1993) – in accordance with the potential identified by Kutay (1990, p. 38) in the provision of experiences that change the focus of tourism for both visitor and host community. Volunteer tourism could thereby offer new mechanisms for the tourism industry to develop approaches to address development and sustainability issues.

It is hoped that in exploring the specificity of a particular tourist experience in depth, it may be possible to provide an understanding of not only the significant divergences and convergences that exist between both mass tourism and alternative tourism, but also the subtle nuances that subtend these tourist experiences. Therefore, it is not simply a matter of differentiating, in a binary fashion, between a general category of tourism and the derivation of niche elements within it. As MacCannell (1992, p. 1) notes: '[T]ourism is not just an aggregate of merely commercial activities; it is also an ideological framing of history, nature, and tradition; a framing that has the power to reshape culture and nature to its own needs'.

In differentiating the volunteer tourism experience from both mass and mainstream tourism and from the broad conceptualization of 'alternative tourism' as identified in the literature, it is argued here that the conceptual basis underlying the analysis of tourism – in relation to both alternative and mass tourism[6] – must be expanded in order to encompass the notion of experience as demonstrated in the social science literature (see Wearing and Wearing, 1988). A focus on the tourist experience more effectively illustrates the conceptual, theoretical and practical differences and similarities between mass tourism and alternative forms of tourism, thus moving towards an understanding and elaboration of the potential benefits of alternative tourism experiences such as volunteer tourism.

MacCannell (1976, pp. 23–29) accords to the tourism experience a considerable degree of complexity in his analysis of it as a subclass of cultural experience, thus opening it to the intellectual and ideological debates of sociology. It is, therefore, essential in the examination of tourism experiences to analyse their social construction in order to understand the complexities of the experience and its relationship to culture. MacCannell (1976, p. 23) suggests that tourism experiences are culturally constructed, having two basic components which must be combined in order for the experience itself to occur. The first he terms a 'model' (an embodied ideal); the second an 'influence' (the changed, created, intensified belief or feeling that is based on the model). In this way, the volunteer tourism experience needs a 'model' to explain the experiences it provides for the participants, and where the tourist and community are the 'influence'. The 'medium' (MacCannell, 1976, p. 24) corresponds to the agency that connects a model and its influence, in this case the face-to-face interaction that occurs at the destination site. The outside interest groups that exist in the community and tourism industry he calls a 'production'. Thus, the tourist experience is a cultural production that is shaped by significant power groups who have a stake in the experience.

---

[6] It is not the purpose of this book to focus on the dualism of the positive or negative impacts of tourism. Its focus is, however, on developing an approach that recognizes the interdependence of the tourism experience, culture and ecology, and explores ways of enhancing the sustainability of the experience, and eliminating or ameliorating negative consequences. Tourism itself is regarded by many social scientists, and many tourists themselves, with increasing scepticism. It is increasingly seen to have a poor environmental record, negative cultural impacts, and to provide unsatisfactory benefits such as intermittent, low-level employment for members of the host community.

The tourist as an entity is seen by MacCannell (1976) as enjoying a privileged western middle-class leisure activity. While this may be true in a macrosocial sense, to explore fully some of the structural differences suggested through the examination of organizations involved in volunteer tourism, there is a need for models that enable the inclusion of more subtle elements that influence and contribute to the understanding of tourist experiences.

> Modernisation simultaneously separates these things from people and places that made them, breaks up the solidarity of the groups in which they originally figured as cultural elements, and brings the poor liberated from traditional attachments into the modern world where, as tourists, they may attempt to discover or reconstruct a cultural heritage or a social identity.
>
> (MacCannell, 1976, p. 13)

Initially, it would seem that the investigation of the alternative tourism experience needs to move into a sphere of theory that allows the face-to-face interaction of everyday life to be followed (Goffman, 1974; MacCannell, 1976). This book does not attempt to diminish the relevance of macrosocial influences on the tourist experience, but seeks to expand the relevance of the microsocial elements which contribute to make up the tourist experience. As MacCannell (1976, p. 10) suggests: '[A]ll tourists desire this deeper involvement with society and culture to some degree; it is a basic component of their motivation to travel'.

MacCannell (1992, p. 3) suggests that critical theory has prepared us for the absence of the subject, for an empty meeting ground including an empty signifier. He suggests that deconstruction gives us access to the realm of absolute possibility in theory, in the imagination and, where it exists, in life. However, he maintains that an allied sociology of interaction or dialogue is still necessary to gain access to the realm of contingency and determinism, and especially resistance to, and struggles against, determinism.

An understanding of this involvement can only come through a better explanation of the relational elements that the tourist experiences within and with the destination site. Goffman (1974), for example, structurally analysed social establishments in what he termed 'front' and 'back' regions. The front is the designated meeting place of hosts, guests, customers and service persons, and the 'back' is the place where members of the community retire between performances to relax and to prepare. MacCannell (1976, p. 94) suggests that being one of the 'locals' is being able to experience this 'back' region. However, if tourists enter this back region, is the experience similar for all involved? This region may offer the ability to work beyond the images the tourist has of the site which have been presented by the media or advertising in the attempt to sell a destination rather than the reality of what is there: 'once a person, or an observer, moves offstage, or into the "setting" the real truth begins to reveal itself more or less automatically' (MacCannell, 1976, p. 95).

> I have claimed that the structure of this social space is intimately linked to touristic attitudes and I want to pursue this. The touristic way of getting in with the natives is to enter into a quest for authentic experiences, perceptions and insights.
>
> (MacCannell, 1976, p. 95)

Rojek (1993, p. 133), in this respect, raises significant questions about the relationship between 'authenticity' and experience. In relation to tourism, he states that the modernist quest for authenticity and self-realization has come to an end and is now equivalent to a mere consumption activity. However, in placing contemporary touristic practices within post-modernism, Rojek (1993, p. 126) states that post-modernism emphasizes the discontinuity of change and the irregularity of association and practice, leading to 'the rejection of modernist universal categories of ontology and epistemology'. Rojek's suggestion that tourism can become generalized and de-differentiated places emphasis on the different meanings and elements that arise. It questions the current order but, significantly, allows for tourism as a form of spectating and consumption.

Situating Volunteer Tourism Within the Context of the Alternative Tourism Experience

Tourist development has not progressed without controversy. Disillusionment with 'mass' tourism and the many problems it has engendered has led many observers and researchers to criticize the past methods and directions of tourism development and to offer instead the hope of 'alternative tourism'. Pearce (1990) notes that the term 'alternative tourism' has been adopted to denote options or strategies considered preferable to mass tourism. As Butler (1990, p. 40) states: 'Alternative to what? Obviously not to other forms of tourism, but rather, an alternative to the least desired or most undesired type of tourism, or essentially what is known as mass tourism, such as the "Golden Hordes" of Turner and Ashe (1975), or the "mass institutionalised tourist" of Cohen (1972)'.

However, the term 'alternative tourism' is interpreted by various authors in widely differing and sometimes openly contradictory ways. J. Butler (1990), for example, places alternative tourism as up-market package tours of rich people to exotic destinations, mostly wilderness areas, whereas others define it as rucksack wandering by young people with limited financial means (see Cohen, 1972).

The term 'alternative' logically implies an antithesis. It arises as the contrary to that which is seen as negative or detrimental about conventional tourism. In the domain of logic, an alternative is based on a dialectical paradigm that offers only two possibilities: a conclusion that is either one or the other. Therefore, the terms alternative and mass tourism are mutually interdependent, each relying on a series of value-laden judgements that themselves structure the definitional content of the terms.

Thus, the common feature of 'alternative tourism' is the suggestion of an attitude diametrically opposed to what is characteristically viewed as the 'hard' and, therefore, 'undesirable' dominant forms of tourism. Like 'alternative tourism', this form itself has been designated by varying terms including conventional mass tourism (CMT; Mieczkowski, 1995) and mass tourism (J. Butler, 1990), of which alternative tourism exists in fundamental opposition by attempting to minimize the perceived negative environmental and sociocultural impacts. Various other descriptions can be found in the literature to allude to environmentally compatible tourism. Examples include green tourism (Jones, 1987) 'nature-oriented tourism' (Durst and Ingram, 1988), 'soft tourism' (Mader, 1988), community-based tourism (CBT; Dernoi, 1981, p. 253) and 'defensive tourism' (Krippendorf, 1982, 1987).

In this way, the concept of alternative tourism can itself be as broad and vague as its diametrical opposite. Many divergent leisure types can be classified as alternative tourism, including adventure holidays, hiking holidays or the solitary journeys undertaken by globe trotters.

The term itself encompasses a wide range of connotations: tourists characterized by particular motivations; touristic practices; a touristic product; levels of technology; solutions to planning; local, regional, national and international politics; and as a strategy for development. In the last case, alternative tourism is the application to tourism of sustainable development practices in regions where tourism has been chosen as a factor in economic development.

Dernoi (1981, p. 253) initially defined alternative tourism by accommodation type: 'In alternative tourism the 'client' receives accommodation directly in, or at the home of, the host with, eventually, other services and facilities offered there.' However, he then went on to list a number of other features by which alternative tourism might be distinguished from 'mass tourism': 'Simply stated, alternative tourism/CBT (community-based tourism) is a privately offered set of hospitality services (and features), extended to visitors, by individuals, families, or a local community. A prime aim of alternative tourism/CBT is to establish direct personal/cultural intercommunication and understanding between host and guest' (Dernoi, 1988, p. 89).

Moving on from a supply-side focus, and acknowledging the inextricable role of participants, for the ECTWT (Ecumenical Coalition of Third World Tourism): 'alternative tourism is a process which promotes a just form of travel between members of different communities. It seeks to achieve mutual understanding, solidarity and equality amongst participants' (Holden, 1984, p. 15). The stress here is on the facilitation and improvement of contacts between hosts and guests, especially through the organization of well-prepared special interest tours, rather than on actual development of facilities. As noted, however, such definitions are elaborated on by way of a systematic contrasting of the features of alternative tourism with those of what is perceived to be the dominant or mainstream variety. The distinction is usually between polar opposites, and there is scarcely any recognition of variations in the mainstream nor any evidence of the existence of intermediate cases. Another body of literature dealing with tourism typology gives greater attention to these variations with classifications between three or more categories that are not uncommon. Moreover, 'alternative tourism' as variously defined above, rarely occurs specifically as one of the classes in the typology literature.

Thus it would appear from the literature that all forms of tourism exist side-by-side, each playing an important role in the tourist spectrum.[7] Both mass tourism and alternative tourism can be viewed at corresponding extremes of such a spectrum and, as Mieczkowski (1995, p. 463) states, they should remain there. The relational elements of ecotourism, volunteerism and serious leisure, as definitional components of a specific alternative tourism experience, exist as modalities of tourism experience along many divergent and convergent points of this spectrum. By elaborating upon each of these elements as specific components of the volunteer tourism experience in the context of an alternative tourism experience and, thus, exploring the impact of such experiences on individual subjective experience, it is envisaged that the analysis of tourism experiences can achieve a clarity of focus through the recognition of the particular elements that contribute to the specific market segments of tourism.

The diagrammatic representation following (Fig. 2.1) – adapted from Mieczkowski (1995, p. 460) – is designed to provide a framework in which to locate the volunteer tourism experience. Mieczkowski (1995) initially divides tourism into two broad categories. The first is CMT, which has prevailed on the market for some time. The second broad category is that of alternative tourism, a flexible generic category that contains a multiplicity of various forms that have one feature in

[7] The idea of a tourist spectrum can be related to the 'recreation opportunity spectrum' as established by Clarke and Stankey (1979) or more recent work such as the 'indigenous peoples' cultural opportunity for tourism' by Sofield and Birtles (1996).

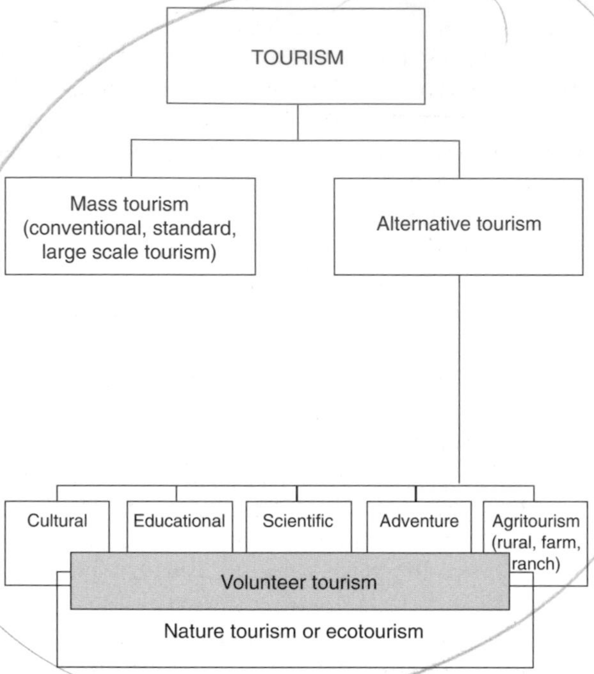

Fig. 2.1. A conceptual schema of alternative tourism.

common, i.e. they are alternatives to CMT. This means that, they are not associated with mass large-scale tourism but are essentially small-scale, low-density, dispersed in non-urban areas, and they cater to special interest groups of people with mainly above-average education and with good incomes. This category also includes the 'explorers' and 'drifters' identified by Cohen (1987).

Figure 2.1 demonstrates the general relational aspects of the different forms of tourism identified in the literature and how serious leisure and volunteerism lie in relation to these forms of tourism.

This conceptual model identifies and includes the elements of serious leisure and volunteerism. These elements are fundamental to the construction of volunteer tourism experiences and allow for, as Fig. 2.1 shows, the elaboration of the overlaps and divergences of tourism forms or markets through viewing the specific elements that comprise them, and their relation to the experiential reality of those participating.

As to the specific forms of alternative tourism, Mieczkowski (1995) distinguishes such forms as cultural, educational, scientific, adventure, and agritourism with rural, ranch and farm subsets. Significantly, there is some overlap with CMT (see cultural tourism in Smith and Eadington, 1992), but the main criterion of distinction is the scale and character of the impacts. Another overlap occurs between the various types of alternative tourism themselves. Cultural tourism, for example, is to a large extent educational. Ecotourism, also called nature or green tourism, is nature oriented and nature based but is not always necessarily practised in wilderness settings. Mieczkowski (1995) finds it difficult to place ecotourism in the context of alternative tourism because, while not coinciding directly with cultural tourism, it overlaps with the educational, scientific, adventure and agritourism forms.

The distinct characteristics of 'alternative tourism' are schematically outlined in Table 2.1, and, although not considered to be exhaustive, are included here to provide the underpinning of the conceptual framework that underlies the basis of the movement towards elaborating the specificity of a particular touristic experience.

Alternative tourism then, generally, is a modality of tourism that pays special attention to environmental and social carrying capacity.[8] Krippendorf (1987, p. 37) notes that the guiding principle of alternative tourists is to put as much distance between themselves and mass tourism in trying to establish more contact with the local population, without a reliance on tourist infrastructure, in utilizing the same accommodation and transport facilities as the local population.

This is directly related to sustainability – and, by implication, sustainable development – which is, despite its ambiguity, fundamental to the positioning of any touristic experience as alternative. Sustainability

Table 2.1. Features of alternative tourism.

- The attempted preservation, protection and enhancement of the quality of the resource base which is fundamental to tourism itself.
- The fostering and active promotion of development, in relation to additional visitor attractions and infrastructure, with roots in the specific locale and developed in ways which complement local attributes.
- The endorsement of infrastructure, hence economic growth, when and where it improves local conditions and not where it is destructive or exceeds the carrying capacity of the natural environment or the limits of the social environment whereby the quality of community life is adversely affected (Cox, 1985, pp. 6–7).
- Tourism which attempts to minimize its impact upon the environment is ecologically sound, and avoids the negative impacts of many large-scale tourism developments undertaken in areas which have not been developed previously (Saglio, 1979; Gonsalves, 1984; Kozlowski, 1985; Travis, 1985; Bilsen, 1987).
- Tourism which is not exploitative of local populations and where the benefits flow to local residents (Yum, 1984).
- An emphasis on not only ecological sustainability, but also cultural sustainability. That is, tourism which does not damage the culture of the host community, encouraging a respect for the cultural realities experienced by the tourists through education and organized 'encounters' (see Holden, 1984).

requires the establishment of baseline data from which change and rates of change can be measured (World Commission on Environment and Development, 1987; World Wide Fund for Nature, 1992). The polemic Bruntland Report (World Commission on Environment and Development, 1987) brought the concept of sustainable development into the international arena, somewhat contentiously defining it as: 'development that meets the needs of the present without compromising the ability of future generations to meet their own needs' (Mieczkowski, 1995, p. 457). In the present context, environmentally sustainable tourism has come to be identified fundamentally with alternative tourism (see Chapter 1). Similarly, Butler (1991) defines it as a 'form of tourism that supports the ecological balance', suggesting 'a working definition of sustainable development in the context of tourism as: tourism which is developed and maintained in an area (community, environment) in such a manner and at such a scale that it remains viable over an indefinite period and does not degrade or alter the environment'.

Thus, in its most general sense, and for conceptual clarity in what follows, alternative tourism can be broadly defined as forms of tourism that set out to be consistent with natural, social and community values and which allow both hosts and guests to enjoy positive and worthwhile interaction and shared experiences.

Commodification and the Tourism Industry

The system of production within the tourism industry (see Stear *et al.* 1988, p. 1 for definition of the tourist industry) is now considered one of the world's most powerful driving forces.

---

[8] The processes of interaction and impact that occur through the two-way social exchange occurring between the community and the alternative tourist (see Colton, 1987; McNeely and Thorsell, 1989; Kutay, 1990; Mason, 1990; Sofield, 1991) is presented as an important element of the tourist experience. While there are a number of methods to determine impact – the most common are those which determine 'carrying capacity' (see Stankey *et al.*, 1985; O'Reilly, 1986; Shelby and Herberlein, 1986; Smith, 1989; Cronin, 1990; Chan, 1993) – the concept is still problematic. Methods need to be developed which are able to identify areas of major social and biological components and determining methods for measuring specific parameters of capacity for tourist, host community and protected areas.

UCB Summer Row Library
Tel: 0121 243 0055
Birmingham B3 1JB

Borrowed Items 03/10/2012 11:58
Ogundipe, Temilola Oreoluwa

Item Title	Due Date
111783	
Volunteer tourism experiences that make a	24/10/2012

Thank you for using this unit
www.ucb.ac.uk

Stear *et al.* (1988, p. 1) provide this definition of the tourism industry: '[a] collection of all collaborating firms and organizations which perform specific activities directed at satisfying leisure, pleasure and recreational needs. It includes only those firms that are purposefully performing specific production and marketing activities which are directed at the particular needs of tourists. To be a firm within the tourism industry the firm must have a vested interest in tourism [and] do things to cause tourism in terms of both its volume and its qualitative aspects'.

Through mergers and concentrations, companies considered a part of the tourism industry have become agents of an interconnected network penetrating many sectors. The transnationals of tourism utilize strategies of capital internationalization in a system of tourist production that has evolved into network companies who operate globally (Dunning and McQueen, 1983). Decisions for whole regions or countries are made inside one company. This system aids the integration of regions and communities into the international whole, as the host culture, society and identity become mass products when this form of tourism enters a country. These forms of international tourism are a powerful force in the universalization of culture and society. To accept it means not only the welcoming of foreign vacationers and their currency, but also access to international planning, technology and finance, entering the world economy and approaching world modernity. One cannot understand volunteer tourism without this view of reality.

Marketing articulates supply and demand within a market economy, and societies embracing international tourism are plunged into this international system. Unlike other industries, the 'products' of the tourist industry are a pastiche of formerly homogeneous elements amalgamated by advertising for tourist consumption. Combined symbiotically, they include: services (lodging, dining, transportation and recreation); culture (folklore, festivals and heritage); and less palpable things such as hospitality, ambience and ethnicity. International tourism promotion, aimed at economic development, requires every location to offer something unique. By this logic, each country or region must produce and publicize its unique identity, with each 'new recognition' signifying superiority. Widespread marketing research determines what this image should be, matching aspects of local identity with the desires of its potential clients. The seduction of identity defines the seductive attributes and crystallizes them in an advertising image such that even locals may eventually recognize themselves in it (see Carpenter, 1973).

Significantly here, it must be asked whether contemporary tourism offers an overdetermined capitalist form of escape or a site of struggle and resistance. Is it folly in this respect to view tourist experience as paving the way towards self-realization or 'consciousness raising'? (Rojek, 1993, p. 212). The separation of this problematic notion is fundamental to the conjunction of tourism and its commodification in the consideration of personal development as an element of alternative tourism. If the subject, 'the self', and 'consciousness-raising' are themselves open to contrasting and changing interpretations, the opportunity may exist to move beyond consumerism, commodification and determinism in looking at volunteer tourism experiences.

Mass tourism appears to operate efficiently in the market system particularly where there are few or no regulations to infringe on operations. Lea (1993, p. 702) suggests that this is leading to unacceptable impacts on social and cultural values in some developing countries, thus threatening the sustainability of tourism itself. If the market system is seen as dominating the entire process of tourism, then all experiences may be predicated on this approach. However, if areas of difference can be identified, then the possibility exists for approaches to, and provision of, alternative forms of tourism and for its attendant infrastructure to be explored.

In a market system, economic principles provide the primary means of measurement and the organizational epistemologies which orient and subtend the tourism system as a whole, despite varying regional differences in emphasis. In contrast, but operating necessarily within such a system, alternative forms of tourism re-prioritize these operational principles. It is the conflict of interests engendered between these approaches that can often lead to a mutually exclusive operating environment. Fundamentally, tourism in the market economy uses and exploits natural resources as a means of profit accumulation in the commercialization of the human desire to travel.

The arguments surrounding modernity suggest that in the capitalist society of the late 20th century, commodification of experience occurs to an overwhelming extent, and in this respect the promise of obtaining intrinsically satisfying experiences habitually eludes us. Commodification, within this argument, constructs needs which are fundamental in a consumer society, relying on and constructing unsatisfied need in order to foster demand.

Simmel's insights into the modern metropolis illustrates this process. The 'metropolis' for Simmel (1978) is the epitome of industrialized society, characterized by a personality type, the division of labour through production and consumption, and dominated by monetary exchange. Human beings living within it are subjected to an increase in nervousness requiring the development of psychological defence mechanisms to distance the shock experience of urban existence, including, for example, the encounters with innumerable persons in the course of a day. As a consequence, individuals become 'blasé', experiencing all things as being of an equally dull and grey hue. However, there is a thirst for increasing amusement and greater excitement which has not been satisfied by the fleeting, intense stimulations of the city (Simmel, 1978).

Against this background, Simmel (1978) is critical of those 'fillings-in of time and consciousness' which lie outside the sphere of work and which constitute leisure. Individuals in the city still wish to assert their individuality and differentiation through leisure pursuits, while seeking to belong to their own social group and its lifestyle (Frisby, 1989). New fashions for old distractions and stimulations constitute an essential part of leisure consumption, and this rapidity of turnover in fashions is ever increasing. Sites of entertainment in all modes are devoted increasingly to the titillation of the senses and intoxication of the nerves by colour, glamour, light, music and, above all, sexual excitement. Simmel (1978, p. 376) suggests that a range of sites, such as world exhibitions, trade exhibitions and large shopping malls, are where this predominantly occurs. The effect of the concentration of a world of commodities in a confined space is to overpower, disorientate and hypnotize the individual whilst the ostentatious presentation is appropriate to the stimulation of over-excited and exhausted nerves.

The ultimate commodified leisure escape today can be seen in specific forms of tourism, where travel to far distant and different places is held out as 'paradise gained' (the return is never presented as 'paradise lost!'). Perhaps the ultimate example of this commodification is the photographing of such experiences in an attempt to possess them and make them desirable. The image becomes all important, the personal experience of secondary consequence. As Jamieson (quoted in Bennett, 1988, p. 17) points out:

> The American tourist no longer lets the landscape 'be in its being' as Heidegger would have said, but takes a snapshot of it, thereby transforming space into its own material image. The concrete activity of looking at a landscape – including, no doubt, the disquieting bewilderment with the activity itself, the anxiety that must arise when human beings, confronting the non-human, wonder what they are doing there and what the point or purpose of such a confrontation might be in the first place – is thus comfortably replaced by the act of taking possession of it and converting it into a form of personal property.

It is within the context of contemporary touristic practices that questions arise as to the possibility of alternative forms of tourism, as leisure in modern society is conceived not only as 'free time' but also as 'freely chosen activity' (Roberts, 1978) and as 'self-enhancing experience' (Kelly, 1982). However, as Clarke and Critcher (1985, p. 232) argue, its commodification constrains rather than enhances freedom.

'Broader questions of freedom and control', they say, 'have been narrowed around the right to consumer choice'.

Glasser (1976) applies a similar argument to the notion of identity itself. He claims that the overriding compulsion governing actions and attitudes of individuals is the pursuit of a desired identity. In earlier societies, an ideal culturally constructed identity was promulgated and facilitated by religious observances or shamanistic practices. Today, the pursuit of a desired identity, he says, has been channelled into consumerism through the circulation of an ideal consumer whose main 'freely chosen' leisure activity is consumption.

The tourist, in this view, can therefore, never achieve what they seek and the experience becomes a tranquillizer rather than raising awareness in attempting to cancel out the stress of life. The individual is left with an unsatisfactory and unending search for some form of identity. Glasser (1976, p. 43) claims that:

> While the high priests of old aimed at an unchanging model of an ideal identity, the new priesthood aims to mould an *ideal consumer*, one who willingly makes the changes in his (*sic*) life-style demanded by competing marketing policies, accepting too, the idea that his (*sic*) immediate anxieties can be assuaged by buying new and more products, imagining that each piece of emotional comfort so obtained will be long lasting.

Thus, under the guise of a legitimate conservation activity leading to awareness and appreciation of nature and the exploration of the relationship between nature and the self, alternative forms of tourism, such as ecotourism, may themselves be underpinned by the consumption of nature in modern society.

Campbell (1983), following Weber, argues that the 'spirit' of modern consumerism rests upon an attitude of restless desire and discontent which produces consumption as an end in itself. Romanticism, he claims, conceived of as a 'cultural movement which introduced the modern doctrines of self-expression and fulfilment', is the most likely source of an ethic which legitimates such a spirit. Thus the 'romantic ethic' of the enlightenment provides a contradictory and compensatory ethic to the self-disciplinary future orientation of the Protestant work ethic, but one which is necessary for perpetual consumption. Campbell (1983) suggests that the two contradictory ethics have been accommodated in contemporary society by separating out the sphere of leisure, with its emphasis on self-expression and fulfilment, from the sphere of work, with its self-denying disciplinary ethic. In this respect, alternative tourism experiences, such as those provided by ecotourism, may not in themselves legitimize nature as an entity but may simply provide another avenue for overtly consumptive leisure practices.

These ideas provide a key tension for this book. They are unlikely to be answered conclusively but they will be explored necessarily with a view to providing a better understanding of the difficulties that exist in moving towards an understanding of volunteer tourism experiences.

The following section examines several of the underlying tenets and structural principles of the tourism industry in order to provide a specific context for tourist experience at the industry level. This analysis will provide an inclusive context for the idea of volunteer tourism.

Volunteer Tourism and the Tourism Industry

A range of institutions and organizations, such as Earthwatch, Community Aid Abroad and Youth Challenge International, play a role in providing tourism experiences that fall outside the boundaries of what is generally considered to be mass tourism. The type of organizations that fall generally in the volunteer category of experiences often provide international support and sponsorship for the implementation of research projects and community development. These organizations have operating philosophies and processes that use resources that may not otherwise be available to mass tourism – such as fundraising – as their infrastructure requires and uses different resource bases. Such a focus allows for the provision of experiences that are not generally encompassed in the analysis of mass tourism experiences – such as volunteerism, community development and personal development. Whelan (1991), for example, identifies organizations that recruit participants with free time and money to spend on sustainable development efforts, and it is such organizations that provide the boundaries for examining alternative tourism experiences.

Against this background, a United Nations study stated: 'international realities today and in the foreseeable future, therefore, point to the importance of paying increased attention to programmes fostering the participation of youth in development' (United Nations, 1975, p. 34). Therefore, the tourism industry may gain from having an understanding of the history of these types of organizations that have contributed to the provision of the tourism experience being sought by the youth who become involved.

An examination of the impacts of tourism industry practice[9] can shed some light on how the provision of alternative tourism experiences relate to it. The power relationships present in modern mass tourism practices, and the emerging resistance to these practices, provide a useful arena to discuss the context of alternative tourism.

While Stear *et al.*'s (1988) definition of the tourism industry (p. x) defines firms as private companies or enterprises whose existence is focused on profit motives, the definition itself is broad enough to encompass organizations that operate with other objectives. For example, organizations can operate with a focus on achieving such objectives as conservation, community development and personal development, offering a range of experiences that engage the tourist in experiences aimed at developing values that are not focused simply on the pleasure of the experience, or the desire to escape from day-to-day existence. Therefore, the definition is inclusive of organizations such as Earthwatch and One World Travel, whose primary focus is beyond normal profit motives and potentially differs from the mass tourism operators such as Thomas Cook Travel.

However, it often becomes difficult to differentiate alternative tourism modalities in terms of industry organizations. Ecotourism, for example, has been labelled pejoratively as 'green imperialism' and as an 'eco-missionary' by Dowden (1992), as 'eco-colonialism' by Cater (1987) and 'eco-imperialism' by Hall (in Cater and Lowman, 1994). In this respect, ecotourism, in its development and infrastructure, might be considered not to be differentiated significantly from other forms of tourism development and it could be argued that it falls into the range of commodified tourism products as explained in the preceding section. As an industry and a leisure activity, tourism generally revolves around the production and consumption of cultural difference and so the thirst for 'nature' and other 'cultures' can be viewed as an endless attempt to commodify them by capturing an 'essence', but never really succeeding because it is an experience that provides only a fleeting gaze (see Urry, 1990).

Post-industrial patterns of consumption have enabled the use of mass tourism as a vehicle for the packaging of developing nations' cultures as 'commodities of difference', filling a commercially created need in the mass consciousness through the effective ability of developed nations to monopolize market forces, thus changing the shape of developing nations' communities.[10]

Authors, such as Fussell (1982), have talked of the artificialities of this type of tourism experience, and Turner and Ash (1975) describe it

---

[9] The infrastructure the tourism industry establishes, in the provision of tourism experiences, causes a variety of effects on the natural, social, cultural and economic environments of destination areas and host communities. Lea (1988) maintains that tourism has stimulated growth in these environments with obvious economic benefits for the host community. However, the negative physical, social and cultural impacts are often ignored by host communities and operators pursuing economic returns. Butler (1991), in aligning the effects of tourism growth with Hardin's (1968) *Tragedy of the Commons*, argues that the tragedy which befell common resources was the inevitability of destruction due to the lack of assigned responsibility. This was brought on by each individual user standing to benefit, in the short term at least, by deliberately exceeding the limits of the resource. This is true in the case of tourism experiences as the resource is the major factor on which the experience is built. If the physical, social and cultural environments decline, significant impacts on the individual experience of the tourist will occur, depending on the specific microsocial influences, background and type of tourist (or the niche market into which they fit).

[10] Crandell (1987, p. 374) argues that indigenous cultures that have changed little for centuries are threatened by the powerful influences of western culture that often accompany the arrival of mass tourism in the developing world.

as a 'plague of marauders', with other authors commenting on its consumptive focus (Murphy, 1985; Krippendorf, 1987; Urry, 1990) in the construction of 'commodities of difference', which are created through the re-arrangement and trivialization of cultural ceremonies, festivals, and arts and crafts to meet the needs and expectations of the tourist. Culture is consumed, photographed and taken home as a memento of the tourist's brush with difference. Affluent 'cultural tourists' visit 'exotic' destinations in relatively poorer countries or developing nations[11] and, in doing so, often quite inadvertently cause considerable damage to the ecology, cultural lifestyle and economies of the host communities.

Failure by some operators to change their operating philosophy and general behaviour has seen not only the ongoing degradation of already overburdened developing nation tourist destinations, but a move by the promoters of mass tourism to the comparatively pristine environments found in many developing nations. Greenwood (1989) suggests that this form of tourism initially establishes footholds in developing countries by promising increased prosperity for the government of the day and the host communities; this, however, seldom results. Culture becomes a pre-packaged commodity, priced and sold like fast food and room service, as the tourism industry inexorably extends its grasp (Greenwood, 1989, p. 179).

Conversely, it is argued that the promotion of tourism experiences to developing nations is a form of global income redistribution. Money is made available to developing nations through tourism, thus allowing developing countries to acquire the foreign exchange needed to purchase technology, resources and infrastructure from developed countries (Wasi, in Srisang, 1991, p. 54). Ascher (1985) and Lea (1993), however, suggest that much of the income and perceived benefits generated by mass tourism 'leaks out' to the large, multinational companies in the developed countries from which the operators come. This occurs through the corporate industry structure that is both vertically and horizontally integrated, for example where one multinational corporation owns an airline, the tour buses, the hotel restaurant and recreational facilities. Profits in many of these cases are returned to the multinational's 'mother' country (Trask, 1991). It is generally accepted

[11] 'Developing nation' is taken in the context of this book synonymously with the usage of 'Third World'. Developing nations (see Sachs, 1995 on underdevelopment) are seen generally as those nations with very little political or economic power in the world system, and within which the majority of the communities have little financial or other means to satisfy much more than the most basic of human needs. These nations can be seen to be marginalized and disempowered from, or peripheral to, the system of international relations in which the wealthy, industrialized, western nations of the world participate. It is through the recognition of their disempowered status that many host communities, particularly indigenous ones, can be seen to have developing country status.

by these authors that only a minor percentage of tourist expenditure remains in the country.

Thus, multinational organizations have the power and resources to control the tourism industry on a global scale. Profits to local communities are reduced further through the importation of specialized goods and services which cater to the needs of the tourists. Key management positions are often held by outside management companies, subsequently reducing the career opportunities and control local people have over their resources. Hong (1985, p. 25) contextualizes this further and suggests that international tourism requires high capital investment and expensive infrastructure necessitating heavy borrowing for developing nations in order to finance these projects.

To date, few of the rare organized resistances by locals against foreign-owned, often multinational organizations, dominating all aspects of the tourist trade, have been effective. The apparently attractive, definitely sophisticated offers by corporations such as 'Holiday Inn' and 'Club Med' all too often result in little real financial benefit to the host communities (Ascher, 1985; Lea, 1988, 1993).

Responses to the effects of mass tourism have been seen in the limited formation of local lobby groups. However, existing local laws and government legislation within affected host nations would seem either non-existent or ineffective in controlling 'protagonist'-designed tourism and its impact on the local populations. There are numerous examples of ways in which developers have used their power bases very effectively. In Costa Rica, foreign investors in tourist hotels can enjoy tax exemption, import all building materials and equipment duty free and have also been the beneficiaries of aid money to help establish business. This is one example of a developing nation's government aiding powerful corporations while siphoning and diverting precious resources which could have been used to improve the quality of life of the local people (Hong, 1985, p. 21).

The literature discussed above indicates that corporations promoting inappropriate tourism development in developing countries often have little regard for the ways in which their practices impact upon local communities. These corporations are utilizing commodification of destination cultures so as to serve their profit purposes better, often with limited regard for the local community and their culture. This has the concomitant effect that tourist developments often cause displacement of local communities. In relation to privacy, cultural protection, prostitution and environmental protection, there is little evidence of local communities having the education, knowledge or resources to have any effect in protecting their country as a tourist/leisure site, for either themselves or more responsible visiting tourists.

Tour operators from developed nations could be said to view tourism as an arena where individuals have certain autonomy over their lives, free from the disciplines of work and the responsibilities of home. However, as Clark and Critcher (1985, p. 16) classify it in politico-economic terms, the choice of what appears to the consumer as a multiplicity of tourism experiences is fundamentally only competing brands of leisure goods.

It must be asked whether it is possible for alternative tourism experiences legitimately to incorporate an ethos that diverges from the forms of tourism discussed above. If demonstrable alternatives to market-driven tourism ideologies are identifiable, there may in fact then be a considerable scope for the provision of forms of tourism experience with significantly divergent outcomes. These may take the form of alternative infrastructure and pricing mechanisms, increased community involvement or lower forms of impact. It is within this context that this book desires to place volunteer tourism.

To a large extent, individual preconceptions of travel destinations are based on information found in a variety of media utilized in the marketing of destinations, such as television or print advertising in the form of brochures. Many organizations that fit within the volunteer tourism context, however, rely on interactions with people actively involved with the programmes. Therefore, in both instances, socially constructed and culturally determined perceptions of 'difference' appropriate to specific social arenas are shared through the internalization of the representational forms. As Urry states: 'Their Western-centred discourses, their wide-eyed cameras, construct the rest of the World as there for us,' serving to exemplify how 'the consumption of cultural difference is socially organised and systematised' (Urry, 1990, p. 1). Thus, what is portrayed as seemingly natural is in fact in the process of historical and contemporary construction through a complex system of mass media and social interaction. When this process becomes dominated by operators focused on selling by volume, as in the case of mass tourism, there can be a distancing of the tourist from the reality of the visit, particularly visits to developing countries on which they have little information.

Of course, where large numbers of tourists are involved, more indirect communication of information is achieved through various forms of mass media. In the case of mass tourism, a code of ethics for tourists could possibly be sent to the intending tourist to ensure a better awareness of the issues surrounding their travel destination (see Weiler and Johnson, 1991, p. 125) and this could be evaluated using macrosocial methodological approaches focusing on media and information technology. For volunteer tourism and the organizations that are involved, we often see information transferred through direct contact and so an understanding of the social interaction, particularly the microsocial elements of the experience, may provide information that can assist in providing an understanding of the value of direct interaction.

Shifts are occurring in the understanding of tourism. For example, some communities have realized that tourism has negative impacts (Santosa, 1985) and are actively opposing mass tourism. If alternative forms of tourism can be developed and implemented, communities may be able to communicate the reality of their situations through the social interaction that occurs between themselves and the tourist. Again a subtle shift may occur in which alternative tourism practices may be embraced and come to affect travellers' choices that accord with the messages received from communities. For example, in the case of volunteer tourism, the returned participant (tourist) who has spent time within one of these communities may then talk to someone interested in obtaining information on volunteering (which is often the case for volunteer organizations). A transfer of information is effectuated that is more direct than through a brochure, possibly conveying messages about impacts in a more profound way.

In this respect, it has been found that Aboriginal people as host communities feel that direct interaction with the tourist could become a powerful tool in enabling the explanation of their culture, political motivations, objectives and problems to the broader community (see Altman, 1987). Bates and Witter state:

> It is the tourists who actively seek out Aboriginal people, places and things. They are our greatest audience. Overseas tourists can apply international pressure, and Australian tourists can provide internal political support . . . [t]he tourist industry which presently exploits our culture is big business. It is very important that we have some influence over this industry, especially in national parks. We must work towards having real control over our sacred places and have a say about what information is given out about us.
>
> (Bates and Witter, 1992, p. 219)

The notion of communication through direct contact creating change was recognized as far back as 1980 when the World Council of Churches decided that alternative ways of travel were needed to return tourism to the people so that the experience of travel could enrich all (Holden, 1984). Organizations have since been able to provide alternative tourism experiences that do not necessarily fall into the general ideas that surround mass tourism, such as working for more altruistic goals.

This chapter has explored alternative tourism experiences within the context of wider discussions about culture and society, arguing that alternative tourism could be best defined by the experiences of the alternative tourist. Some of the subtle differences that exist between the ideas inherent to mass tourism and those of alternative forms of tourism such as volunteer tourism have been explored.

While it is possible to provide alternative tourism experiences (such as those potentially promised by volunteer tourism), based on ideologies that purport to differ from those inherent in mass tourism, these ideologies are in contrast to those provided by an industry premised on consumer capitalism operating within the 'world' market economy. The alternatives are available to offer a wider range of socially, environmentally and economically sensitive options for the industry itself and society as a whole to explore and support. This may take the form of alternative infrastructure and pricing mechanisms, increased community involvement or lower impact types of tourism and so offer new directions for tourism.

The examination of the commodifying practices of the tourism industry has illustrated how the provision of alternative tourism experiences may achieve some change in practice in this industry, especially with the power relationships present in modern mass tourism and the emerging resistance to these practices.

Alternative tourism is not only a part or subset of mass tourism where tourism operators are using an alternative tourism label such as ecotourism to market conventional ventures. A focus on the symbolic meanings and values they associate with alternative activities shows that alternative tourism can be differentiated from mass tourism through organizations such as Contours, Community Aid Abroad, ECTWT and YCI. It is the latter of these that provides a background for an analysis of the elements of volunteer tourism in the next chapter.

Chapter 3

Volunteer Tourism Experiences

Youth Challenge International (YCI) is a youth and community development non-profit organization committed to undertaking projects and programmes in developing nations. The programme has evolved from a tradition of overseas volunteer organizations that work on projects of community service, medical assistance and scientific discovery. This organization will be used as a case study to develop a better understanding of alternative tourism experiences.

Youth Challenge International (YCI)

The YCI programme evolved from the concept developed by Operations Drake (1978–1980) and Raleigh (1984–1989) which originated in England with the patronage of Prince Charles and administered by Colonel John Blashford-Snell. These programmes provided the opportunity for over 4000 17- to 25-year-olds from all over the world to work on different projects of community service, medical assistance and scientific discovery in over 30 countries.

These types of programmes focus on the personal development potentiality in tourism which, in the past, have not been construed specifically as tourism organizations. However, the programmes and approaches of Operation Drake and Operation Raleigh provided outdoor group activities, focusing on scientific study, community and health projects. Prince Charles hoped that 'apart from making a modest contribution towards encouraging conservation of our natural resources', it would give volunteers the opportunity, 'to work and live amongst people of other countries and contribute towards a better understanding of one another' (Chapman, 1982, p. 7). Specific elements of the programmes are fundamentally aligned to tourism, with rafting trips, mountaineering, and scuba diving included, usually led by skilled military or civilian staff from different nations.

YCI projects seek to be locally identified and sustainable, while providing the participants – 'challengers' – an opportunity to learn about and be involved in development issues. These projects incorporate many of the key elements considered essential to the underlying concept of volunteer tourism:

- the long-term involvement and commitment of host countries in identifying projects and involving local participants;
- specialist staff involved in implementing training courses on language, culture and development issues for staff and participants in their home countries and during projects; and
- the on-going encouragement of youth to be active, responsible participants in local and global development.

YCI has offices in Guyana, Costa Rica, Australia and the Solomon Islands that are staffed by local representatives. Johnson (1992), in an independent review of Youth Challenge's early projects in Guyana and Costa Rica, indicated that these projects were implemented effectively and provided a valuable learning experience for participants. The funds for YCI projects are generated by the fundraising of the participants, which is supplemented by corporate donations and grants from government and other organizations. YCI has involved over 1200 people in approximately 216 projects throughout Costa Rica, Guyana, the Canadian and Russian Arctic, and the Solomon Islands.

A number of authors (for example, Young, 1973; Hong, 1985; Lea, 1988; Smith, 1989; Urry, 1990) express major concerns about the impact of international tourism, particularly on developing countries. A range of organizations operate into these countries and could be considered across a spectrum encompassing high volume tourism to niche market tourism. It would appear that organizations such as Contours, Community Aid Abroad and ECTWT – as examples of organizations corresponding to niche markets given their operating philosophies – require differing infrastructure support from that of mass tourism, which is generally associated with the negative impacts on the sustainability of the destination. This chapter contextualizes YCI within this spectrum,[12] enabling the creation of a framework that allows for the elaboration of the relevant elements that contribute to the provision of the experience itself.

The adoption of a broader conceptual framework for the understanding of alternative tourism practices, in relation to an operator like YCI, allows for the complexity of interactions that make up the touristic relationship, specifically those between developed and 'other' cultures

(Silver, 1993) found in international tourism, to be better understood. The complexity of cross-cultural issues inherent to the tourist experience are often omitted in the analysis of tourism. The adoption of a broader conceptual framework may allow the exploration of these relational issues and their consideration in the tourist experience.

Silver (1993, p. 305) suggests that marginalized communities have rarely (if at all) had their 'voices heard' (Spivak and Harasym, 1990), i.e. the host communities who are the recipients of mass tourism have little or no ability to influence its construction. Crick (1991, p. 7) and Said (1976) provide particular critiques of this position from what could be characterized as a 'Foucauldian' (see O'Hanlon and Washbrook, 1992, p. 172) in the analysis of the centrality of power whereby the exchange between discourse and power is fundamental to the way in which developing countries are advertised and sold in the tourist literature.

YCI is a non-profit organization, seeking, as one of its primary goals, community development by attempting to encourage support at the local level. This includes both the place of origin and the destination; thus its operating philosophy seeks joint venture approaches which are community based, driven by local needs and encourage equal exchange and shared learning. In this way, there is a concerted attempt at establishing a practice that attempts to provide some equity in the exchanges of power for those in developing countries while still providing viable experiences to the participants involved.

Introducing the Interacting Elements

The ecotourism element

Ceballos-Lascurain (personal communication, 1987) is widely acknowledged as having first coined the term ecotourism in 1981. He used the word in 1983 in discussions as president of PRONATURA, a conservation non-government organization (NGO) and as director general of SEDUE, the Mexican Ministry of Urban Development and Ecology. At the time, he was lobbying for the conservation of rainforest areas in the Mexican state of Chiapas. One of the arguments he used for maintaining the integrity of the forests was the promotion of ecological

[12] Organizations such as YCI, Contours, Community Aid Abroad and ECTWT provide specific forms of tourism experiences. However, other organizations that operate in a more commercial manner, such as World Expeditions and Adventure Travel, often can be aligned by some overlap in the elements of the experiences provided — such as group size or in attempts to meet sustainable and ethical criteria — thus demonstrating the subtle differences that may influence the alternative tourist experience. If looked at in terms of an (Recreation) Opportunity Spectrum, all these organizations fall toward the alternative tourism end of the spectrum and so offer useful information on industry scope and structure and the type of experience provided, thus enabling specific contextualization of YCI.

tourism in the region. He emphasized that ecotourism could become a very important tool for conservation.

The first appearance of the word in the written form was in the March–April 1984 edition of *American Birds* in an advertisement for a tourist operation initiated by Ceballos-Lascurain. His definition first appeared in the literature in 1987 in a paper entitled 'The Future of Ecotourismo' which was reprinted in the *Mexico Journal* of 27 January 1988 (Ceballos-Lascurain, personal communication, 1987) and this definition was expanded upon by Boo:

> We may define ecological tourism or ecotourism as that tourism that involves travelling to relatively undisturbed or uncontaminated natural areas with the specific object of studying, admiring and enjoying the scenery and its wild plants and animals, as well as any existing cultural aspects (both past and present) found in these areas. Ecological tourism implies a scientific, aesthetic or philosophical approach, although the ecological tourist is not required to be a professional scientist, artist or philosopher. The main point is that the person that practices ecotourism has the opportunity of immersing him or herself in nature in a way that most people cannot enjoy in their routine, urban existences . . .
>
> (Boo, 1990, p. 10)

Unfortunately, the last sentence of Ceballos-Lascurain's definition was omitted by Boo and by others who have since quoted him. It reads:

> This person will eventually acquire a consciousness and knowledge of the natural environment together with its cultural aspects, that will convert him (*sic*) into somebody keenly involved in conservation issues.
>
> (Ceballos-Lascurain, personal communication, 1987)

The first part of the definition has been widely discussed and interpreted within both the conservation movement and the tourism industry. After much discussion at international conferences held in 1992,[13] conservationists and responsible tourism operators now believe that conservation is an essential part of the definition. This definition has evolved as a result of these discussions. A popular definition used by The Ecotourism Society in the USA describes ecotourism as 'responsible travel that conserves natural environments and sustains the well-being of local people' (Ecotourism Society, 1992, p. 1).

A number of important basic ecotourism concepts have emerged in recent years. The notion of movement or travel from one location to another is a fundamental component. This travel should be restricted to relatively undisturbed or protected natural areas as ecotourism focuses on the promotion of nature (O'Neill, 1991). Such natural areas offer the

[13] In 1992, three worldwide conferences were held: The United Nations Conference of Environment and Development, Earth Summit; The International Union for Conservation of Nature and Natural Resources (IUCN); and IV World Congress on National Parks and Protected Areas.

'best guarantee for encountering sustained natural features and attractions' (Ceballos-Lascurain, 1990, p. 2). Naturally, some degree of travel must be undertaken in order to reach these areas and must be included in the definition. Thus in 'travel [ling] to unspoilt natural environments . . . the travel has to be for the specific purpose of experiencing the natural environment' (Jenner and Smith, 1991, p. 2). Ecotourism would then seem to exclude such activities as business travel, travel to cities, conventional beach holidays and sporting holidays, where the experience is not focused on the natural environment of the area visited.

Ceballos-Lascurain (1990, p. 1) suggests that 'the pressures of urban living encourage people to seek solitude with nature' and therefore, 'the numbers of visitors to national parks and other protected areas continue to rise'. Ecotourism is considered nature dependent, and some argue that it should involve active nature appreciation, education or interpretation (see Mieczkowski, 1995 for a general overview of definitions). Other activities occurring in natural environments, such as hunting and white water rafting, are more difficult to locate within this context and require further evaluation before consideration. The ecotourist generally expresses a strong desire to learn about nature on their trips (Eagles *et al.*, 1992), hence some authors place greater emphasis on nature appreciation, education and interpretation, and the explanation of 'concepts, meanings and inter-relationships of natural phenomena' (McNeely and Thorsell, 1989, p. 37). Ecotourism also seeks to generate revenue while at the same time protecting vulnerable natural resources (see O'Neill, 1991, p. 25; Wheeler, 1992).

Specific nature-based experiences within the western market economy may be delicately balanced and difficult to differentiate. For example, the intrinsic pleasure which comes from being closer to nature, focusing on the education/interpretation elements rather than equipment-based activities such as rafting, and contributing in some way to conservation, does not necessarily mean that the visitor is having less impact (see Williams, 1990; Butler, 1992; Pigram, 1992; Mieczkowski, 1995).

Ecotourism, therefore, is conservation led and, as a segment of the tourism industry, it has emerged as a direct result of 'increasing global concern for disappearing cultures and ecosystems' (Kutay, 1990, p. 34). Fundamentally, the central concept revolves around people experiencing natural areas and their respective local communities first-hand, thus the potentiality exists that they will be more likely to be concerned with preserving them (O'Neill, 1991). Mass tourism, on the other hand, historically errs towards 'inappropriate tourism development . . . and can degrade a protected area and have unanticipated economic, social or environmental effects on the surrounding lands' (Ceballos-Lascurain, 1990, p. 1).

Boo (1990) uses the term 'nature tourism' synonymously with ecotourism. However, it is argued here that the terminology is not so easily transposable because not all nature tourism endeavours to preserve natural ecosystems, whereas a fundamental defining principle of ecotourism is this very issue. In addition to this, some forms of volunteering can be considered ecotourism but the focus of volunteering is not necessarily on the natural environment. The establishment of a conceptual framework that explores these inter-relationships may help clarify the correspondences between the two and their relationship to mass tourism.

Additionally, it is believed that ecotourism will 'contribute to a sustainable future' (O'Neill, 1991, p. 25) in the form of equitable economic returns. It is intended that the ecotourist who is affected by the experience will want to ensure that the environments visited are maintained sufficiently for the benefit of others. In this way, 'ecotourism has the potential to foster conservation of natural resources by increasing the awareness in people of the importance of the natural resources' (Swanson, 1992, p. 2), and for this reason the notion of conservation must be included in a definition of ecotourism. Ecotourism, therefore, 'promotes a greater understanding and respect of cultures, heritage and the natural environment – and people usually protect what they respect' (Richardson, 1991, p. 244).

Finally, ecotourism must have an educative role. This educative role refers not only to the tourists themselves but also to industry operators and local communities. As Swanson (1992, p. 3) recognizes: 'Most ecotourists expect discovery and enlightenment from their ecotourism experience' and this is brought about by such factors as; communication, culture, knowledge and information, which have to be conveyed effectively in order to become educative. By their active participation in the experience, ecotourists may be able to be educated to appreciate the importance of natural and cultural conservation. 'The need to disseminate information to tourists on appropriate behaviour in fragile social and ecological settings' is being recognized increasingly as the responsibility of industry operators (Blangy and Epler-Wood, 1992, p. 1). Guidelines presented to tourists before commencing a trip are an example of this. Ecotourism can also provide local people with the opportunity to learn about and use the area and its attractions (Wallace, 1992). It may also stimulate renewed appreciation of the 'unique value of their own cultural traditions' as a result of the interest shown by tourists (Kutay, 1990, p. 40).

According to Williams (1990), excellence in mass tourism is measured by consistency, predictability and uniformity of experience. This benchmark is in fundamental opposition to ecotourism where excellence is measured by discovery, the unexpected and the opportunity to appreciate the diversity of the natural world and human cultures.

The profile of an ecotourist is said to differ in matters of degree and purpose from the profile of an average conventional tourist. Ecotourists are 'relatively affluent, well educated, mature and environmentally-focused' (Williams, 1990, p. 85). Also, according to Eagles *et al.* (1992, p. 1): 'Ecotourists are interested in seeing as much of their money spent on conservation as possible' and they will pay a little extra for a more acceptable product. Some common characteristics in the varying definitions of ecotourism do exist, such as higher income levels, tertiary education, environmental concern and awareness, the desire to travel in small groups and the desire to learn about nature (Kerr, 1991; Eagles *et al.*, 1992). Generally, the scale of ecotourism differs from that of conventional tourism, with most ecotourism operators averaging fewer than 300 clients per year (Ingram and Durst, 1989), rather than an equivalent number per day, or per week, which is the case for some larger conventional tour operators.

The volunteer element

The development of organizational volunteering has occurred without it having been considered as a form of tourism. The modern phenomenon itself appears to have begun in about 1915 (Gillette, 1968; Clark, 1978; Australian Volunteers Abroad, 1989; Beighbeder, 1991, pp. 109–110; Darby, 1994) and has involved a variety of organizations and groups throughout the world, with Australian Volunteers Abroad operating in Australia and similar types of organizations such as the Peace Corps USA, Voluntary Service Abroad NZ and a range of others operating in other countries.

The Organization for Economic Co-operation and Development (OECD) estimates that in 1990, over 33,000 overseas volunteers were involved with projects, primarily in developing countries. The investment in over 18,000 volunteers for 1986 was US$389 million, a growth of 400% since 1976, according to OECD figures (Beighbeder, 1991, p. 103).

International volunteerism generally involves some form of travel and, as this brief outline will demonstrate, the underlying concepts comprising both alternative forms of tourism and organizational volunteering significantly overlap, thus providing for a more specific form of ecotourism which:

- falls outside the context of mass tourism; and
- within a conceptualization that involves altruistically motivated travel.

Significantly, there are a number of organizations in the area of volunteering that have programmes relating closely to the age groups of those involved with YCI. The number of studies (see Dickson, 1976; Clark, 1978; Darby, 1994) that focus on the range of volunteer programmes for the 17- to 25-year-old age group provides a perspective that allows for the elaboration of the relationship between the volunteer and the ecotourist experience (for a detailed account of volunteerism, see Darby, 1994).

It is generally agreed that the volunteer is one who offers service, time and skills to benefit others (Beighbeder, 1991, p. 109), voluntary personal aid for developing communities (Clark, 1978), and gains mutual learning, friendship and adventure (Gillette, 1968). The YCI programme, when viewed as both a volunteer and ecotourist experience, is able to provide a macrosocial context for the SERR experience.

However, it is not suggested that the alternative tourist experience under examination is a panacea or that its simple adoption by mass tourism practice, even if feasible, will lead to equity and sustainability in post-industrial societies' provision of tourism experiences. There have been suggestions that there are enough developed nations already working in developing countries (Chavalier, 1993) and increasing this level through alternative tourist activity, such as ecotourism programmes, is not going to help resolve local problems. One fundamental danger is that volunteers can reiterate the ethos of the 'expert', thus promoting deference in the local community to outside knowledge, therefore contributing to the curtailment of self-sufficiency.

However, a tourist experience that allows for the opportunity to live and work with people of another culture may provide a modality of alternative tourism that is able effectively to meet some of the concerns raised by destination communities about the impacts of tourism. Younger tourists are more likely to use the knowledge gained from their volunteer tourism experiences to influence other areas of their lives, such as the choice and development of career paths, particularly if these experiences allow for inclusiveness of issues and impacts that relate to natural environments and destination communities.

The research in the area of volunteerism has shown that people working and living together on jobs of social significance develop understanding and friendships that are more important to them than the physical construction (Clark, 1978, p. 13). Whatever the genesis of the programme, it is the personal encounter between the volunteer and the community that is essential (Clark, 1978, p. 4). For example, Beighbeder (1991, p. 104) has identified the dynamic of: 'Helping others to help themselves', and has recognized the need to involve those with problems as a part of the process. Many of these ideas are supported in the discussion of ecotourism in the earlier section and will be elaborated upon with specific reference to the data in later chapters.

Additionally, research on international volunteer organizations has demonstrated an orientation towards reviewing the issues around personal development. The links between volunteering and ecotourism possibly can be made more apparent when viewed as leisure experience, and the research on personal development and international development volunteer programmes initially provides us with some background for the idea of alternative tourism experience. These programmes share a number of common features with YCI, including the cultural exchange and international peer exchange/group experience.

In reviewing the international volunteering literature,[14] there is a focus on personal development and the role of learning in changing or influencing the self which introduces to the alternative tourism experience issues relating to self-identity and change. It is proposed that the concept of international volunteering as an element, within the context of the alternative tourism experience, and particularly in relation to the YCI experience, highlights learning as a central element of the interaction with the destination culture and environment. It is this symbiosis of interlocking concepts stemming from the research that has contributed to the second question that orients the book: that is, does this experience influence their (the YCI participants) sense of self and identity?

The research of Weinmann (1983, p. 16) and Carlson (1991), in considering exposure to a new culture, found personal development related to: greater tolerance; a more compassionate understanding of other people and their individual differences; and the gaining of a more global perspective and insight into new values, beliefs and ways of life. Learning components within this exchange included academic learning, the development of personal knowledge, self-confidence, independence, cultural awareness and social abilities.

Stitsworth (1987) similarly indicated that participants, as part of a group for 6 weeks, contributed to their own personal growth and development while gaining a better understanding of the role of developed countries, particularly the issues surrounding development, in experiencing another culture. 'The AFS Impact Study: 1986' (American Field Service, 1986) of over 1000 high school students found that

---

[14] The studies considered the more widely researched area of personal development and the university student, or college experience (Terenzini and Wright, 1987; Kuh *et al.*, 1988; Karen, 1990) as well as personal development through culture shock (Weinmann, 1983). These studies were followed by research on university student study abroad (Kauffman and Kuh, 1984; Carlson *et al.*, 1991); youth programmes and national service (Thomas, 1971; United Nations, 1975); and international youth exchange (American Field Service, 1986; Stitsworth, 1987). Studies of international development experience include, specifically, youth-based Canadian Crossroads International and Operation Raleigh USA (1989) as well as government-based volunteer programmes: United States Peace Corps (1980, 1989), Winslow (1977) and Volunteer Service Overseas (VSA) (Clark, 1978).

participants' greatest amount of positive change was in awareness and appreciation of the host country and culture, and foreign language appreciation and ability. In this way, these studies of volunteering provide an added dimension to the examination of alternative tourism experiences.

Serious leisure element

The time contributed to the participation in international volunteering can be considered voluntary leisure (Stebbins, 1982, 1992; Henderson, 1984) and many organizations rely on this 'free' time in order to operate (Bishop and Hogett, 1986). It is evident that the travel component of volunteerism in YCI and other similar organizations is an essential component of the appeal of organizations operating in developing countries. Rather than travelling simply as a 'tourist', the volunteer may regard travel 'as an activity for the stimulation and development of character' (Foucault, 1983, p. 115). The appeal of travelling with a purpose, working with communities in developing countries and spending time to assist in saving natural environments provides a strong platform for expanding the conceptualization of tourist experience.

Definitions of volunteers necessarily include the recognition that they are those who provide assistance, or unpaid service, usually for the benefit of the community (Australian Bureau of Statistics, 1986). This may be through formal involvement as a volunteer in an organization, and/or independently as an individual. For the purposes of this study, the concept of volunteering is defined as an action perceived as freely chosen, without financial gain and generally aimed at helping others (van Til, 1979; Stebbins, 1982, 1992).

Stebbins (1992), in defining 'serious leisure', uses the fields of amateurism, hobbyist and volunteering to encompass the range of specific characteristics. Similarly, Parker (1992) links 'serious leisure' to a range of activities such as volunteering, suggesting that this affects individual values. Two distinguishing features of volunteering identified by Stebbins that may contribute to our understanding of the YCI experience are that volunteers are usually motivated by a sense of altruism, and that they are often delegated tasks to perform, making them a 'special class of helper in someone else's occupational world' (Floro, 1978, in Stebbins, 1982).

Stebbins (1992, p. 18) suggests that the major characteristics of volunteering can be summarized as:

- a motivation based in altruism and self-interest;
- an institutional role of delegated work; and
- a contribution of helping and satisfaction.

Stebbins (1982, p. 257; 1992, p. 18) also identifies a number of components that contribute to volunteerism, including:

- demonstrated perseverance;
- significant personal effort based on special knowledge;
- training or skill; and
- durable benefits relating to;
  - self-actualization;
  - self-enrichment;
  - recreation or renewal of self;
  - feelings of accomplishment;
  - enhancement of self-image;
  - self-expression;
  - social interaction and belongingness;
  - lasting physical products of the activity; and
  - a unique ethos demonstrating a subculture with intrinsic beliefs, values and norms.

Research (Stebbins, 1982, 1992; Parker, 1992) indicates that some volunteers do not perceive themselves as being 'at leisure', but rather involved in a sense of 'good citizenship concern for the community'. The addition of volunteering to the analysis of alternative tourism experiences enables us to differentiate it from forms of mass tourism that are inclined towards a focus on relaxation and excitement. This is not to deny that relaxation and excitement are not components of alternative tourism experiences, but allows for volunteering as a significant differentiating component.

In order to align the participant in the YCI project to volunteerism in accordance with the outline presented above, it is useful to examine the motivations involved in seeking a volunteer experience. Neulinger (1982, p. 30) and Henderson (1984) both note that volunteerism and leisure fulfil higher level needs such as self-esteem, belonging and self-actualization. In addition, Stebbins (1982, 1992), in examining 'serious leisure', sees 'career volunteering' as a specific example. In his consideration of 'serious leisure', Stebbins points out that it is an important part of people's lives in its relationship to personal fulfilment, identity enhancement and self-expression (Stebbins, 1982, p. 253).

The research[15] on volunteerism which focuses on individual motivation acknowledges that volunteers seek to gain considerable personal benefits from their endeavours, including self-satisfaction and social and personal well-being (Henderson, 1981, 1984; Stebbins, 1982,

[15] A range of research exists in this area (see Phillips, 1982; Allen and Rushton, 1983; Rohs, 1986; Independent Sector, 1990; Luks and Payne, 1991; Darby, 1994).

1992; Frank, 1992). Motivations, such as: (i) being useful (Independent Sector, 1990); (ii) altruism and being needed (Beighbeder, 1991, p. 106); (iii) personal satisfaction; and (iv) being cared for by the organization (Tihanyi, 1991) are all considered important by the volunteers. The YCI experience could be studied within this construct, as a fundamental motivating element for the participant is the desire to assist communities in developing countries.

Volunteer experiences often include long-term educative impacts: '(T)hough not often articulated in a formal sense by participants, learning in these community settings is nevertheless real and substantive' (Whitmore, 1988, p. 53). Whitmore's study outlines a variety of learning statements by community volunteers relating to self; external (outside the community group) knowledge and skills; and internal (within the community group) knowledge and skills. While the motivation to volunteer may imply an altruistic, or 'helping' perspective, the potential learning from such an experience (as shown by Whitmore's 1988 study) can be diverse and influenced by a range of factors.

The literature supports that the consideration of serious leisure – with its component of volunteering – is a defining factor for the alternative tourist experience, and thus becomes an element that provides a significant broadening of the context for the analysis of the YCI experience. For example:

- the time to travel – often the reliance of the participant support to operate organizational elements (see Bishop and Hogett, 1986 on the leisure profession);
- serving communities through leisure (Neulinger, 1982; Henderson, 1984);
- the provision of purpose for leisure (see Roberts, 1981, p. 61 and Stebbins, 1992, p. 19);
- the high correlation between an individual's description of their volunteer efforts and their perception of leisure (Henderson, 1981);
- the degree of involvement and its correlation to commitment and more satisfying and rewarding experiences (McIntyre, 1994).

The early literature that attempted to clarify the concept of leisure (see Wearing and Wearing, 1988) does so without adequately considering the relationship between leisure and natural environments. It focuses instead on the ideas of non-work time and individual activity. It is this limited perspective that serves to obscure elements of leisure, such as volunteerism. A more inclusive approach beyond the simple paradigm of work/non-work serves to query the construction of leisure as individually conceived, arguing instead that it should be built around the microsocial dynamic exchanges that are a part of the participant's experiences. Such an approach allows the incorporation of the interaction of cultural or social influences, such as those between the host community, the participant and the site. Budowski (in Valentine, 1991) draws attention to the two-way interaction between ecotourists and the environment upon which their experience depends, in that the environment consists in part, of the dynamic social exchange that establishes much of the experience of the natural environment. What is at issue here is, fundamentally, the dynamic social exchange between and within social groups (the host community and the tour group) which forms the basis of the participants' experience and the way they construct their ideas of the experience.

Therefore, the consideration of alternative tourism experience must move beyond a conceptualization of it as either simply volunteering or as a leisure activity that is reliant on the polarization of the work/non-work distinction (see Wearing and Wearing, 1988). This does not allow for the complexity of interrelating elements, such as ecotourism, volunteerism and serious leisure. For example, if it is accepted that protected areas such as the SERR are socially constructed and that the organizations and agencies using these areas (and the communities associated with them) in the provision of tourism experiences are social institutions, then it follows that they derive their meanings from social interaction. These interactions may be indirect (through the media for example) or direct (through individual experiences of them).

The elements and interactionism

The alternative tourism experience, contextualized in relation to the differential elements of volunteerism, serious leisure and ecotourism as discussed in the preceding section, promotes interactions within the destination area. Therefore, the destination area (in this case the YCI site in the Santa Elena Rainforest Reserve) and the relational construction of meanings (expressed in this book as social value) allow an analysis that ascribes to protected areas, such as the SERR, boundaries that relate to a process of dynamic social exchange. This may lead to the exploration of new areas, in moving towards approaches to protected area management in developing countries that enable an expansion of the conceptual ideas to include the daily life experiences of the communities outside the protected area boundaries. Research in this context can contribute to future policy as it is able to examine protected areas, local communities and (eco)tourism as socially constructed institutions in the wider social constructs rather than simply as an escape to a natural environment isolated from the social boundaries that construct and define it.

A number of theoretical approaches to tourism indicate the need for a research direction with a more social focus (van Raaij and Francken, 1984; Colton, 1987). As an example, McCool *et al.* (1984,

p. 4) acknowledge that social contexts are a more significant factor in recreation choice processes than generally recognized and understood. A theoretical approach with an interactionist perspective suggests that each group will negotiate the meaning of the natural environment in order to establish the types of experiences they may expect to have when visiting there (see Glaser and Strauss, 1967; Berger and Luckmann, 1981; Strauss and Corbin, 1990). In relation to the YCI experience in particular, this meaning is represented as the social value held by the participant and the host community for the protected area.

The essential premises of interactionism are that human society is characterized by the meanings inherent to cultural exchange. The meanings of various social and non-social objects (symbols) are derived through the social interaction process and modified by each individual. The ecotourist and community member act toward the natural environment (as a symbol) on the basis of the meaning that environment has for them (social value). Furthermore, situations, roles and audiences, including others and reference groups, have meaning and provide the context in which the action or behaviour occurs (Blumer, 1969). The reality of the SERR experience, whether it be interactions with animate or inanimate objects, is enmeshed within the meanings that people assign to the objects in their world.

The community member and the participant experience the world differently and, therefore, ascribe different meanings to their corresponding realities. However, through any social exchange (interaction), there is a subsequent communication of meaning (within a particular field – the experiences of a protected area in this case), and thus the individual perception of reality becomes a socially shared phenomenon. This can be taken further when viewing culture as a consensus norm (agreed upon by the participant and the host community), which is socially produced through the convergence of meanings assigned to common experiences. Objects (such as the protected area itself) are symbols of meaning, and become culturally significant through the communication and assimilation of the meanings assigned to the common experiences that the ecotourist and the host community have with that protected area. Therefore, one key to understanding the experience within this perspective is to explore how individual members (participants and community members) view themselves, their relationships with others, their roles and their construction of the situation. This enables us to explore, for example, how the participant and community member can come to have a shared social value of the protected area, where the community may originally have viewed it as a source of income alone while the participant viewed it as a place to be conserved.

An interactionist perspective, therefore, enables an examination of the individual experience in particular, exploring how this experience is derived from the social values surrounding them – originating in part from the social interaction of the participant and the community members. The need for research based in social psychology and research based in sociology is facilitated through an interactionist approach which significantly elevates the status and significance of the 'other' (such as the host community or the protected area) to the pre-eminence of dominant construct while allowing for the transfer of attitudes between individuals and its effect on identity within a specific temporal and spatial location.

This chapter has described and linked the elements of ecotourism, volunteer tourism and serious leisure in the context of the YCI experience. Through synthesizing these via an interactionist perspective, it can be seen that the role of participants is paramount in all alternative tourist experiences. The next chapter provides an empirical exploration of the volunteer tourist experience.

Chapter 4

Exploring the Experience

> I bring it back down to something a lot more selfish. I did it for me. That aim changed when I got there, with the experience I was having, there was a lot more focus on the people. My original reason for going wasn't the environment or anything else, it was for me, it wasn't even for the experience. It was just to get away and to have a different experience, to take on a risk or changes, just something different. My attitudes and the importance of Santa Elena and the rainforest came home to me a lot more when I was there and when I was doing it. But my original expectation wasn't anything like that.
>
> (Kim, focus group participant)

This chapter presents some first-hand insights gained from interviews with volunteer tourists. It provides information from the volunteer tourists' stories and experiences, and constructs the volunteers' views of their experience by reviewing their recollection of the experience.

The analysis of the volunteers' understanding of their experience requires a definition or framing of the experience in their own words. Before confirmation of the respondents' perception of the main areas of the experience, the volunteers were asked to define the experience in their own terms. From this, a number of themes were constructed that allowed the volunteers' stories to provide the framework for the examination of their experiences.

Their motivations for being involved in the programme were also reviewed to gain some idea of the background each brought to the experience. Motivation is seen as one of the contextualizing elements of the alternative tourism experience, examples including: (i) the motivation to travel as an escape from the workaday world (Rojek, 1993); and (ii) a desire to go 'sightseeing' or gaze at objects either authentic or unauthentic (MacCannell, 1976; Urry, 1990).

For the alternative tourism experience to be established as different from mass tourism experiences (see MacCannell, 1976, 1992; Urry, 1990; Rojek, 1993), it is necessary to examine the elements and themes in the stories of the volunteers. This section seeks to explore the process and learning experience through the stories of the volunteers. The starting point within the literature suggests that the experience should enable the volunteer to experience the 'other' in relief, and often in fundamental opposition to the usual images presented to them in their everyday life. While a developed country provides specific role models and a culture that will allow them to fit into existing social structures, the volunteers' experience itself should allow the examination of the subtle differences that may exist in this experience as opposed to those of mass tourism.

The volunteers' 'stories' have been used to identify the aspects of the experience that they perceive as important in creating clusters and subcategories which help to group together common and repeated outcomes to give an overall perspective of the experience. A discussion of the volunteer is provided to contexualize the experience through the presentation of background, motivations and definitions of the type of experience. The overall aim of this chapter is to establish a general understanding of the volunteer experience, how volunteers constructed it and the assessment of outcomes perceived by volunteers through their recollection of the experience.

The chapter does this through the use of interviews at the recollection stage of the experience, in order to facilitate an understanding (as per Clawson and Knetsch's (1966) process for the recreation experience) of pre-departure elements that relate to anticipation and motivation.

The Volunteers

As with most other social analysis, the personal characteristics of volunteers are considered significant. Table 4.1 provides a list of elements considered of importance to an analysis of the volunteer tourism experience.

The study group consisted of past Australian YCI representatives who participated in the SERR project. They were generally tertiary students with an average age of 21–22 years. The majority of volunteers involved in the study were members of a nuclear family, with their original parents living together (only one participant had separated parents). Family size ranged from one to five siblings, with family and friends generally being supportive of their participation. Experiences of growing up varied widely from country to city environments. The

Table 4.1. Sociodemographic data to be considered.

Age:	On the project
Family status:	Parents and number of siblings
Education:	Type and level of achievement
Growing up:	Key aspects or memories of growing up
Environmental contact:	Things remembered about the environment
Overseas travel:	Travelling experiences
Cultural experiences:	Memories and experiences with other cultures

volunteers were asked to discuss the important influences that led to their becoming involved in YCI.

Parents

> My parents have been another huge influence in this area. Mum and Dad have been a bone of support; having that family structure is incredibly important for wanting to go on and do worthwhile things.
>
> (Jen)

> My family has always travelled and gone camping. They've always encouraged me to be independent . . . my Dad has always been really supportive.
>
> (Pen)

> So after my parents supported me for 4 years throughout university and then when I told them I was going to work in another country for 3 months, they thought that was pretty stupid.
>
> (Ann)

> My parents were also a big influence, they were always very strong dependable people and loving parents . . . so I guess my wanting to go out and help others was generated from my family background.
>
> (Sue)

> My parents were against it when I first wanted to be involved, there was no support . . . and it was just great to say 'I can do it if I want to, this is not you influencing me to do anything'.
>
> (Lil)

The volunteers' parents varied in their support and attitudes to the programme; two of the volunteers felt that their parents did not support them going, three did not comment on the influence that their parents had, while six felt that their parents were very supportive.

Environmental context

We lived right by the coast. I love the sea, being by the water, the nature and I love the life lived, we backed onto a reserve . . . sucking honey dew as they were growing up, that might have influenced them to go down in the bush finding pet snakes. I really loved nature'.

(Jen)

My family has always travelled and gone camping.

(Pen)

I did a lot of bushwalks, we used to disappear into the bushland and make cubby houses.

(Ann)

We lived in a semi-bush, I'm very happy with places like Santa Elena. They're naturally beautiful and I like them probably because I have lived in various places . . . a reasonable amount of time in the bush doing trekking, camping, things like that.

(Mic)

Being on the Murray I'd go on a lot of canoeing trips. A great pasttime was to get Dad to drive up in the car with your lilos and he would drop us there and we would float home, that was a weekend pasttime. Lots of outdoor stuff, playing outside and bike riding . . . trips with Dad. Dad, being a geography teacher . . . he would point out really interesting trees, rock formations and mountain formations, so I had an appreciation of those kinds of things when I was quite young, which was good. He made sure that we had some kind of knowledge of those kinds of things, natural geography and an appreciation and respect for them. Dad was big on plants as well. I don't think we ever had a holiday that was in a motel room or in a caravan. Every holiday was in a tent.

(Meg)

When we were kids, we would go walking and camping . . . definitely a big influence was taking me camping every holiday. I don't think I would be doing what I am now if I hadn't had that exposure when I was a kid. We have always gone to Fraser Island where we learnt a lot about the sand mining and I've always been exposed to that sort of stuff.

(Sue)

I think it surprised a few people how inventive we could be when we were over there. When we were kids, we would make our own cubby house, or make a dam in the creek, we were always playing and looking around trying to find things to do or create.

(Kim)

We went on the annual holiday up the coast, we did a little bit of camping when we were kids, it was a good lifestyle.

(Amy)

Generally, the volunteers appear to have spent time with their family in activities such as holidays or trips in outdoor environments; only one participant did not really spend time in his youth in these environments.

Overseas Travel

> . . . my parents took us on a trip, I wanted to see this volcano, my father said if I go and find the tour and book it, I can go on it, so I did and went. I have done a great deal of travelling as a child . . . all those countries were fantastic.
>
> (Jen)

> When I finished sixth form, I spent a year in England, which included 3 months back-packing with a friend through Europe. In 1989, I left and went to Asia, I had 3 months in Thailand, 4 months in Pakistan, 4 months in India, a couple of months in far western China. Then flew to Hong Kong and worked there for 4 months. I then enrolled for university and went back overseas for 4 months until university started. I went back through Singapore and went to Borneo. I was very interested in going and living in the rain forest . . . I travelled back to Brunei, then to the top of Australia and travelled overland from Darwin to Sydney.
>
> (Mic)

> I've done a fair bit of travelling. When younger, as a family, we did America, Noumea and Europe.
>
> (Lil)

> I've been to New Zealand on a school excursion . . . I lived in Brazil for a year.
>
> (Pen)

Four of the volunteers had overseas travel experience with the family group, while two travelled independently. For the remainder, the YCI programme was to be their first trip overseas.

Cultural experiences

> They had so much to teach you in a very basic sense. From climbing up coconut trees, to living on very subsistence-type foods. In the missions in New Guinea, to see places that were only accessible by foot, you had to wade through rivers to get to them, to see these people giving up their lives to help small communities in terms of medical needs and religious needs. They're all great experiences. I've always taken away with me an admiration and respect for these wonderful people that have given so much and obviously get so much out of doing it. From that point on, I spent about 4 months in Africa, a place of much cultural diversity. In

> Africa I guess you see the other side that you don't so much see in native islands. In Africa, you see how people can be abused by the position they're in, by brute force and coercion, the underdog can be severely disadvantaged, like prostitution, lack of real authoritarian basis and real solid grounds of justice. It's their own system of justice. It's disheartening when you see an innocent person brutalized for no good reason at all.
>
> (Jen)

> Cultural experiences, basically within Australia. The differences between people in Adelaide and people in Queensland are quite different. The way they speak, the way they go about doing things. That's sort of sub-cultural but that was quite noticeably different, they way you speak. Being exposed to Aboriginal people and Torres Strait Islanders in schools, you never see them in Adelaide, so going up there was good. Then as a nurse I got the opportunity to travel to Aboriginal communities. It was good to get involved in that way.
>
> (Ros)

> . . . the big thing for me was living in Brazil, that was when I really got to appreciate a different culture that wasn't westernised.
>
> (Pen)

> A lot of that stems from going to places like Thailand, India or Guatemala and spending time in the natural areas, trekking in rainforests and jungles, spending time around ruins in these areas. So I guess that had all been built in my head; with each experience I was taking more on board as regards to what cultural ideas and values I have, through coming in contact . . .
>
> (Mic)

> I suppose I find other places really challenging and exciting and different. I love different things, different places. The places I have been to were still quite similar – the western culture. I suppose from doing that travelling it did teach me to be culturally sensitive, not to offend people and all those sorts of things. Just the experience of being in different places, but I don't think that any of the places I went to were that amazingly different that it blew me away, there was still that similarity.
>
> (Lil)

> I've had a lot to do with the Aboriginal culture, not because I've gone into it, but because I grew up with it. Other cultures though, not a lot other than living in Sydney, knowing people from other cultures and trying to find out about their cultures.
>
> (Kim)

Generally, the volunteers had a knowledge of other cultures. Those volunteers who had travelled mentioned the cultures they had contact with in those travels, while a number of others mentioned Australian Aboriginal culture.

Similarities and Variations

In order to analyse the data further, a matrix was developed that allowed comparison between all volunteers' personal development and their motivation and backgrounds. A variety of elements were considered for similarities or variations in the outcomes.

Common reasons for participating in the programme (termed motivations in this chapter) consisted of travel and adventure, with the more commonly identified area of personal development, confidence in self and interpersonal awareness/learning. Quite a number of the volunteers considered confidence in themselves and their abilities a main form of personal development. The majority of the volunteers had experience of the outdoors through family, and some had cultural contact that had created an interest. One participant was involved only for the reason that a friend was involved and his background had no notable features that may have motivated him in the way that others were – little travel, minimal cultural contact and no family holidays in the bush.

Decisions to participate in YCI were strongly influenced by past experiences and established patterns of recreation behaviour. These patterns could be traced to the influence of families and friends. These past experiences were characterized by shared perceptions of what YCI might satisfy in their leisure needs (although often variable).

Motivation

Motivation for being involved in the YCI programme and SERR project was reviewed to gain some idea of the background each brought to the experience. In considering the responses, it should be noted that many volunteers acknowledged that they did not have a full understanding of YCI prior to application or any idea about the SERR project. It would appear that many were merely responding to an application form provided for them, and some just arrived in Santa Elena because they were allocated it. However, others saw it as their primary focus:

> Santa Elena was the first thing I heard about in YCI. It was the bit they used to describe YCI and the sheet that they sent out with the information. My background is in landscape/architecture and I wanted to get into all that sort of stuff, ecotourism, and use my landscape architecture in an environmental way. So that definitely sparked it all off and the whole experience of doing community development and volunteer work. Before, I didn't really know much about it, so I went with the idea of helping other communities and stuff like that. It really interested me

> because I was interested in Australian Volunteers Abroad (AVA) but I was too young for that.
>
> (Sue)

The primary source of information on motivation came from the interview question: what originally interested you or motivated you to apply for the YCI programme? The responses to the question were then categorized according to the schema outlined below.

Motivation categories

Altruism

This category included differing levels of idealism relating specifically to concepts such as saving the world and 'doing good', but generally related to helping others. It was based on past community service experience, media images of the development and/or a wish to be involved in community work for the first time in an effort to 'give something back'.

> That was the trigger which made me think I would like to do something of a worthwhile nature and I think the cause is good.
>
> (Jen)

> . . . do something that was worthwhile.
>
> (Ann)

> . . . to do something for another country.
>
> (Meg)

> . . . doing something constructive or helpful, rather than just going and looking.
>
> (Mic)

> . . . doing community development and volunteer work. I'd always thought about doing volunteer work.
>
> (Sue)

> . . . going to a foreign country and doing volunteer work.
>
> (Pen)

> . . . working with them and trying to improve their lives.
>
> (Kim)

Travel/adventure

This category related to the excitement of travel and/or the adventure of going to new places and meeting new people.

> . . . the opportunity to travel.
>
> (Meg)

I was going to travel and see the world sometime.

(Sue)

. . . gave me the opportunity to go somewhere.

(Ken)

I thought about going to Europe and then I decided that I wanted to do something really different.

(Kim)

I think it was the experience of doing something entirely new and entirely different.

(Amy)

. . . was to go somewhere adventurous and come away alive.

(Pen)

. . . wanted to do something like working overseas in a developing country, some sort of adventure or something different.

(Lil)

. . . wanted to go overseas and just see what it was like.

(Mic)

Personal growth

This category related to the participant's wish to seek growth and learning on a personal level. It included the opportunity for cultural exchange or learning along with professional interests.

. . . building my own character, confidence and self-development.

(Jen)

I like to push myself to see what my limits are.

(Ann)

. . . there was that personal development aspect.

(Lil)

I guess to get a sense of achievement at what I was doing.

(Ros)

. . . it was a bit of a growth thing.

(Meg)

. . . more independent and self-assured and sure about who I am.

(Sue)

Cultural exchange/learning

This category was primarily concerned with experiencing local communities along with the sense of sharing the experience with other challengers.

To see local people was another objective.

(Jen)

. . . the other cultures and the difference of being in different cultures.

(Mic)

. . . work with people from other countries.

(Ann)

. . . living and working with people from other countries and forming friendships.

(Sue)

. . . learn about another country.

(Meg)

. . . totally different culture.

(Amy)

. . . get a taste of different culture.

(Kim)

. . . working with communities.

(Lil)

. . . living in a community and live with people.

(Kim)

. . . to take myself out of my own cultural environment and put myself somewhere different.

(Ros)

. . . converse with locals.

(Sue)

. . . learning a lot about other people.

(Sue)

. . . learning about different people's life experiences.

(Kim)

Professional development

This category highlights desire to gain experience of or simply sample a specific field of expertise, and the consideration of development or volunteer work in more detail.

I had done a teaching degree before I left. I wanted to see if I could apply what I learnt while working with kids there in the primary health clinic.

(Ann)

. . . it was the whole area of development, working with communities. I wanted to get some experience with development groups.

(Lil)

I am really keen on outdoor education and the whole thing about working in an outdoor environment. I thought that I would gain experience in that area, that whole outdoor, basic living skills situation.

(Meg)

. . . it was to get experience in the field that I would like to end up working in. So professionally, it's more just involvement, field work experience.

(Ros)

I really thought it would help my course.

(Lil)

I wanted to get experience in community development work, because I was still really keen to do something like AVA and have a career in development work overseas.

(Sue)

The YCI programme

This category gives an indication that it was the structure of the programme and the people involved in the organization which generated the interest.

. . . this really interested me, because it was 3 to 4 months and I was prepared to resign from work or leave work for that period of time . . . working as a team, cooperation versus competition for instance.

(Jen)

I was mid-way through university, I suppose I saw it as an opportunity to go overseas. It fitted in to my 3 months off, I didn't have to defer studies.

(Ros)

Four friends went the year before.

(Meg)

. . . it was for 3 months, which was over my university break.

(Pen)

A friend of mine, Kate, a friend of hers had done it. She mentioned she was going and it just sounded something interesting to do.

(Ken)

I guess for the intensive experience. I wanted to live in a community and live with people.

(Kim)

Right time/right place

A range of personal and social factors led volunteers to believe it 'was the right thing for them'.

> . . . time frame is good.
>
> (Jen)

> It was something that I really wanted to do. I really wanted to get involved in it.
>
> (Pen)

> It was also really well timed because it was the end of university, so it was something to do.
>
> (Ann)

> I was pretty well 100% on the look-out for opportunities of that nature, which involved travel and also work experience and things like that.
>
> (Mic)

> I suppose I was at a point in my life where you are just trying to see things, experience new things, meet new people, go to different places – learn about the world basically.
>
> (Lil)

> I was at that stage of my life where I wanted to move out of home and do things on my own.
>
> (Sue)

However, it is this final quote which serves to encapsulate the complexity of responses:

> I think most people would be lying if they didn't say there was some selfishness in why they were going. Because it was really to benefit themselves, not just the environment and community in Santa Elena, even though it is really important. And that's one of the things I had trouble with at first. I thought that it was really selfish on my part, because I just wanted to go over and see what Costa Rica was like. Helping save a pristine rainforest in Santa Elena as well as helping the community in developing their ecotourism, which is helping save the rainforest ultimately – they were secondary things. But, as you say, when you come back, you think how you benefited a lot out of it and it was really great. When you look at the whole picture, you think well maybe we have affected this community and have possibly saved a cloudforest.
>
> (Ken)

Summary of motivation

A range of reasons emerge that provide information on the motivation of the volunteers for undertaking the programme. The volunteers consistently mentioned altruism and travel/adventure as significant motivational influences. The majority of volunteers previously had been involved in a volunteer capacity. Those who had actively volunteered in the past identified these experiences as being an influence, and the consideration of professional options in this area was similarly a motivating factor. Of the volunteers who had not been overseas before, travel was not their main motivation. Those who had travelled before were keen to repeat the experience due to the learning and adventure that they associated with past trips. The other category of motivation mentioned by the majority of the volunteers related to details of the YCI programme itself.

The participants' motivation can be categorized by the following terms: altruistic, travel/adventure, the YCI programme, personal growth and right time/right place. The participants' background indicated a tertiary educated group with an average age of 21–22 years, predominantly from the Sydney metropolitan area.

Generally, there was considerable diversity in the expectations of the project. For example:

> I didn't have any expectations of what the project was going to be like.
>
> (Ken)

> I think I imagined the cultural experience, the mix of people and the type of food and the type of lifestyle, that was more or less how I expected it to be. The actual landscape and the forest in Santa Elena was more or less how I imagined it.
>
> (Ros)

> The rainforest itself, I didn't expect it to be anywhere near as beautiful.
>
> (Amy)

> I suppose I had a vision that Santa Elena was going to be the most beautiful place.
>
> (Lil)

> I didn't know what to expect.
>
> (Kim)

The volunteers came with relatively high expectations in many cases, and many post-project reactions illustrated these expectations: 'the rainforest itself, I didn't expect it to be anywhere near as beautiful'; 'I thought that the community would appreciate our presence, they would be grateful that we were there, for wanting to help in their country and in their town, in the middle of nowhere'.

Some volunteers adjusted to the failure of their initial expectations being met:

> We got there thinking about a community project and it wasn't that. We were thinking, 'oh my god this is just manual labour, we've come from all around the world and raised all this money and we're going to be lugging sand up a hill for the next month'. Once we saw that it was basically up to us to do what we could do, to look at and problem solve ourselves, it allowed a lot of scope for thinking about what is required as well.
>
> (Mic)

Expectation levels are relative to each individual. However, one of the underlying expectations appears to have been a desire to see 'nature in its natural state' as Sue's comment demonstrates: 'I guess the remoteness was as I expected it to be and the lushness of the forest'. However, even with a high level of expectation, the site still managed to have an impact:

> Walking, sitting at one of the views that you can see the volcano. I loved it, I would just sit there, it was so peaceful. I used to sit there thinking about how I was in a rainforest in Costa Rica and no one at home would have any idea where I am. I was in the middle of nowhere, that used to blow me away. I would just go up there and sit and think and stay there until it was too dark and run down the trail thinking the panther was going to get me.
>
> (Lil)

This underlying motivational theme of a desire to experience nature would appear to be consistent with the general literature in that the nature experiences gained on ecotours are fundamental motivational reasons for undertaking such tours, thus generating a high degree of demand. In this respect, we can situate the type of experience that relies on nature on a continuum, with some ecotours being quite expensive, such as an all-inclusive African safari or an Antarctic cruise, while some styles of nature-based tourism (the SERR for example) are relatively inexpensive. Therefore, cost and demand do not necessarily correlate with nature-based tourism experiences. Nature as the pre-eminent component of these experiences provides a link which enables us to view expectation across a wide spectrum, therefore removing expectation and price as the key factors in differentiating alternative tourism from other forms of tourism. It is possible, for example, to satisfy expensive and inexpensive nature-based tourism with fewer developmental costs. Valentine (1992, p. 113) states: 'There are few nature tourism experiences so intense and rewarding as stalking a tiger on elephant back and it is highly likely that consumer surplus remains very high'. Comparatively, Sue suggests a similar intensity in experience in the SERR project:

> . . . it was certainly incredible rainforest, the greenness and lushness of the place. It was dripping wet and there was a lot of mist, you couldn't see any of the tree trunks. I thought the beauty of the place was amazing . . .. I guess the fact that it was so vast and in one little patch in the forest there can be so much going on and it will always be going no matter what happens in your life, these sort of things will keep on living . . .

Mic responds similarly:

> One of the things that I really liked about Costa Rica was the monkeys, the wild boars and all the different types of birds and things: Santa Elena is famous for the quetzal and there are also a few other birds. I really

> enjoyed having the time by myself, to sit out there, and to do something like read or write and also use that as a chance to get a feel for the forest. The animals would just pass by, if you weren't moving. If you sat down they would often come to you.

Expectations of challenge and excitement may be sought on certain types of ecotours. Safaris through African game parks, trekking through the Himalayas, shooting the rapids and exploring the ancient Inca civilizations promote these type of adventures. Mohanlall's (1992) description of his 2-day trek and climb starting in Kinabalu National Park in Sabah illustrates the confluence of factors that contribute to such an experience: the active pace of the trek was somewhat softened by the authorized guides (their hiring was required by the National Parks) who could also be employed as porters by those who lost their initial bout of enthusiasm. Although the activities pursued on this trip were fairly strenuous, in addition to challenge and excitement, tranquillity and solitary impressions were also experienced through rainforest walks and a mountain sunrise. Meg, who was an SERR participant, similarly encapsulates these views in the following:

> I can't remember what my expectations were. I knew it was going to be wet because we were told to buy gum boots. In terms of having showers, eating food, or the sleeping arrangements, I didn't really think about those things a lot. I knew it was going to be hard and probably one of the hardest projects that I would do because of the environment that I was in. I thought there would be a big welcoming party, but they were my expectations.
>
> I used to wander off by myself a bit and write letters, just because it was a nice place to be.

Although initial expectations of the tourist may not be met, the ecotourist may not, however, be entirely disappointed with the expedition. Whale watching has become a large part of local tourist industries in areas which are fortunate enough to be near to the habitats or migratory paths of these creatures, and although the tourist may hope to see a whale they may recognize the potential disappointment of not seeing one. Alternatively, seeing several pods up close, or perhaps a mother and baby, will generate excitement and probably exceed the expectations of the tourist. Valentine (1992, p. 119) comments: 'although the whale-watching activity seems neither aesthetically pleasing nor recreational, nevertheless the excitement of the volunteers is obvious'.

> The rainforest itself, I didn't expect it to be anywhere near as beautiful. I didn't expect to like it so much because when we first arrived, it was so muddy and horrendous, but by the end of it, you were really sort of attached to the place because the time there was so good.
>
> (Amy)

In preparing for the project, nine of the of the 11 volunteers undertook Spanish courses, while one made no attempt to learn Spanish and the other had already acquired Spanish proficiency. Two volunteers went further to improve their skills and understanding of the project before departure: one studied the area and researched widely while the other talked to people that had been on the project.

The volunteers spent from 10 to 35 days on the project, depending on which year they participated, and when they departed the project site had worked on tasks ranging from: trail design, construction and stabilization including cutting up logs with chainsaws and carrying and installing them, carrying gravel to surface the trail, building steps and gullies and redoing the trail; building the interpretation centre, clearing and levelling land, constructing the building and also doing the same for the science centre; designing and planting a scientific garden, carrying out a community survey; fundraising; organizing a community day; and designing and printing a self-guided trail brochure.

An additional activity was the community survey work which was organized by the author and another participant, and then run by the volunteers of two project groups back to back in January 1993. The two volunteers who had the most input to the survey have been interviewed in the respondent group and have both completed ecotourism projects subsequent to the SERR project as part of university courses being undertaken.

How Do the Volunteers Define Themselves?

The analysis of volunteers' reflection on their experience requires a definition or framing of the experience in their own words (Glaser and Strauss, 1967; Denzin, 1989a). Before confirmation of the respondents' perception of the main areas of the experience, the volunteers were asked to define the ecotourism experience in their own terms. In defining the ecotourism experience, some respondents struggled with the term, while others used common terms associated with the area including 'nature-based' and 'helping communities' as well as drawing upon personal explanations: others admitted that their definition, or awareness of the ecotourism experience as a concept, had changed in itself due to the experience.

The volunteers defined ecotourism as a tourism activity that 'is about seeing a forest or whatever, in a more or less reasonably pure sort of form' (Ken) which, 'in doing so, is helping the community' (Jen).

Four major themes that appear to relate to the elements of ecotourism identified in the literature came from their definitions.

Nature-based

. . . do something that's not harmful to the environment, and enhancing the environment.

(Jen)

. . . see a forest or whatever, in a more or less pure form.

(Ken)

. . . maximizes the environment without destroying it.

(Ann)

. . . to go to a relatively undisturbed area or a natural area.

(Lil)

. . . visits some kind of natural place, natural environment, working with it and not trying to alter it in any way that's detrimental.

(Meg)

. . . not degrading the environment in any way.

(Pen)

. . . wilderness experience.

(Sue)

. . . combined the environment with tourism.

(Kim)

Community involvement

. . . helping the community bring in money, education.

(Jen)

. . . the communities involved.

(Lil)

. . . economically viable for the community with it.

(Ann)

. . . that will be going back into the community.

(Pen)

. . . income-based centre for the community at large.

(Jen)

. . . actually putting something into the community.

(Amy)

Process

. . . that the ecotourist is someone who is participating in that venture.

(Jen)

. . . where the tourist was actually putting something into the community, learning from the community and learning from the rainforest.

(Amy)

. . . someone who creates that sort of environment or is a part of it in some way.

(Ann)

. . . gives more of a sense of going and either participating or giving something back to the place.

(Mic)

Learning experience

. . . learning from the community and learning about the rainforest.

(Amy)

. . . learn about and appreciate the natural environment.

(Lil)

. . . actually learning.

(Ros)

The emergent themes are underscored by the participants' identification of interaction/exchange.

Interaction/exchange

. . . we did interact with the community.

(Sue)

. . . interacting with Costa Ricans.

(Jen)

. . . two-way project, you put in effort and we'll put in effort.

(Jen)

. . . interaction between the challengers and the community.

(Ken)

. . . quite a good interaction between the community and youth challenge.

(Jen)

. . . there was a lot of social exchange.

(Ken)

The following definition provided by one of the volunteers encapsulates the interdependency of the thematics:

> An ecotourist is someone that has specifically in mind to go to a relatively undisturbed area or a natural area. They want to learn about that area, the nature and things like that; I think they also have an interest in the conservation, the communities involved or whatever, or just a desire to learn about and appreciate the natural environment.
>
> (Lil)

In summary, the definition of the concept of ecotourism as provided by the volunteers involves a tourist experience that is nature-based and involves a process that puts something back into the community and the natural environment while being a learning experience for those involved, which would appear to come very close to Ceballos-Lascurain's definition:

> We may define ecological tourism or ecotourism as that tourism that involves travelling to relatively undisturbed or uncontaminated natural areas with the specific object of studying, admiring and enjoying the scenery and its wild plants and animals, as well as any existing cultural aspects (both past and present) found in these areas. Ecological tourism implies a scientific, aesthetic or philosophical approach, although the ecological tourist is not required to be a professional scientist, artist or philosopher. The main point is that the person that practices ecotourism has the opportunity of immersing him or herself in nature in a way that most people cannot enjoy in their routine, urban existences.
>
> (Boo, 1990, p. 10)

The link between ecotourism and the participants' recollection of their experience is now investigated in more depth; particularly in elaborating upon the participant's qualification of the experience in relation to ecotourism and the experience's alignment to volunteer experience. This demonstrates the complexity of alternative tourism experiences in the difficulty in breaking it down into specific categories.

Qualifying statements included:

> It was fun and a holiday as well. It was work but it wasn't work.
>
> (Meg)

> I was working, which the average ecotourist wouldn't be doing.
>
> (Ken)

> I guess it is, but it is also volunteer work as well, which is a little bit different.
>
> (Mic)

Negative participant response to ecotourism included:

> I don't think I was an ecotourist at all, because we were there and we were doing the building of it, we weren't there to sightsee. But as a wilderness experience, it was definitely that, being so isolated.
>
> (Sue)

In exploring the volunteers' comments about the differences between their definitions of what an ecotourist is and their experience in Santa Elena, the following comments were made:

> I guess the extent that we were working. For me personally, I thought what I was doing was ecotouristy [*sic*]. I don't mind using my free time to work really hard. I was more preparing it for the ecotourist.
>
> (Meg)

It was a lot more rewarding than staying in the Hilton and then going off on a hike.

(Ken)

In terms of working in this environment:

We gained a lot from the experience, just getting up in the morning and actually being in it, and walking through it in its natural state, which was fantastic.

(Amy)

I guess the definition entailed that the host community are quite happy to have you there, and I thought in Santa Elena they were still going through the process of trying to accept why we were there. I guess in that way, more from the community side of things, the host/visitor relationship is probably different than maybe what I'd anticipated.

(Ros)

. . . but at the moment it's all outsiders making the SERR work. The community might benefit . . . but on the large part, they don't. It is mainly the hoteliers. I don't think much is going back into the community. It's reported as being an ecotourism project, and it might be more of one in a few years, but at the moment I don't think it is.

(Pen)

You tend to think of tourism as short term, a couple of weeks, or more structured holidays, whereas, in a lot of ways, Santa Elena was also a work and personal development type thing. It wasn't just a holiday.

(Mic)

We weren't just looking. We were there building . . . we didn't just come for a day . . . we tried to maintain the forest. If I had gone to Santa Elena in a day, had gone for a walk and went away again, the experience would have been so different to living in the rainforest and working for the 4 weeks.

(Kim)

From the focus group, it is possible to identify that the volunteers had the opinion that they were different from tourists:

I felt that when tourists were up there, it was not an intrusion but something that you could do without, but then that's why you were there. There was one German group who came up and they went for a walk. They weren't being very quiet, they came back and were all smoking in the interpretation centre and flicking their butts out. They don't have that same sense of value for the place, they're just there passing through, they have 100 other things on their itinerary, so it's just one more thing to see. You get upset that these people don't have the same sense of that really deep-felt appreciation for where you are. I guess that comes from living there, being a part of it and helping that place to try and grow. We walked around and picked up their cigarette butts in front of them.

(Ros)

> We had it a little bit different, because we didn't have the tourists up there. But there was one occasion we came down and went over to Monteverde, we were there having a look. It was like, look at the tourists, look what they've done, look at how promotional it is. Then you sit back and realize that we are doing exactly the same thing in a neighbouring village. Maybe not to the same extent, but to recreate itself in another area, to bring in the tourists' dollars. While we were over there, we were being the tourists and it was a really yucky situation. We were part of it and we didn't realise it at the time, but, looking back, we were developing this tourist chain that eventually we would have no control over. The little bit that we were doing, would have absolutely no impact on the outcome.
>
> (Amy)

> Sure it's an unpleasant sight. At the time, it was probably something that people felt ill towards these tourists coming in. But it's something we shouldn't be feeling guilty about because the option was that they fell all the forest and have dairy farmers there. I don't think we should be feeling guilty about what we are creating, because at the same time we are saving something that is still there, which might not have been. So I don't think it is something we should feel too bad about. It has to be there, it is the economic reality.
>
> (Ken)

> Sure we are saving a cloudforest, but then that's not taking into the equation the community who live there, who may have clear-felled that forest. By bringing in ecotourists, and us choosing to bring ecotourism into their area, we can put them way off centre, and all of a sudden they're in a situation where they've got no idea. The impacts aren't just physical. If you look at other resorts, like in India, there are drugs and prostitution in the towns, all of a sudden it's just exponential for the people who live there. We can go in and walk away, but they're left with not just the result of us saving some land, but their culture just takes a complete U-turn.
>
> (Mic)

An overall view that might sum up the differences suggests:

> I see myself as working in the area; it was more part of the YCI thing, me working there. I look back now, and it was an ecotourist experience. Before, my perception of an ecotourist was someone who went in daily, whereas I didn't consider myself an ecotourist because I was living there and working there. Now looking back at it, there is no set definition for an ecotourist, they can be the people going in and out, but my experience was more substantial, living and working there, it was more intense.
>
> (Lil)

MacCannell (1976, 1992) suggests that tourists who consider themselves culturally or environmentally aware do not like to be labelled as (mass) tourists as they see it as a predominantly negative term. The volunteers fit within this idea as they are self-conscious about the label and also about contributing to the future of mass tourism in the area. Urry (1990, p. 2) has argued that each single tourist will construct a different idea of what is experienced, according to non-tourist forms of social experience. It is not surprising, given the similarity in backgrounds that the volunteers have, that they have relational opinions and they form these opinions based within their social group (as volunteers in YCI) and in contrast to those they consider (mass) tourists. The appeal of travelling with a purpose, working with communities in developing countries and spending time to assist in saving natural environments provides a strong platform for volunteers to be defined as alternative tourists.

The research (Stebbins, 1982, 1992; Parker, 1992) in Chapter 2 indicated that some volunteers do not perceive themselves as being 'at leisure', but rather involved in a sense of 'good citizenship – concern for the community'. Mass tourism appears to have a more self-centred approach focusing on relaxation or excitement, while forms of alternative tourism such as ecotourism appear to relate more to volunteering and could include as a major part of its approach the more common term, 'community work', being applied. The responses of the volunteers would seem to indicate that they fall into this category and again reinforce the idea of them being alternative tourists.

Constructing a Framework to Examine the Data

Based on the concept of the ecotourist and the ecotourist experience related by particular volunteers involved in the Santa Elena project, Table 4.2 has been constructed to provide a schematic overview of ecotourism in relation to participants' experience. These experiences are grouped into four main categories: process, nature-based, learning experience and interaction/exchange. Subcategories within these clusters have been taken from the volunteers' comments to define the structure further. The two research questions are also reviewed to construct Table 4.2.

It is recognized, however, that the clusters are obviously interrelated in many ways as the personal experience of the volunteers and the definitions they have can produce a range of variations. However, it is possible to broadly differentiate the elements that form the experience and to establish a relationship with the ideas in the ecotourism experience. The data, or quotes, could, in some cases, readily apply to a number of the areas elaborated upon below following the preceding schematic outline.

As one participant noted:

> So as far as Santa Elena, I think when I was actually there, I didn't really think too much about it, apart from I knew that an ecotourist was someone that came to enjoy the natural areas. I didn't know all the things that

Table 4.2. Framework of categories of participants' experience related to the SERR experience.

Process
Nature-based
Awareness and appreciation of natural environment
Interaction with the natural environment
Valuing the natural environment
Learning experience
Learning from the community and the natural environment
Exchange/interaction
Process of exchange/interaction between participant and natural environment
Process of exchange/interaction between participant and community
Process of exchange/interaction between participant and group

> were surrounding it. It wasn't until afterwards, when I did the elective and when I did my chapter, that it sort of all came together. That's kind of the way I'm going now with my career.
>
> (Lil)

Process

This cluster identified that some exchange/interactive process had to occur between the participant and the community/natural environment/group. It could not be short term and should be 'intense'. This process should have some effect on the participant and involve the notion of 'living there'.

Nature-based

This cluster reinforces the idea that ecotourism must be based on the natural environment with 'pristine', 'wilderness' and 'relatively undisturbed' describing this process.

Learning experience

This cluster saw that the result of the 'process' should involve learning about the community and the natural environment.

Interaction/exchange

This cluster was derived from the participants' belief that some form of exchange would occur in their definition of this type of experience and has been reinforced while examining process and learning experience, and thus is considered to need further highlighting (this is an acceptable practice when using grounded theory).

The outcomes of the data suggest that the volunteers' experience and backgrounds fall within the scope of ecotourism and the parameters that define it, and the experience of the volunteers as they defined it strongly relates to the original definition of Ceballos-Lascurain (personal communication, 1987; Boo, 1990; p. 10).

The next chapter examines the themes that emerged from the volunteers' definitions of the experience and links them to related information in the interviews and to the literature. As noted, the major themes are those of process, nature-based, learning experience and exchange/interaction. It is particularly focused on the elements of the experience the volunteers discuss, and attempts to present an overall picture of the experience they have had with YCI on the SERR project. Under consideration is the variety of elements that affect the experience of the volunteers and which are context-specific (Denzin, 1989a,b; Henderson, 1991) in relation to the literature and related studies.

The following model, based on the information outlined in Chapter 2 and adapted from Hamilton-Smith's (1994, p. 80) '[m]odel of the role of the participating individual in shaping the character and quality of the experience', Kolb's (1984) adaptation of Dewey/Lewin's (see Dewey, 1960) experiential learning cycle and Clawson and Knetsch's (1966) notion that each recreation experience involves a number of phases or stages, provides a schematic overview of the interrelating elements and processes that have been identified in this chapter and that contribute to the alternative tourism experience.

Hamilton-Smith (1994) refers to personal characteristics as 'personal baggage', including such aspects as social position, previous experience, preferences, values and beliefs. As outlined in the studies identified (de Carlo and McConchie, 1980; Rohs, 1986; Beighbeder, 1991; Tihanyi, 1991), personal characteristics incorporate social background, and personality and attitude factors. The experience is also shaped within the broader constructs of the experience, or 'management regime' (Hamilton-Smith, 1994). This is the political, administrative and resource base by which the experience is provided by an organization, or under which the individual undertakes the activity. Hamilton-Smith (1994) outlines four elements, or constructs (relating primarily to a wilderness setting) including personal/social relationships, location in time/space, physical–aesthetic characteristics of setting, and behaviour and action. Rohs (1986) basically refers to this as the structure and operation of the particular volunteer organization or programme.

The interaction of these two areas defines the alternative tourist's motivation and level of involvement. The understanding of motivation, as Iso-Ahola (1989) suggests, is the primary basis for understanding leisure behaviour. Motivation is also linked implicitly with outcomes, or learning, and provided the primary basis from which benefits or personal development have been measured scientifically in the past (Schreyer and Driver, 1989; Scherl, 1994). Involvement, being the 'degree of cognitive, affective and behavioural investment a person has in a situation' (McIntyre, 1994, p. 57), is also determined through

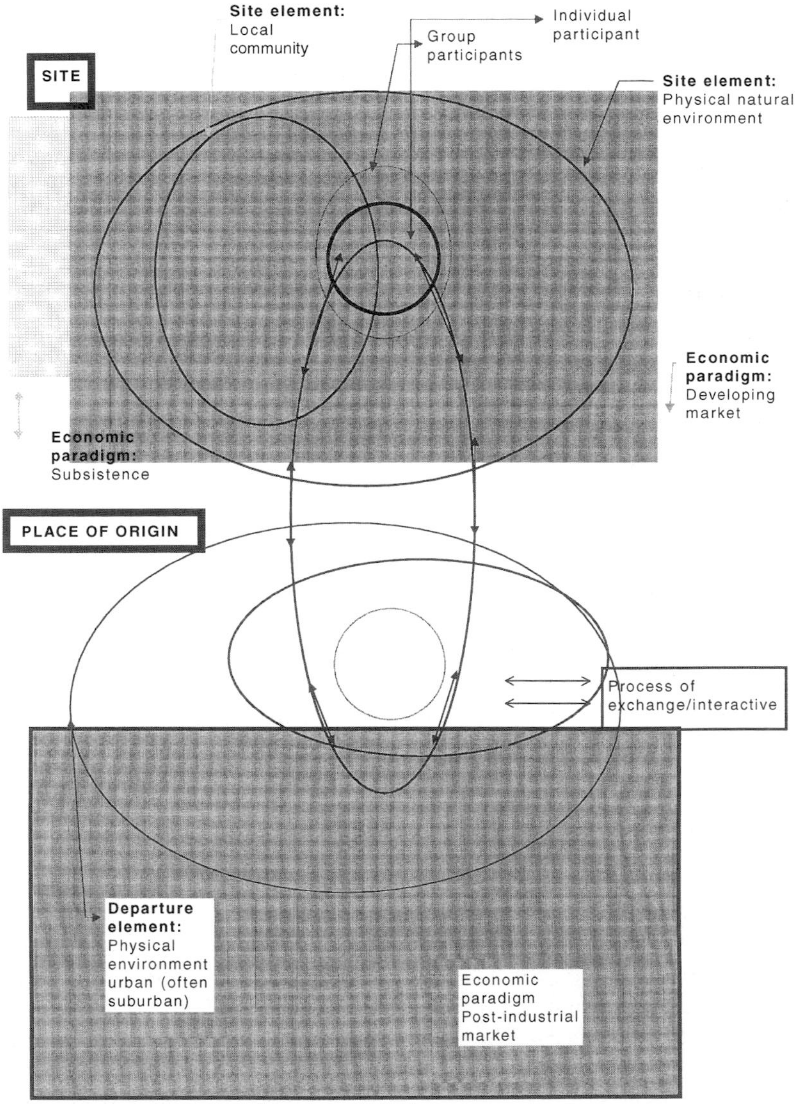

Fig. 4.1. Model of the spheres of influence of the volunteer tourism experience. After Clawson and Knetsch (1966), Kolb (1984) and Hamilton-Smith (1994, p. 80).

the interaction of the alternative tourist and the structure of their experience.

The experiential learning cycle of Lewin and Dewey (see Dewey, 1960) indicates a basic four-stage cycle of an experience: observation; reflection; the formation of abstract concepts or ideas based on this; and the use of these ideas in shaping new experiences (Kolb, 1984). Viewing leisure as an experience, a number of researchers (Henderson, 1984; Scherl, 1988; Hamilton-Smith, 1994) draw on Clawson and Knetsch's (1966) idea of leisure experience involving a number of phases, or stages. This concept of an experience involving a number of phases originally was applied to outdoor recreation. An individual, in order to appreciate a recreation experience fully, potentially would undertake the experience in a number of phases or stages, including: anticipation of the experience, travelling, the actual experience and recollection.

As Henderson (1984, p. 8) suggests, this would indicate that recreation and volunteerism are not activity specific, but 'require aspects which make for a meaningful experience'. This is also true for the alternative tourist. Hamilton-Smith (1994), in reference to Clawson and Knetsch, indicates that within a 'lived leisure experience' there potentially exist a number of aspects with their own impact and value. These perspectives suggest an alternative tourism experience with a wide variety of elements which impact upon volunteers and others, and thus potentially lead to a range of subsequent outcomes.

The preceding model (see Fig. 4.1) schematically outlines the process of the alternative experience as identified in the data obtained from the YCI experience, serving to elaborate the interdependent elements which contribute to the provision of the volunteer tourism experience. Having explored the experience in the context of YCI, the next chapter will examine how that experience affects the alternative tourist's sense of self and identity.

Chapter 5

The Volunteer Tourist's Experience – Self and Identity

> So Santa Elena in particular, I think that's why it stuck in my mind so much, because it seemed to me to represent what could be achieved and what communities can be, and what individual people can do for themselves. I think it was a booster in faith and a hope in humanity. So personally it committed me to what I was doing, it solidified values that I was just starting to change. You are always reassessing your values and effects and morals and what you are actually working for, and what they mean.
>
> (Ros, study volunteer)

> You've been exposed to this up until now, so next time you get exposed to a situation, like whether to do study, write an essay, read that extra paper, your answer is slightly different because you have one more experience, which has had a big effect on your life. I'm now looking for jobs that are meaningful, not just to me, but also that I can see positive social impact from, which is one of the things I guess I gained from Santa Elena.
>
> (Mic, study volunteer)

> I'm a lot more interested in, not so much environmental issues, but in human rights issues, how people cope and where they live and what they do.
>
> (Kim, study volunteer)

In what way does this experience affect the alternative tourist's sense of self and identity? The volunteer tourists themselves suggest that tourism sectors such as ecotourism should be based on the natural environment: 'pristine', 'wilderness', 'relatively undisturbed' describe the type of natural environments suggested. What role does the natural environment of the site play in their tourist experience? The site is examined to explore what other elements of the site may have affected the volunteers' sense of self and identity. This chapter then examines the volunteers' experiences with nature, examining the role of the natural environment in the experience of the volunteer, and analysing how this has influenced their sense of self.

Much of the sociological analysis of contemporary post-industrial social systems, particularly in relation to questions of identity, have focused predominantly on the construction of the self through the distinction between the dominant social modes of work/non-work (leisure). Feminist analysis in particular has critiqued the excessive emphasis on the productive sphere and the work ethic as the basis of identity construction, and this shift in emphasis suggests that identity negotiation and consolidation can actually depend more heavily on the non-productive sphere of consumption – leisure and tourism for example. Examination of the research on activities similar to those undertaken by alternative tourists, particularly for women within the age groups, has shown that such groups of individuals are actively searching for alternative experiences and paradigms; for example, women who participate in outdoor adventures such as rock climbing, canoeing, camping, bush walking and scuba diving report emotional, physical and psychological benefits accruing from participation in these experiential modes that offer a distinct contrast to the socially prescribed roles offered to women in post-industrial society (Miranda and Yerks, 1985; Scherl, 1988; Burden and Kiewa, 1992).

Simmel (1936) has argued that in urban industrial society the variety of groups to which one belongs produces a unique mixture of group affiliations for each person, thus contributing to individuality. The individual's background (class, race, ethnicity, age and gender) will produce attitudes and motivations (see Denzin, 1994) that will be influenced differently through the process and learning experience that occurs on and with the site with which the individual interacts.

Erikson (1971) suggests that identity is a 'process' both within the core of the individual and in the core of her/his communal culture which gives meaning and continuity to individual existence. Erikson maintains that the crucial elements of identities established in youth are autonomy from parents, sex-role identity, career choice and internalized morality. Recent feminist theorists, however, have critiqued Erikson's notion of a unified identity by expanding on the concept to include the potentiality of multiple subjectivities for both males and females (J. Butler, 1990; Braidotti, 1993). It is within this expanded context that the alternative tourism experience can be placed.

Wearing (1998) found that volunteers in formal programmes are subjected to (and by) a tourism experience that is a 'process', involving 'components of learning' about 'nature'. Therefore, it is reasonable to state – and many of the respondents' statements have suggested as much – that the experience itself is likely to impact on the formation of volunteers' 'values' and therefore their sense of identity. This chapter examines the elements of the alternative tourism experience in conjunction with the themes that emerged from the volunteers' definitions of the experience in Wearing (1998).

If the volunteer experience (as an alternative tourism experience) affects the values and identity of the volunteers in the studies conducted by Wearing (1998) and Darby (1995), then certain ideas can be developed. For example, it would therefore suggest that this constitutes a fundamental nodal point in identity formation and construction; crucially, one which is constructed inherently around the notion of value for a physical place, i.e. a site of constellations of values and meanings that are negotiated, constructed and mediated upon, where the identities of individuals can be constructed, developed, rejected and/or refined. Conceptualized in this way, such an approach attempts to theorize as to how leisure and tourism can influence value systems and identity formation. It is then considered imminently possible that if such alternative experiences can be provided, allowing individuals to challenge and resist dominant identarian models and cultural stereotypes and perception and construction of nature/environment itself, then the opportunity arises for a concomitant range of alternative identities and value systems that may be encountered and explored by individuals.

There are a number of theoretical processes that could be explored in order to examine the themes arising from the volunteers' 'stories'. The avenue that this book has pursued is the suggestion that the experience provides an alternative form of leisure beyond those available to youth in developed countries; one enabling youth to explore new cultural paradigms and to create new identities that incorporate the 'other' – this other being the community and natural environments of the area visited. This contributes to the 'value' that individuals place on the environments visited, and this value(s) may be incorporated subjectively.[16]

The volunteers' experience has been examined in the previous chapter, with a specific focus on the nature of that experience as a 'process' in relation to the question put forward, i.e. the experience as having an impact on the volunteers and their values. This section looks at the experience and how the individual – the 'I' – is affected, within the context of a 'learning experience'. It focuses on the process as a learning experience as it relates to the 'nature-base' (natural environment) of the volunteer experience. It should be remembered that as this

---

[16] This idea of 'value' is aligned to the idea of *social value* discussed in Chapter 2 which enables the examination and provision of further insights into the way the community and the participants construct their ideas of the volunteer.

is done within the context of interactionism, where the natural environment is viewed as being a socially constructed symbol mediating the interaction between the volunteers and the key elements of the site they identified as contributing to the notion of social value.

Returning to Ceballos-Lascurain's (personal communication, 1987) definition of ecotourism, it is observed that for the ecotourism experience to have occurred the volunteer must have acquired a consciousness and knowledge of the natural environment while concomitantly becoming involved in conservation issues. This definition leads in part to the initial research questions in that the experience impacts on the volunteers to the extent that it affects the attitudes and perceptions they hold and causes them to change in the process of the experience and as a result of the experience. One avenue that is not explored extensively in this book is the area of personal development as it relates to 'process' and 'learning experience'. Darby's (1994) work on YCI provides a thorough examination of this area, concluding that the experience impacts fundamentally on the perceptions and attitudes of the volunteers. The focus in this study, however, is on the specificity of the experience of the volunteers in the SERR project and the impact it has on their construction of social value as represented in its effects on self and identity. Using grounded theory as the basis for the development of the volunteers, relating their 'stories' provides the basis for an exploration of these ideas. In accordance with studies[17] that have provided support for personal development experiences effecting changed attitudes, the focus here relates to the formation of *values*, specifically 'social value', as it relates to the 'nature-base' of tourism.

The Relational Elements of the Alternative Tourism Experience

Analysis of the data in Chapter 2 has identified the fundamental emergent themes – process, nature, interaction/exchange – as forming an interrelational complex that intermeshes with the environmental factors of the site – nature, community members and other volunteers.

Environment/nature

The most obvious theme identified was the volunteers' response that the ecotourism experience should be based on the natural

---

[17] See Ford and Blanchard (1985), Ewert (1987), Abbott (1989), Pettit (1989) and Darby (1994).

environment, with 'pristine', 'wilderness' and 'relatively undisturbed' describing the type of natural environments suggested.

The general feeling amongst the volunteers was that the project has protected a threatened rainforest. Meg maintains that '[i]t protected that area and that area only I guess. So yes, I think we saved part of a rainforest'. Others, however, aligned it more with the general idea of ecotourism. Sue, for example, states:

> I think that was achieved in bringing awareness to the area. The rainforest is less likely to be chopped down if lots of people know about it. Also, if it has people paying money to come and see it, they're hardly likely to start chopping it down, if the money that the people are paying is more than the money they would get from farming and grazing cattle there. But they obviously seem to think it is worthwhile at the moment. So as protecting an endangered forest, I think it is doing an OK job.

Other volunteers viewed the project as encouraging support for the establishment of protected areas. Ros and Pen suggest:

> The fact that the local community is getting benefits back from them, they're seeing the benefits of preserving. The only other way they could be using the forest would be to physically use it by cutting it down and clearing it, because at the moment it is just sitting there.
>
> (Ros)

> I think it is because people would hopefully see how important it is to have protected areas so that animals can still roam. If they walk into the reserve they can see animals and birds and it's only by protecting these areas that it's possible for people to see that. The more Costa Ricans that come up, the more interest they will take in their own country and hopefully preserving their own. Hopefully, more Costa Ricans will become involved in their own country and do it for themselves.
>
> (Pen)

For many, it facilitated a change towards the perception of the environment and what is happening to the environment at a more global level. Ros expressed the hope that 'the community push is going to be enough to get worldwide action on environmental issues'.

> I think it was being achieved quite well. I guess it's not just Costa Rica or the Santa Elena project that have encouraged that. It's the whole society's view and push for environmental support, for protecting rainforest areas and environmental areas in the last 10 years. After we left, the World Wildlife Fund for Nature came in with a big donation to help Santa Elena and the Reserve and to help build a house for students and scientists who come to research the rainforest. So if they can still get support like that and it appeals to environmental agencies, they will survive. The whole issue of supporting and protecting rainforests and protecting the environmental areas, by its existence, it is supporting it.
>
> (Kim)

From the focus group, we see some support for Ceballos-Lascurain's idea of ecotourism which suggests that for the ecotourism experience to have occurred, the volunteer must have acquired a consciousness and knowledge of the natural environment and become involved in conservation issues.

> Made me a lot more critical of a consumer's society. I think there are a lot of things here that are all very nice and convenient and are good for status. But there are a lot of things we just don't need. If something is broken, we go down the shop and buy another one, or buy a dishwasher instead of doing it yourself. I have become more critical of my environment, because each time I buy something, I have to really justify to myself, do I need this or is it just something to do with the money I'm spending my life earning? A lot of people have an identity, their car or their job is their identity. So when you meet them, in the first couple of minutes, they're telling you, 'I do this' or 'I have this'. It shrinks your identity, but I'm not sure if it shrinks it as much as it defines it. It takes away all the things that aren't you and leaves you with just the core, so it is really just chopping away at the unnecessary bits.
>
> (Ros)

> A lot of rainforest had been cleared to raise money to have a better life-style. It happens all around the world, and rainforest has been considered as something that you can get rid of, so that you produce and therefore raise money. In ecotourism, especially in Santa Elena, using the rainforest to get the money for the community, especially in the last 5 or 10 years, is quite a normal approach, turning it around so the rainforest isn't gone in the next 10 years.
>
> (Lil)

Since the industrial revolution, many cultures have become increasingly urbanized. This has led to a growth in demand for the use of natural areas for recreation and enjoyment. As more people get caught up in the complex web of urban life, they look to natural areas as a means of escape from the pressures and stress of modern living. As Welton contends,

> The only way to counteract the unnaturalness of urban life is to periodically renew oneself in the wilderness.
>
> (Welton, 1978, p. 30)

The societal benefits derived from leisure experiences in natural areas show that there is a need to preserve natural areas not only for their environmental qualities, but for the 'quality of life' benefits that humans can experience from recreating in these areas. Schreyer and Driver (in Jackson and Burton, 1989, p. 388) suggest that a benefit denotes a desirable change of state, i.e. it is a specified improvement in condition or state of an individual or a group of individuals of a society or non-human organisms. If we consider, as Pigram (1992, p. 1) does, the anecdotal and empirical evidence which suggests that the intrinsic values derived from experiencing leisure are perceived as being more in keeping with natural environments than with human-dominant landscapes, then these natural environments become an important part of travel and the ecotourism experience.

Given the widespread appeal which nature seems to have for society, the growth in ecotourism should come as no surprise. Pigram (1992), in reviewing research in this area, found that Stankey and McCool's (1985) work suggests that natural settings are of major importance to recreation users: even big game hunting revealed a pre-occupation with nature, with two-thirds of the hunters interviewed stating that enjoying nature was important (Allen, 1991). Kaplan and Kaplan (1989) report that experiencing nature is a central issue for visitors to natural areas. Studies on recreation motivation by Shafer and Mietz (1969) and Fly (1986) suggest that 'enjoying the natural surroundings' and 'experiencing nature' are the strongest reasons for visiting these environments.

Research on white water rafting by Hall and McArthur (1991) reveals that although adventure and excitement are significant motivational factors, the most important motivation cited was the opportunity to experience the natural environment. Research by Gold (1973) indicates that the need for outdoor recreation is directly proportional to the degree of urbanization due to the biological need for nature and a psychological need for contrast and change in spatial surroundings. Brightbill (1960) suggests that nature becomes a means of escaping the pollutants and pressures of modern living by giving us a kind of inner peace. Proshansky's (1973) research offers a valuable insight into key independent variables that are central to understanding the effects of urbanization on life and leisure choices. Urbanization has become the norm and, not only are we adapting, but we are adapting too well. Proshanksy's fears are that this overadaptation may reach a point where characteristic human values are destroyed.

Iso-Ahola (1980) advocates that if we see the environment as self, we are more likely to experience the environment as self. Therefore, by separating humans from the environment, we are separating humans from themselves, hence an attraction to natural areas. It is thought that natural areas represent the past. Natural areas in this respect are a living embodiment of the past, contributing to our present sense of duration and identity. For Aboriginal people, this sense of identity is maintained through totemism which accomplishes not only the kinship and cooperation of humans with nature but the continuity between past and present (Levi-Strauss, 1964).

Humans are interacting constantly with their environment, adapting it to suit intrinsically human ends (Proshansky, 1973). Response to the environment is often obtained through feedback from 'others' in relation to the natural environment. In some natural areas, however, the environment cannot be changed to suit one's needs. In these cases, the human agent must focus on adapting the self rather than the environment. In this way, the interaction between the individual and the surrounding environment is founded on a relationship of self-control. That is to say that the behaviour modification resulting from the apperception of an unmalleable and often hostile environment is one that fundamentally questions the ontological and existential status of the agents themselves: in short, the very make-up of the value system of the individual is brought into relief.

A process of self-control that necessarily shifts the focus inward enhances self-consciousness. As this attention shifts from the environment to a physiological state, it gravitates to other aspects of the self. This in turn produces a feeling of self-reliance resulting in a positive feedback of the self. Slosky (in Scherl, 1988) explains that natural areas create a greater awareness of the self, because there is no escape from experiencing the present. The enhancements of these emotional and physical sensations increase an awareness of one's inner capabilities, which in turn increases self-confidence.

It is thought that some people who constantly seek identity images, such as being adventurous, find that a natural area can reinforce identity by allowing the individual a closer understanding of their individual strengths. Simmel (1965), however, views the excitement derived from the gamble with the forces of nature, in contemporary social systems, as being an excitement not from the gamble itself, but as symptomatic of the modern fetishization of stimulation. This may be the initial motivating force, but the psychological benefits that result from natural area experience go beyond simply the drive for stimulation. The heightened physiological state occurring when natural environments are used purely for their functional utility, i.e., for the stimulation as a physical end in itself, produces a distancing effect by taking one's self away from the self. Natural areas, however, can facilitate a reconnection with the self through a process of self-control resulting in an increase in self-confidence, an increased awareness of one's emotional and physiological sensations and enhancing perceived freedom. Self-control enhances self-feedback, resulting in positive self-image.

Now that we are beginning to understand human affinity with nature, we can understand why humans look for ecotourism experiences in natural areas. Driver *et al.* (1991, 1996) found that there are benefits that are derived from outdoor recreational experiences and that in understanding the physiological and psychological changes that occur within an individual, through experiencing nature, a range of personal benefits could be seen to result. It is not the purpose of this book to examine these, but it is an area that would warrant further research in the future.

The ecotourism experience research in this book has been able to incorporate Scherl's (1988) and Hamilton-Smith's (1990) work, in suggesting that by collecting data of the experience, we are able to develop an understanding of the process related to any leisure or, in this case, ecotourism experience. The understanding developed from such a research design and its link to existing research provides a framework for analysing the interaction of the ecotourist and the host community.

The individual ecotourism experience within this context can now be examined. Iso-Ahola (1984) suggests that the need to 'escape' from one's everyday life circumstances and 'search' for personal meaning are dimensions which are central to leisure motivation. Wearing (1986), for example, emphasizes the rewarding effect of achieving both physical and psychological separation from work, which contributes to the popularity of nature-based experiences in more remote regions of the world, while Scherl (1988) reminds us that the search for challenging outdoor environments is not new. Wilderness as a natural environment has always been explored by individuals in search of adventure. What is a more recent phenomenon, however, is the availability of structured experiences to the general public in organized groups.

Increasingly, a greater number of people are using commercial-based companies to take them on their experiences. Scherl (1988) finds that such trips/programmes typically are packaged so that it is not necessary for volunteers to get involved with extensive expedition preparations and that the use of programmes and excursions into wilderness nowadays is rarely determined by the amount of labour required for their organization; rather, 'their value is a function of the quality and quantity of the experience they provide' (MacCannell, 1976, p. 23).

Even if benefits of these types of experiences are exaggerated somewhat, they offer some potential for direction of possible lifestyle changes for those who participate. Although the ecotourist experience cannot be performed on an everyday basis, as other leisure activities can, Simmel (1965, p. 248) points out that the adventure entails a dropping out of the turmoil of everyday existence to experience anew 'something alien, untouchable, out of the ordinary . . . an island of life which determines its beginning and end according to its own formative powers'. Ecotourism experiences can present challenges, the achievement of which bring satisfaction and a sense of personal control. As such, Simmel claims that the experience extends beyond the island of the adventure to everyday life through reflection. It is this reflection that the questions put forward by this book seeks to examine.

Ecotourism, when examined as experience, can provide the opportunity to learn through experiences (see Ewert, 1987; Whitmore, 1988), and the benefits accrued from such experiences can fundamentally influence identity (see Schreyer and Driver, 1989), and subsequently affect groups and communities. Thus, while the individual is important in research of this type (Darby, 1994), it is important in understanding ecotourism experiences that the social environment is given significant recognition. Factors that relate to social development include responsibility for others, group cooperation and leadership (Abbott, 1989; McRae, 1990; Darby, 1994).

Ecotourism experiences (contexualized as leisure experiences) coexist with personal development.[18] Scherl (1994) notes that it has long been suggested that recreation should be studied as an 'experiential state' and that understanding this state is important in itself (Ingham, 1987; Mannell and Iso-Ahola, 1987). Understanding the experience and its components, or the process, is essential for research (Scherl, 1988; Schreyer and Driver, 1989; Hamilton-Smith, 1994).

As leisure is a socially and personally constructed concept, changes over time and occurs in differing environments (Kaplan, 1975; Hamilton-Smith, 1992), it is perhaps best defined 'by those engaging in it' (Stebbins, 1982, p. 254). In summary, then, the 'some essential elements' of ecotourism experiences are: that the ecotourism experience is a personal experience which generally incorporates the perception that it is chosen for its difference and involves intrinsic motivation; potentially benefiting the person's life; meaning is given to this experience through social interaction which may involve a re-negotiation of the individual's identity.

Therefore, it is essential that the framework for ecotourism experiences incorporates a method of providing the tourist with an experience that enhances ecological awareness and appreciation. Guided tours, written pamphlets and interpretative signage are all means of heightening an ecotourist's experience to achieve this. The social exchange between the guide or the host community member is likely to reinforce this, possibly even representing the most important part of the experience.

Boo (1990) found that the majority of tourists who visited parks and reserves in Central and Latin America wanted more educational and interpretive material during their visits. Nature tourists are fairly well educated and increasingly are looking for conservation messages and better interpretation services. It is obvious that high-quality, local interpretive services are the key to tourist satisfaction, as they provide a learning experience that is understood by the ecotourist, but still contexualized within the local culture.

---

[18] See Csikszentmihalyi (1975), Roberts (1978), Kelly (1982), Kuh *et al.* (1988), Iso-Ahola (1989), Roggenbuck *et al.* (1991) and Hamilton-Smith (1992).

Educating tourists is a key way of eliciting public support for an area and assisting in its conservation. Tourists can write to politicians, talk with their friends or contribute financially to a protected area. They are more likely to do this if they have a heightened awareness and appreciation of the area. Therefore, underlying the idea of ecotourism, is the belief that people will benefit from the experience of the natural environment, and that the environment will benefit from the support of these people, both financially from the visit and socially from a change in their attitudes and values.

The ecotour guide acts as the main connection between the environment and the tourist. As such, the performance of the guide in responding to the tourist's emotional and informational needs largely affects tourist satisfaction.

> [T]he visitor's need for authenticity and contact with the environment, the unique and authentic features of that environment and the interface between the tourist and the environmental setting, which is necessary to achieve the kind of experience the tourist seeks, while preserving the setting for others.
>
> (Pearce, 1982, p. 115)

Insensitivity, communication problems or an authoritarian style of guidance may decrease the value of the ecotourism experience, thus reducing the potential for information to be influential on behaviour.

> It definitely does, but I think it could be very much improved. I heard from a few visitors that they were very disappointed with the tours they were given because the information provided was very brief. A couple of the guides didn't have very good English. They really didn't say much at all, they just sort of walked them around and when they asked questions, they weren't answered. So in way, from a tourist's point of view, I think it could have been improved a lot. I don't know how much involvement the school kids had, I never saw them up there. I never saw the community members up there. The fact that it was there, and made a Reserve, I guess is going some way towards educating the people that it is important.
>
> (Sue)

It is apparent that volunteers' experiences have provided opportunities for the volunteers to gain an increased understanding of the Santa Elena rainforest as well as the community and their group. Their evaluation of the SERR project expresses a recognition that they have become connected through the group and the demonstration of a concern for the social and cultural environments of Santa Elena. This aligns itself strongly with Pearce's (1988) idea that a connection between attitudes and behaviour is possible only when the opportunity to perform the behaviour exists and where the attitude was formed by direct experience (thereby strengthening the attitude).

Ceballos-Lascurain's definition of ecotourism (see Chapter 2) suggests that for the ecotourism experience to have occurred, the volunteer must have acquired a consciousness and knowledge of the natural environment and become involved in conservation issues. This definition led in part to the questions put forward, which suggest that the ecotourism experience impacts on the ecotourist to the extent that it affects the attitudes and perceptions they held before the experience and causes them to change after the experience. It suggests that a foundational principle of ecotourism is experiential integrity. Ecotourism must satisfy the need for both conservation and for quality experiences in natural areas.

Interaction/exchange/group

Research indicates that outdoor recreation activities contain an important social component (Manning, 1986; Colton, 1987; Heywood, 1991). The experience of leisure in outdoor settings reflected the meanings of those activities developed by volunteers through social interaction (Unger, 1984; Shaw, 1985a,b; Samdahl, 1988). The place of social interaction in these outdoor activities can, in this analysis, be understood on two levels. The first is that these activities provide opportunities for social interaction in their own right, in a context of freedom, where interaction is not as constrained as in other, non-leisure settings (Colton, 1987). The second involves the meaning of the activity as 'leisure' as also constructed through social interaction – although this construction is not necessarily confined to any particular setting (Kelly, 1983).

The data presented under this theme relate to the first type of social interaction, i.e. one which is essentially sociable and which has its own inherent qualities of enjoyment and satisfaction for the volunteers (Wolff, 1950, p. 43). This first type of interaction was evident as an aspect of the social exchange between the volunteer, representatives of the host community and the volunteers group. Volunteers consistently reported the main setting for social interaction as the SERR project site, with the secondary setting being the Santa Elena township – the manifestations of such being with their group, co-workers from the community, families in the community and elements of the natural environment.

> First we were living closely with people for that amount of time and becoming incredibly good friends with them and being like family. Santa Elena itself, personally I think gave me a lot of peace.
>
> (Mic)

> We all went up the mountain as individuals, with our own sets of goals and our own way of doing things, and when we came down from the mountain as a group I felt Santa Elena was our own.
>
> (Sue)

> Whereas in city life, people tend not to focus so much on the relationship, it's the job they're doing, which they focus on, then other people revolve around that. Whereas in Santa Elena and youth challenge, you revolve with the people. You're looking at a task that the main focus is how you get on with the other person. I think that's what I enjoy and why I keep seeking out that sort of experience. I think it heightens your resolve to do something and, maybe because of the group skills, you're focusing on the consideration of others.
>
> (Mic)

In the secondary setting (the Santa Elena township), socializing appeared to be the main form of interaction:

> Another time was socializing at Belvades, which is a bar in town, where we got together with the community in a sort of free-flowing nature. That was a lot of fun mixing with them in a social environment, rather than a working environment. I think they appreciated us being around to provide some entertainment. I guess that was my only real experience, socially and at the workplace with the Santa Elena community. The Costa Ricans are fantastic, fun loving, full of vibrancy and they really know how to live life to the full. On a one-to-one nature, trying to battle my way through Spanish, because some of them didn't speak a word of English, was a really lovely experience. Those sort of moments were day-to-day, nothing really stands out as being one-off. They were always quite memorable, trying to communicate with various Costa Ricans.
>
> (Jen)

The importance of the group and co-workers from the community and these interactions were central to many volunteers' perspectives on the nature of the ecotourism experience. One volunteer summarizes a typical instance of the social interaction experienced:

> My involvement with the group was great. That was the beauty, you're working with Costa Ricans, Canadians, fellow Aussies and working with experts in the field. Just the basic things like getting together for dinner, and for Australia Day we cooked up a batch of lamingtons and Anzac biscuits. We had a couple of sing-along nights and everyone from different countries would get up and do their bit and sing and dance and carry on. You're doing this in a wooden shack with a sheet of plastic over the top of it, but nevertheless it was a really homely environment. A different group would be cooking, particularly of an evening; those times were really special moments with the group. When you had finished a hard day's work and you're looking forward to a bite to eat and something to drink, chatting over dinner about the way of the world, the problems of

> the universe or whatever. Also interacting with Costa Ricans and getting them to teach you more about their culture, the way they do things in contrast to the way we do things, and likewise with the Canadians. Really discovering their sort of views on various topics in contrast to your own views and getting to know a bit more about each and every race that you're working with. I loved the group situation, I loved getting to know all walks of life. Most people come from very different backgrounds. I really enjoyed that aspect. By the same token, there were some people that I probably wouldn't bother spending too much time with, but I think on the whole, the people that I spent time with, I learnt a great deal from them. Even in the workplace, the locals coming up from the community, a lot of them were very skilled. Watching them and the way they worked was an inspiration. The Costa Ricans were very happy-go-lucky. Working with them in a group was good fun. Working with the Canadians and fellow Aussies was great too, it was real spirited camaraderie. You could always get a helping hand more often than not from any of your fellow work mates and that was touching, especially in times when you were dead-set tired and frustrated. You would often be helped out, or likewise you would be giving a helping hand to someone else in the same situation or in a difficult situation. Group interaction at work and socially was great.
>
> (Jen)

This statement reflects both the importance of the SERR as a setting for the interaction and the importance of the group and representatives from the community as elements of this.

> Another thing was having big festival-type nights where we would make up cocktails. The locals and the challengers used to drink them about once a week. Because I couldn't speak with them very well, that was a fun form of interaction. I got along quite well with them on that level. The people from the local community would always come up and work their guts out, then at the end of the day they would have to walk back through all the mud.
>
> (Meg)

It was evident that social interaction with the group was different from that experienced with the representatives of the host community. Such an observation illuminates the need to broaden the examination of elements that make up these experiences and the importance of the specific types of social components associated with it. There is also a difference in the emphasis between the character of social interaction in SERR and the community. The volunteers reinforce this perspective:

> By the time we got to Santa Elena we were like a family. Probably as a group, the thing I really enjoyed was comfortability with each other.
>
> (Mic)

> The person in charge of the project also owned the bar, so that was the only interaction we had with the community at that stage. I didn't feel

> like we had a great deal of connection with the community when we first arrived. I remember they used to look at us a lot and wonder who we were, but not much else. They may have been a bit nervous, I don't know, but it wasn't a very positive feeling, except for those who were actively wanting the project to happen. There were a few younger teenage boys who would come up each day and work with us in the rainforest, they were pretty friendly. They were actually showing us what to do up there, showing us how to find the right wood and that sort of thing. So they were memorable moments with the community.
>
> (Ann)

Each of these statements suggests that social interaction established, even if limited, can be very memorable, even though the experience may vary from positive to negative. This expectation or shared meaning about the role of enjoyable social interaction in the SERR experience was common amongst the volunteers. Meeting the community and doing things (with other volunteers) that are not normally done reflect the character of these occasions and the nature of the shared meanings. Approaching and talking to strangers (community and tourist), singing and telling stories with them are all essentially social behaviours, and enjoyable social behaviours from the perspectives of those interviewed. The satisfaction derived from these occasions was evidently intrinsic in nature (Neulinger, 1982, p. 74) and this is the main motivation that can be discovered for participation in these occasions.

The data support the idea that the experience participated in by the volunteer on the YCI SERR project involves a process of exchange/interaction between the volunteer and social and environmental factors of the site such as representatives of the community, the natural environment and the volunteer group. The ecotourism experience offers a chance for some degree of cultural exchange and opportunities for social interaction, with both the volunteers' group and representatives of the host community. With this exchange came changes in the value held for the social and physical environments of the SERR and the community, evidenced through the responses of the volunteers.

> You may not agree with the way someone lives or someone else's value system, but you've got no right to sit there and judge it, or try and change it unless you really see some benefit in re-educating people to another way of thinking. It doesn't matter that they have a totally different system to the way we do things, just enjoy the differences.
>
> (Amy)

The natural features of the SERR and its aesthetic qualities contribute to this increase in value in a range of ways. The SERR provides a physical and psychological distancing from the normal 'home' lifestyle, with solitude and contemplation identified by the volunteers as an important aspect. Social interactions with the group and community are fundamental elements and contribute to the social exchange (seen as a process) of the experience. The SERR also provided a range of other opportunities that allowed 'social interaction as leisure' as a component of the sociocultural exchange which contributed to the attitudinal shift in the way the volunteers felt about themselves, their lifestyle, and the way in which they regard the social and natural environment. All of these factors contribute to the valuation of the site, and this valuation in relation to natural environments in general has been attenuated demonstrably as a result of the process of the experience.

The operation of social interaction in this aspect of the experience emphasizes the connection between the data and related studies of outdoor recreation behaviour which find that social groups and the family stage are important determinants of outdoor recreation participation (Manning, 1986, p. 16; Roggenbuck and Lucas, 1987, p. 204) illustrating the development of a common meaning for the SERR as a setting which accommodates the variety of leisure needs of the volunteers, while allowing for the similarities and differences which may be determined by common family and social backgrounds.

There was substantial evidence of shared meanings of SERR as an enjoyable experience. This meaning was reflected upon and developed by the volunteers through the experience of SERR. It is evident that the parents of these volunteers had an important influence on the reason they chose YCI. This is consistent with Colton's findings that there is a relationship between patterns of childhood socialization and outdoor recreation participation and that patterns of recreation in childhood were related to adult recreation behaviour (Colton, 1987, p. 353).

In each of the situations above, social processes have contributed significantly to the development of meanings about the ecotourism experience. These meanings were derived through social interaction with family and friends and reflect Stryker's observations about the development of meanings as they affect behaviour:

> Behaviour [in the symbolic interactionist perspective] is largely governed by the individual's social definition of the situation, interaction with others in the social milieu, and the self concept [which is] governed to a large extent by others in a social process.
>
> (Stryker, 1980, p. 27)

These data reinforce the utility of the interactionist perspective in understanding the observed patterns of behaviour. They recognize the status and significance of others in a social group as a dominant construct, as opposed to research based in psychology and social psychology, which regards the influence of others as peripheral in relation to individual decision making.

A theoretical interpretation of these observations suggests that macrosocial phenomena, such as an ideology of environmentalism[19] as it influences individual roles in wider society, is variable in micro-social contexts such as the ecotourism experience (see Clarke *et al.*, 1975). According to Foucault (1981), social institutions (such as the family) constitute and govern individuals through hegemonic discourses (such as those surrounding environmentalism). In the future, an understanding of the discourse of environmentalism may assist in understanding the ecotourism experience particularly as expressed by the volunteers here. For these volunteers, the discourse of environmentalism creates a belief of what can be achieved in projects such as the SERR.

The styles of interaction apparent here involve intimate relationships with the group, sociable contact with representatives of the community and elements of the natural environment. There was a clear expectation of this interaction as a component of the ecotourist experience, with social interaction identified as an important aspect of the experience among the volunteers interviewed.

Primary Influences on the Self and Identity

Meaning will be constructed according to individual volunteer's cultural and social backgrounds, but it appears that the individual/group interaction in the interrelational nexus between elements of the experience fundamentally impacts upon the volunteer's sense of self and identity. The preceding section explored the relationship between the interactions that occur with the natural elements of the site and the influences this has on self. The present section seeks to elaborate upon this relational interchange, specifically with respect to the emergent thematic areas of influence in the volunteer's experience.

The data reveal that the experience impacts fundamentally upon the volunteer's degree of learned experience in that an awareness is created or enhanced in their future actions (see Ewert, 1987; Whitmore, 1988).

> It inspired me in one area to do the ANZSES trip up North. I got involved in the ANZSES trip because I thought it was a lot like Youth Challenge but within Australia. All I knew was that it was rainforest and I thought of Santa Elena and that maybe the two would gel, but I didn't have any specifics.
>
> (Jen)

---

[19] For an outline of the history of modern environmentalism, see Pepper (1984) *The Roots of Modern Environmentalism*; for its relationship to society, see Eckersley (1992) *Environmentalism and Political Theory*; for its effects on individual identity, see Fox (1990) *Towards a Transpersonal Ecology*.

> Awareness, I suppose from being in Santa Elena and study afterwards, I have a much broader understanding, an awareness of a practical ecotourism project, how it works, the impacts it can have because I have lived there, I think about the positives and the negatives.
>
> (Lil)

In this way, the experience has initiated a change or reorientation in life direction. Meg suggests that: 'I think it's reinforced why I'm doing the work that I'm doing, as in outdoor education'. Whereas Ros states: 'In the last week, I have been working out ways I can actually give something else back to Santa Elena, I visited the Seaacres Centre, which is setting up a sister relationship with Santa Elena, with some people from Youth Challenge to give a talk'.

Similarly, Mic finds: 'You can see why you're recycling, it gives you practical focus of why you're doing things. I've noticed I'm swinging towards careers that are going to be socially beneficial'. With Sue suggesting: 'It hasn't changed my direction at all, it's just strengthened what I already felt or motivated me more to get involved in what I'm interested in'.

Information from the focus group tended to reinforce the above views. Ken, for example, maintains that:

> I don't know if it hits you in the middle of the day sort of thing. Conditions of living were different and were probably totally alien to us middle-class Australians, so we really got a lot out of it. It is an experience which everyone has taken away something. It is something that they have never done and probably never will do again. I suppose the values we brought away from that are what we are talking about now, tolerance and patience, because they were really stretched to the limit. I wouldn't say that I'm home in New South Wales, chaining myself to bulldozers and that sort of thing. But I think in your own way, you still like to affect the whole thing in some way. I would also like to think that I had an appreciation through my work. A lot of the projects that I've worked on are environmentally contentious, and I would like to feel that my input would have some effect, in the respect of the environment and that sort of thing. I think that's a positive influence that I've taken away from Costa Rica.
>
> Everything we do, we know what happens to it. We know where all our waste products go, we know where we throw all our rubbish. Since Santa Elena, one of my pet things now is to use a strainer when I'm washing up, so when I let the water out all the crap doesn't go down the sink, because I think I'm going to be swimming in that.
>
> (Ken)
>
> How much toilet paper do you use? You can use a whole roll, it doesn't matter, because you just go down to the shop and buy some more. But when you've got limited resources you value them, you use them. One of the first things when I got back, was I had a really hard time

getting used to being able to leave the shower tap on for the whole shower.

(Sue)

That's something that we could do here to help our environment. Every time I go to the toilet at night, I refuse to turn the light on, because I always think about how many times I went in Santa Elena without light, and you adjust, you can see without light. These are basic things that you don't experience until you've done something like Santa Elena

(Ros)

The changes effectuated in relation to lifestyle and life direction varied considerably for each individual; many related to family:

In Costa Rica and Santa Elena, there was a sense of family, and Israel really focused that. In Australia, we have a really different society. Coming from a split family, it was really wonderful to see the importance that people put on families in the community, to have a community that works as a whole family unit is really important over there. I was single and never wanted to get married, never wanted to have kids, but I came back with a real sense of what a wonderful thing it is to have a family. It's something that is really basic, and you kind of almost think because we are such consumers, it almost defaults it. But it is such a basic part of life, and such a natural thing to have that family life. To put yourself out for your kids and your family. I don't necessarily want kids, but I would rather kids than a house. I'd rather live in a tent in Santa Elena than have a house.

(Ros)

I came from the country. Over the years, especially when I left school and got into business, I lost a lot of contact with my three younger brothers. They all said the school I was going to really changed me. There were about four or five policies that you make for yourself when you come back from Costa Rica and you usually get through about one to one and a half. One of them was, I had one family, they're my blood relations and they're wonderful, and I have three younger brothers and I don't know them very well. In the last few years, I have made the hugest effort to make them a large part of my life again and I have. It has been the most rewarding experience. It has been unreal, I've loved every minute of it.

(Kim)

I came back and took off 6 months so I could go and visit my family. I hadn't seen my grandparents for 5 years. I wanted to go and see my grandfather for Christmas this year, it was to get that increased sense of family.

(Ros)

The following statements reflect the range of areas, upon return from the SERR project, that were impacted upon:

It definitely affects what you do. I had a bit of an ethical problem going overseas and working, but it was all worth it because it gave me a comparison, it gave me an appreciation of another culture and another environment. Coming back to Australia gave me a real focus of what I was doing. It really made me want to get in there and finish university, do really well and do justice to Costa Rica. I did ecotourism as my following project, and although I didn't do phenomenally well, for me it was a great way of going through it all and putting it all into context. I went walking last week with the environment centre. We had been doing stuff on storm water drains, so I thought we would go for a walk to the top of the hill at North Head and appreciate what's there. I was struggling all the way to get them to have an interest, but once they were up there, they thought it was amazing. It took me a long time to encourage them to come back. To have an appreciation for something in Sydney, you're in this metropolis, but it can still be unique and very beautiful. It certainly changed the way I want to travel, it changed the way I appreciate what I've got.

(Ros)

It puts you in such a radically different environment. Over the years, you've got used to the environment and it doesn't change much, like what car you drive, what clothes you wear, etc. You get there, and that all shrinks in because there is none of that there, it's just you, and no-one really gives a stuff what car you have back home. So it really shrinks your sense of self. You've got to get down to yourself and it's not all these other consumer things which we tend to take for granted. Then when you then step back into this society, your sense of self, or your identity has shrunk a fair bit. You're not as attached to those things that were slowly growing over you like a parasite. So when you come back, you just naturally adjust yourself with all the attachments that you used to have. So I think it does make quite a large difference. I work sometimes and I don't work others, but I'm not too worried about the money I make. I may have been before I went there, but now I'm more likely to do what I think, rather than think about what my attachments are, or think that I need more money for my car, or to buy clothes or CDs. It just shrinks you down until you're just you.

(Mic)

I really don't remember what my tolerance level was at the time, with going into a new community and accepting the way that people work, but my tolerance levels are so different now. You can have an attitude towards it, but you don't have to judge it.

(Sue)

I guess I'm one of the least changed people since I came back. I could definitely say that Costa Rica and Santa Elena and everything else were probably the most significant 3 months and could compare it to almost 3 or 4 years of other times in my life, because of the intensity of it and what went on. The experience was so huge. So the effect it had on me was more a fantastic memory, I guess.

(Kim)

I think the biggest impact was what I was talking about earlier, and the way that the experience affected me. I think my tolerance level and my acceptance levels, aren't as black and white any more. It doesn't necessarily have to be about environmental things, just generally. You may not agree with the way someone lives or someone else's value system, but you've got no right to sit there and judge it, or try and change it unless you really see some benefit in re-educating people to another way of thinking. It doesn't matter that they have a totally different system to the way we do things, just enjoy the differences.

(Amy)

What you were saying about doing something for a friend or business partner. I think the thing about Santa Elena is that you weren't doing it for anyone, but you were doing it for nature. It's not like I'm doing it for person *x* or *y* or whatever, you're sort of doing it for no reason, the reason is the whole environment around you.

(Ros)

The experience has impacted on the volunteers in giving them a larger view of the world and by generally having a pro-active effect on their daily lifestyle at home, which is in accordance with research on outdoor recreation.[20] Also, as Ittelsen *et al.* (1974) suggest, it changes to a degree their relationship with the environment in that environmental awareness means that they now perceive their role within the environment in a different way from before the experience.

If I had that time over again, I would never get back and get into that same routine and structure. No one can see the difference, but things have changed. You need to have some sort of recognition in yourself that you have changed as a person. Not even so much a debriefing, just sort of on your own terms, just to be able to synthesize afterwards.

(Kim)

I think the grooves are pretty deep too. So if you come back and jump back straight into your other life, you might have changed a bit, but then you just slot back into the old grooves. When you said you had to step back into the old grooves to stay sane, I wonder if that's to stay sane or so that you didn't change too much. Because if you hadn't stepped straight back into the grooves, then the path you were on, might have led to a different outcome. I think the other debriefing in Costa Rica wasn't useless but that was in another country and it can't do a lot for you. Maybe if you had the same thing here, that allows you to be that different person in your own environment. I think you can be a different person in a different environment, but coming back here you've got the choice of either stepping straight back into the grooves, or like you say, being off your mind for quite a while, you're not sure how to work it.

(Mic)

---

[20] See Heimstra and McFarling (1974), Kaplan and Talbot (1983), Scherl (1988) and Hartig *et al.* (1991).

> No I don't think I would have gone back into accounting anyway. I think the thing that it gave me was a sense of what I'm capable of, I now have complete faith in myself. If I did decide to start running a nursery and a horticultural place, I'd know I can do it. The thing I learnt over there was that I could probably do anything. I did things that I'd never done before and you realized that every single time you could do it. So I haven't broken away as much as I wish I had the guts to, but I now have complete faith in my own ability.
>
> (Kim)

> That's why I think it is a long-term process. You asked about the change in ourselves and our identity, I think it is a really long-term process. I think it is just one experience, it is a pretty big peak I guess, it leads you slowly but gradually off to a different path.
>
> (Mic)

Other volunteers found that it gave them a greater appreciation of Australia. Ros who went to school and had 'a lot of day-to-day contact with Aboriginal people' would prefer to spend time in their community rather than travel overseas. Similarly, Kim, who 'grew up in an Aboriginal community' felt that 'getting an Aboriginal community to meet people like Canadians, Ticos [Costa Ricans], etc., would be amazing, especially if you're really helping them'.

Change to self and identity often related to family impressions:

> There was no recognition from my parents that changes were made, it was like coming back into this structure that you just didn't fit any more, you didn't understand where you were coming from so much any more, let alone trying to fit a mould that you just don't fit.
>
> (Amy)

One area where a change in attitudes and values would be expected to occur is in the perception that the volunteer has of a developed country. Direct experience is one of the fundamental reasons for setting up international volunteering (see Dickson, 1976; Clark, 1978). It is apparent that the majority of the SERR volunteers changed their perception in some way. Meg said: 'Yes, I now have the basic knowledge. I guess it has made me more aware' while Amy states that 'they [attitudes] were formed because I went over there with the question, "what is it like?" So a lot of those questions were answered for me to an extent in that area'.

Focus group evidence also broadly supported this perceptual and attitudinal change:

> I think it is part of a universal pattern, there are people everywhere in the community who care. That was the good thing about travelling. You often wonder what you're doing, it is because there are people and communities that make it worthwhile to go there; in Australia, Costa Rica or wherever, you're going to meet more people that have that same sense of

> appreciation for the environment. It was good to realize that even in developing countries people still have that sense of what they've got.
>
> (Ros)

Sue, who has travelled to Nepal and Thailand since the project, suggests:

> I didn't really relate to the experience at all, because we were tourists coming in, looking and going again. I just couldn't really get into that, because of my experience in Santa Elena and Costa Rica, we were part of the community, we were giving something back to the community. In Thailand, I almost felt like a thief in a way. I was taking and not giving anything back. And the same in Nepal, I wasn't giving anything back. I wasn't taking the time to get to know the people. Costa Rica was the first time I had been overseas and I think that has really laid the groundwork for me in what I want when I travel, because I didn't see myself as a tourist when I was in Santa Elena, I was living. A tourist is someone who just comes and goes without giving anything. But I felt in Costa Rica and in Santa Elena, at the time it felt like we were really doing something that was benefiting the community, and I think that's an experience you can get by doing that sort of thing. Next time I travel I will take time to find out about the culture.

The above comment encapsulates a view held by many other respondents who suggested that they would never travel again for short periods, particularly on 'Contiki-style tours', for example. Instead, they would take more time to appreciate fully the diverse cultures and the rhythm of the place visited. Kim suggests:

> I'm happy not to travel if I can't do it on the terms that I want to do it. You can get a photo of the Eiffel Tower any time. But the people who work in the environments like Santa Elena, that's the sort of way I want to know a country, not just taking pictures of buildings.

The potential strength for ecotourism to change attitudes and behaviour lies in the creation of interest (mindfulness) through the ecotourist's perception of the experience as being an unfamiliar or unique one. This potentiality is elaborated in the stories that the volunteers have to tell. The ecotourist, as is shown in Chapter 6 and supported by Crompton (1979, p. 420), is seeking new sights and experiences, a sense of adventure, moral obligations and/or to benefit educationally from the unique environment.

Behaviour is believed to be a function of attitudes, social expectations, beliefs about the consequences of such action, the value of the consequences of a behaviour and the knowledge of how to perform the behaviour (Pearce, 1988, p. 145). Therefore, an ecotourist may only contribute funds towards wildlife conservation if they believe that money will actually help save a rainforest species, that such behaviour

BIRMINGHAM COLLEGE OF FOOD

is socially endorsed, if they have money to donate and know where and how to donate.

> One example is my attitude towards World Vision and those sort of organizations where you pay $20. Originally I would have never given money to organizations like that, but now you see the work from the money and how it manifested itself in actually working with the different communities. It makes you think through things a little bit differently now.
>
> (Amy)

Pearce maintains that emotional involvement through tourist experiences is another important means of communicating information and altering attitudes and behaviour: '[t]ravel can be viewed as one of the forces shrinking the subjective distance between the observer and international events, thus increasing the emotional impact of such phenomena' (Pearce, 1982, p. 114).

> Having had first hand contact with it you do. You're a lot surer of your conviction, also you have to think things through. When you go down town to a little Costa Rican village and every second place is a restaurant, every third place is a hotel and there are taxis going through town, you stop and think, do the people really want this to be changed? Is this something they really wanted? I think that also goes back to what Santa Elena has given me as a cultural influence and as an environmental project? But I have general fields, and I think Santa Elena's influenced that a lot. Having seen that we're responsible in a lot of ways for what goes on in developing nations, I would think 'if I've had contact with it and I feel like I know what I'm talking about, why don't I get in there and help?'
>
> (Mic)

Pearce explores this idea further using the idea of 'vividness'. He finds that an example of information may be effective if it elicits emotional interest (relates to the individual), is concrete or tangible and has close proximity to the person in time or space (Pearce, 1988, p. 154).

Information which is relevant to the tourist's own situation or interests will be more mindfully processed. For example, Kim stated that:

> My mother and I talk a lot and she's a real gardening freak, so when I found out that I was on the gardening project, I was thinking that she would love to be here right now. They were talking about how there were 200 orchids in the rainforest and how two new ones had been found that year by science, and other botanical bits and pieces. One of the guys had the most beautiful botanical book of Costa Rican orchids. I spent a whole afternoon looking through that one day. Probably one of my biggest feelings was that I wanted to say 'Mum, look at this', I knew she would have been so interested in it.

Within the ecotourism context, such emotional response is often displayed as a result of activities and circumstances experienced.

Ecotourists are at liberty and are encouraged to make judgements and respond to totally new environments, lifestyles and experiences which are usually outside their domain of concern in their home environment. Additionally, persuasive measures are more effective when the audience is in a pleasant setting, which is usually the case in ecotourism (Pearce, 1988, p. 155). A study conducted by Pearce relating to tourist–guide interactions found that although tourists could often only remember a minimum amount of information following a guided tour, the experience had a significant emotional impact on the arousal level, sense of control and emotional satisfaction of the tourist (Pearce, 1984, p. 145).

> Santa Elena was very beautiful too, but as you came down the mountain, you could see the terrible deforestation which had created a really dry environment, where as you knew before it would have been moist, so there are big contrasts. There were areas like the ocean and the coast that were beautiful. I guess I'm comparing it to Australia, the way they urbanize their land, they practically cut down everything. The reserve is so beautiful. That type of reserve is something I'd never seen before. It was really good to be actually working with nature. We don't really get that much of an opportunity to do it here. It was work that was totally different to anything that I would ever do in Australia, so that impacted on me in a big way. As I was doing the work, I felt as if it was beneficial for the reserve. In the long term you hope the work that you were doing in the reserve and the money that went to the school would hopefully bring the children from the school to have the same appreciation that foreigners seem to have of their reserve. So you're always hoping that the work you were doing would eventually attract the Costa Ricans. In Santa Elena, there are different areas, there are primary forests and secondary forests. Seeing the forests that were cut down growing back, is reassuring. You hear about so many places in the world being forested and if they are left the forest does grow back and eventually diversity comes back. There are pockets of primary forest left and that made you feel good, you could actually see that was happening. Just knowing that such a large area of land was left to be a reserve and not to be used for anything was good.
>
> (Pen)

Erikson's work (1971 (see Chickering, 1969; Craig, 1983)) suggests that this type of structured experience – one which resolves challenges and deals with tasks in a staged process – results in the development of a clear sense of identity.

> Personally, in the sense of that we were doing something constructive and productive and it was actually, particularly in Santa Elena, a community project and the benefits were being felt in the community. It gave me a sense that what we were doing was something that was on the right tracks. I came back very positive for university, to finish off my degree, for which I did a comparative study of ecotourism in Costa Rica and Australia. It broadened my ideas of what people were like and that no

matter what country you are in, you all face the same kind of problems to different degrees. I think it is a chance to put your own culture into perspective too.

(Ros)

When I came back I wanted to do volunteer work with other national parks.

(Pen)

It does make you think you want to do things meaningful 'well I don't like this' about what I'm doing now, maybe I should try harder, or get more involved in this sort of thing.

(Mic)

I came back and I was supposed to do a Graduate Diploma in Environmental Studies, but after my experience in Costa Rica, studying theoretical equations in a book didn't seem applicable to my life at that stage. I had just come back from such a real life experience and basic life. If I hadn't had that experience, I think I would be doing a Graduate Diploma in Environmental Studies at the moment. I went on the dole and then I went looking for a full-time job. I'm working as a supervisor/tutor for a bush regeneration project, supervising unemployed youth. In Costa Rica, I said my perfect job would be to come back and do exactly what I'm doing. I don't know if it's my perfect job now that I'm doing it.

(Sue)

I decided that I wanted to have more to do with my family when I came back and I have, and I'm loving it. The reality in Costa Rica is so different from the reality here, you can't combine the two very easily.

(Kim)

The volunteer Liz had a firm idea of what ecotourism was before the project and this was reaffirmed through her involvement in the project which saw her reorientate her studies to focus on protected area management, ecotourism and outdoor recreation. She has returned to Costa Rica with YCI as a staff member and also worked in the USA as a volunteer wilderness ranger. The reinforcement of her original attitudes is very important to consider in studying ecotourist behaviour, as well as understanding the influence of social interactions and prevailing social attitudes on behaviour. In such circumstances, the influencing of these attitudes requires an increase in the level of understanding of the ecotourism experience and the results of the effect of direct experience (increased quality of life for Santa Elena community, for example), the positive evaluation of such an experience and the subsequent changes (either redirection or a more focused direction) in behaviour (i.e. the pursuing of a career in the area).

In situations which are perceived as unexpected, unfamiliar or very relevant and important, individuals will pay much greater attention to the information available and will process it in detail – that is, they will be mindful.

(Pearce, 1988, p. 144)

Now that the impact volunteer tourist experiences can have on the self and identity of participants has been examined, the next chapter explores how important elements of an alternative tourism experience such as group, nature and community can combine within the experience to create a social value of the space for the volunteer.

Chapter 6

The Site, Social Value and the Self

What are the elements of an alternative tourism experience and its process that are important to the alternative tourist? The elements of an alternative tourism experience have now been examined in relation to their impact and influence on self and identity. The present section will provide an outline and discussion of how the different elements of the group, nature and community, through the process of learning experience, create a social value of the space for the volunteers.

> Social value is created through the way people interact in them; spaces such as the site take their meaning from the people who, and elements that, occupy them. The interactive dimension of the site represents a social process where a place acts as a material resource that over time (this can be a short intense period of time) has social significance for a group of people.

The role of 'place' in experiences (see Denzin, 1977, p. 149) is important; the setting that allows for interaction, which, in turn, provides the conditions for encounters. In relation to the SERR experience, the preceding chapters and the data have identified setting as the conjunction between the host community and their natural environment. Ulrich *et al.* found that in natural physical settings:

> immediate, unconsciously triggered and initiated emotional responses – not 'controlled' cognitive responses – play a central role in the initial level of responding to nature, and have major influences on attention,

subsequent conscious processing, physiological responding and behaviour.

(Ulrich *et al.*, 1991, pp. 207–208)

These involuntary or automatic mechanisms may be important factors in influencing reflection on the experience. Similarly, Ulrich *et al.* (1991, p. 75) argue that environmental stimuli, 'pleasant natural spaces', for example, evoke physiological responses and influence preferences for particular types of natural environments. Volunteers may not be consciously aware of these influences but may, however, provide clues to these influences if given the opportunity to reflect on the experience. This serves to exemplify the centrality of the second research question in relation to the ecotourist's increased value for the social and physical environments of the destination area.

It is acknowledged that exploring experience singularly through the reflection of the volunteer can be problematic since the exigencies of experience in everyday events can often leave the individual unconscious of the structural determinants of behaviour. However, if analysis is placed in the context of the actual on-ground experience, a valid and comprehensive understanding can be arrived at.

The interactive dimension of the SERR site represents a social process where a place acts as a material resource which, over time,[21] has social significance for a group of people such as the volunteers and community members.

> That was a wonderful area to spend some time. Like most beautiful spots in the world that I've visited and admired, it just goes in the memory books in my mind.
>
> (Jen)

> I thought the beauty of the place was amazing. I guess the fact that it was so vast and in one little patch in the forest there can be so much going on and it will always be going no matter what happens in your life, these sort of things will keep on living. It was a really calming experience.
>
> (Sue)

> You asked before about whether it hits you being in Santa Elena and I think it does. Any other time I've been in a place like that, it's been for a weekend, you're in the city and you head out and camp or do whatever. Santa Elena was the first opportunity I had to live in the forest. So you're not just going for the recreation and then leaving, you're staying there and basing 6 weeks of your life around it. So when you come back it sometimes seems all a bit fake, like it's all a bit imposed. When I think back, it might just be because it was something I enjoyed and the experience

[21] This can vary from an extended period to a relatively short, intense period of time.

> as well. It was so nice just living in that natural environment without cars or whatever, or the hassles you have with living somewhere like this. I think it does affect you a fair bit. It affected me in that I pay more attention to environmental issues, or maybe I have a pre-thought-out view about which side I fall on in a debate, for example, should we woodchip or shouldn't we. And now I sort of automatically know, because I've been there and it's so beautiful. It might make me dogmatic to some extent, it's a real factor now my decision-making, whereas before I may have thought about it but then not having experienced as much, even the outdoor stuff, it wasn't as big a factor. I guess it changes your views a lot. For me it wasn't the sole cause and only factor, but it was a fairly substantial leap. I guess the only problem I see from that is how do you separate out the environment we were in, from the group we were in, it is sort of a difficult thing. It was beautiful there and it was a fantastic experience and they sort of go hand-in-hand. You can't say that one was the focus more than the other. If you sent me back to that, or if you sent me with a group into a concrete jungle somewhere, whether they would be totally different, I wouldn't know.
>
> (Mic)

Volunteers' responses identify that the Youth Challenge experience does provide an opportunity for a shift in the way the volunteers value the environments they have interacted with. By their definition of the term, the volunteers involved in the SERR study experienced a social valuing that came from the 'social interaction as leisure' between themselves, representatives of the host community, the natural environment and their group.

The concept of social value is linked to the research through the volunteers' experience which they describe as being a process, learning experience and interactive exchange with the natural environment which relates fundamentally to the debate surrounding sustainability which has been discussed by a range of authors.[22] The fundamental point of consensus within this diverse range of studies is inter-generational equity or, as explained by the *Brundtland Report*, what individuals effect in the present must be equitable, not only for those involved, but also for those who follow (World Commission on the Environment and Development, 1987, p. 87).

Equity in the case of the SERR relates to the community in terms of their income, wealth and education. The inequalities effected by tourism, that need to be addressed in order to increase the community's equity, include initiating the implementation of sound practices that enable social structures and processes that the community themselves, if not controlling, at least have direct consultation and input into.

---

[22] See World Commission on the Environment and Development (1987), Cronin (1990), Ecologically Sustainable Development Working Groups (1991), Hare (1991), Sofield (1991) and Curry and Morvaridi (1992).

The SERR is socially valuable in terms of its fundamental role in the lives of the ecotourist and representatives of the community that interact with it. A multitude of factors contribute to the SERR social value, and the volunteers have provided, through the data, the key contributing themes. There is a fundamental sense of the establishment of a different form of community in the SERR site, in that it provides the opportunity for a more equal basis for the interaction of representatives of the community, YCI group and the volunteers, contributing to the establishment of an equitable exchange between the community and ecotourist as it occurs in a setting whose social value is established and mediated through a joint process of exchange between the range of elements identified.

The process of becoming (Kelly, 1994) that is associated with leisure and tourism forms can be enscapulated by interactionism as the provision of space for the development and transformation of the self. The interaction of social value in the space that is created by the SERR through the interaction of the elements of the alternative tourism experience demonstrates the value of creating and/or maintaining these spaces in order to facilitate and maintain intimate relationships with others (see Bella, 1989).

The SERR, then, offers the opportunity for representatives of the community, ecotourist and group members to interact in a space that can facilitate the development and transformation of self in relation to others and nature. This may prove equitable for both the community member and ecotourist as the space is created by both in mediation. If the alternative tourism experience is viewed, in what Seamon refers to as an 'encounter: interaction with the environment in a state of heightened consciousness' (in Brown, 1992, p. 63), the result is the creation of a space that relates to the notion of place identity, place identity then being defined as the connections that people form with places, and the influences places have on their lives. In this context, the SERR becomes for both the community member and ecotourist, as Godkin (1980, p. 73) suggests, a 'reservoir of significant life experiences lying at the centre of a person's identity and sense of psychological well-being'. Buttimer (1980, p. 186) suggests that personal identity and health require an on-going process of centring – a reciprocity between dwelling and reaching – which can find its external expression in the sense of place or regional identity. It is in this respect that the SERR becomes a significant part of the idea of self and identity for the community member and the ecotourist.

The preceding section has provided an understanding of the underlying dynamic between the volunteer and representatives of the host community, the natural environment of the project site and the volunteers/group, and how this interaction is viewed by the volunteer. The exchange between the ecotourist and the community member, even if limited to certain community members, can be seen as an interactive process or a social exchange between 'significant others' which affects the attitudes and values of both; in this case contributing to the experience in the contribution to the social value held for the SERR site.

Volunteer experience has been demonstrated as a social exchange between certain elements of the site and the volunteer. The community is an essential element in providing a context for that experience. In applying interactionist perspectives and assessing their utility for further understanding of this social exchange, it is considered fundamental to contextualize the experience in addressing the limitations of the paradigm (as summarized by Denzin, 1992, p. 47, 1994) and its associated macroorganizational problems.

Denzin (1992, p. 164) has recognized the role of consciousness in determining existence for interactionism as an important point of departure from other sociological theory. For Blumer (and Mead), consciousness determines existence. For Marx, Mills, Sartre and the Critical School, consciousness does not determine existence; nor does existence determine consciousness. Between consciousness and existence reside processes of communication and cultural determinants. These two processes dialectically structure existence and consciousness.

The widely recognized role of consciousness in the critical sociological literature cannot be dismissed as a determinant of behaviour. This departure highlights a further limitation of an exclusively interactionist paradigm. This limitation could be addressed in future research through incorporation of other community studies perspectives, which broaden and contexualize understandings of specific instances of interaction.

In relation to a structural bias, criticisms of the interactionist paradigm relate to its 'microscopic' focus, which neglects historical, economic and political issues and tends to be descriptive rather than critically analytical of the situations which it examines. In Cunneen *et al.* (1989, p. 19), this limitation was addressed by introducing Marxist theory, and Clarke *et al.* (1975, p. 13) suggest that by situating microsocial observations of culture into their 'parent' cultures, a more adequate understanding of cultural phenomena can be developed.

Criticisms of the paradigm in neglecting emotional factors as they influence interaction are similar to the issues present in the foregoing discussion concerning theory and method. Denzin (1992) presents substantial evidence to refute this criticism; however, there is little to suggest that the methods of interactionism are able to capture the neuro-psychological determinants of behaviour. This limitation is acknowledged here in order to focus on the strengths that interactionism brings to the analysis of the data.

In relation to textuality, criticism focuses on attempts to read the key texts of interactionism (for example, Mead and Blumer) objectively. Denzin (1992, p. 69) recognizes that this is not possible and argues that new readings of these texts 'seek to locate a text, its author, and its subject matter within a historical moment and to show how a text reinscribes the dominant ideological and epistemological themes of its historical period'. In presenting this argument, Denzin implicitly recognizes the necessity of situating an observation into its social context.

Research methods such as 'volunteer observation' are essential tools in the process of gaining understanding of individuals within communities, but they themselves do not stand alone: instead, they require complementary methods for assessing and analysing individual behaviour within cultural and historical perspectives. Communities may define, and may themselves be defined by, human behaviour, and it is for this reason that this book needs to address the complexities of human behaviour within communities and within individuals. Interactionist approaches can play a central role in interpreting variance in attitudes and behaviour by placing information in a framework where it can be understood by outsiders to the community. In interpreting such variables, interactionism adheres to a number of basic premises. First, human beings act toward things on the basis of the meanings that things have for them. These things may be objects, other human beings, institutions, guiding ideals, activities of others and situations, or a combination of these. Secondly, the meaning of such things is derived from, or arises out of, the social interaction that one has with one's fellows. Thirdly, these meanings are handed in, and modified through, an interpretative process used by the person in dealings with the things he/she encounters (Chenitz and Swanson, 1986, p. 5).

Interactionism may then be able to be used to explain actions within a different cultural context, and this is an important step towards developing cross-cultural understanding. Such a perspective has significant implications for this research as it suggests that human behaviour, in order to be understood, must be examined in interaction. The setting, the implications inherent in the setting and the larger social forces such as ideologies and events that affect behaviour are analysed. The full range and variation of behaviour in a setting or in relation to a phenomenon is examined to produce self and group definitions and shared meanings. In order to do so, the researcher describes social behaviour as it takes place in natural settings. The actual setting is examined for social rules, ideologies and events that illustrate shared meaning held by people in the interaction and, thus, affect their behaviour in the interaction.

Next, the researcher needs to understand behaviour as the volunteers understand it, learn about their world, learn their interpretation of self in the interaction and share their definitions. In order to accomplish this, the researcher must understand the world from the volunteer's perspective. The researcher, therefore, must be both a volunteer in the world and an observer of the volunteers in that world. Finally, in order for the knowledge to be understood and accepted by the researcher's discipline, the researcher, as observer, must translate the meaning derived from the researcher as volunteer into the language of the research discipline.

Thus, interaction theory, informed by the literature on leisure experiences, has a significant contribution to make to the understanding of the SERR experience. Interaction theory provides insights into the microsocial contexts of leisure and the generic elements which constitute the social occasions that give rise to the SERR experience. Leisure theory identifies the factors that frame the phenomenon of leisure at both an individual and a societal level. In combination, these theoretical perspectives can enable the meanings of the SERR experience to be more fully understood.

Social Value, Identity and the Alternative Tourism Experience

Fundamental themes that have been identified – process, nature and interaction/exchange – form an interrelational complex that intermeshes with the elements of the site – such as nature, community members and other volunteers. This combination can be identified broadly as a symbolic system, which provides a place, or topos, within which the experience impacts upon the self and identity. MacCannell (1992, p. 3) suggests that critical theory has prepared us for the absence of the subject, for an empty meeting ground including an empty signifier. He suggests that deconstruction gives us access to the realm of absolute possibility in theory, in the imagination and, where it exists, in life. However, he maintains that an allied sociology of interaction or dialogue is still necessary to gain access to the realm of contingency and determinism, and especially resistance to, and struggles against, determinism.

The natural features of the SERR project site offered a contrast to the home, city and suburban environments of the volunteers, while the SERR site provided a context for exchange and experience which related fundamentally to the elements of the site. The SERR provided accessible experiences of flora, fauna, scenery and space, and these natural/aesthetic qualities of the SERR reflect one dimension of a change of environment on leisure opportunities and experiences which are important to the ecotourism experience (see Mercer, 1981, p. 41; Scherl, 1988, p. 1). The volunteers surveyed held a common meaning of these qualities of nature in the SERR as contributing to their experience.

The SERR setting had a number of important contributions to make to the volunteers' experience of the SERR when contextualized as leisure. The responses demonstrated a definite value for the SERR setting which can be seen in the responses from the interviews in the previous chapters. In each of these question areas, there was consistent evidence to confirm that experience in the SERR was constructed as an alternative tourism experience (ecotourism) by the volunteers, characterized by underlying ideas relating to freedom (Kelly, 1987, p. 6) and by positive effect (Kleiber *et al.*, 1986, pp. 169–176). Additionally, the volunteers, through the process of the experience, were significantly affected in terms of the value held for the environment in general and the SERR (site) in particular.

While the ecotourist is likely to share meanings of the protected area as a symbolic place, individuals within the group itself will bring to it, and come away with, differing interpretations which will impact in varying ways and to varying degrees on their daily lifestyle. Significantly here, the experience itself, in its very diversity of meanings and interactions, provides a social field[23] that enables the individual to renegotiate and reconstruct their usual roles (Colton, 1987). Hazleworth and Wilson (1990, p. 36) find nine areas of self-concept in which this may occur: physical; moral–ethical; personal; family; social; identity; self-satisfaction; behaviour; and self-criticism, with their overall findings demonstrating significant positive changes in moral–ethical self-concept, identity and self-satisfaction. Similarly, Darby (1994), in considering theories related to personal development (in concordance with Kolb (1984) and Kuh *et al.* (1988)), finds seven general categories that essentially underlie the notion of personal development. These include: cognitive developmental; psychosocial; maturity; typology; person–environment interaction; spirituality; and experiential learning, and they are reflected in the comments of the YCI volunteers.

The social interaction of volunteers with the elements of the site influenced behaviour, initiating impacts on the volunteers' values, the most prominent being an increased value for the social and physical environments visited. Their visit also had both positive and negative impacts on the host community which could, in both the short and long term, affect the long-term sustainability of the experience and thus jeopardize its experiential integrity. Existing studies corroborate these findings but they did not offer a significant contribution towards understanding the social and qualitative dimensions which affect this

---

[23] Social field is used here to designate the complex of meanings and interactions that arise between, and within, the context of a spatio-temporally bound locus.

interaction. An explanation of these dimensions was sought in the sociological literature and applied to the emerging data.[24]

The interactionist perspective, in combination with microsociological research, provided the original theoretical framework for the investigation. This framework was applied to examining the microsocial processes within the project and the wider social influences of the experience. It enabled an understanding of the meanings inherent (social value) in the SERR project. Social interaction was identified as the basis for the development of meanings of the project which places the shared experience of those involved as central to the experience.

It has been argued, and supported by the data, that the volunteers gained a social value for both the social and physical environments as a result of the experience itself. However, the change was not overly dramatic in the context of the physical environment as the majority of the volunteers held a concern for these rainforest environments before their arrival at the SERR site.

The process of change within the community was seen as a key element, and the interaction of volunteers and representatives of the community is in need of further investigation within a sociological context. For example, the mutual interdependence of power and resistance, observed by Foucault (1978, p. 95), can be applied to understanding the nature of this change. In terms of power, the community appear to be accessing more economic power through the ecotourism project, particularly in relation to income and the provision of increasing opportunities for part- and full-time paid employment. Accruing economic, and therefore social power – in relation to the sections of the community interested in conservation – enables the reorientation of the determining social mechanisms and paradigms in which the community operate. The microsocial situation of the ecotourist experience is therefore an important site as this is the location where the exchange of values for the environment occurs, thereby creating a shared social value of the environment interacted with.

The exercise of power in the 'guest' and 'host' relationship (which may give rise to changes in attitudes and behaviours at a microsocial level; i.e. in the ecotourism experience) must also be considered as aggregating to produce changes in wider societal contexts beyond the level of individual exchanges. Doxey's (1976) 'tourist irritation index' is an example of this process. As exchanges between the ecotourist and

---

[24] Initial research for the book in relation to understanding tourist behaviour did not enable a discernment of the behaviours and interactions of ecotourist and host community. The book has developed a provisional framework that can achieve and assess this area. Additionally, as the group is becoming more significant in both domestic and international tourism, this framework will also allow further research and provide further explanations of this type of experience. Frameworks can now be developed to identify the social and qualitative variables which affect the exchanges within these groups.

community member increase, the distinction between tourist and worker is reduced. As this distinction fades, it can give rise to a perception of legitimacy for the ecotourists and what they represent to the community in relation to that of a 'holidayer' status, thus adding credence to their views on topics (such as the environment and what it represents) related to the experience. In a Marxian analysis, it could also be argued that the recognition by the market of the profitability of the ecotourist reinforces this legitimacy through various marketing mechanisms. Through political mechanisms, the rights and entitlements of their attitudes are also embodied in the state. At the level of individual exchange, various processes assist the community to resist dominant discourses, such as those surrounding the profit basis of the tourism industry in a cyclical process which links the microsocial interaction and macrosocial structures as described by Simmel (Wolff, 1950, p. 41). The outcome of this process is a change in the power relationship involving the host community which enables them to influence decisions which materially affect their lives.

Using an example of a specific ecotourism project (the SERR project) and longitudinal observation, the above view can be confirmed in the outcomes of the ecotourist exchange for both ecotourist and the community. Such studies then legitimize the community's claims to control over ecotourism.

Significantly though, the extent to which the findings of this study can be generalized beyond the specific context of the research is limited, as the case study was not sufficiently representative to do so. However, it is considered that rarely will there be a situation in the context of ecotourism experiences where factors combine to allow transferability to occur. Recognizing this fact lends credence to the need to provide more comprehensive, specifically localizable theoretical approaches and techniques. There is scope for further research to apply this perspective in other contexts where microsocial groups, particularly project-based ecotourism, have a significant role in the development of ecotourism in a local community.

> I was saying that we weren't doing it for anyone in particular. We weren't doing it for ourselves or even the community at Santa Elena; they're lucky enough to live there. I guess, overall, we were doing it for everyone, not just specifically the community. I guess the reason you are there helping them is because they have the most need of it, living a subsistence lifestyle. I can see them, more likely than others, to clear-fell their land, because they have much greater need of it than anyone else. But I'm not doing it specifically for them. I'm doing it for everyone.
>
> (Amy, focus group)

In summary, then, the questions that orientate the research design suggest that the development of ecotourism depends not only upon maximizing the influence the experience has on values but also the social value they hold for the social and natural environment visited. This requires shifting the emphasis of travel from one designed primarily for providing pleasure for tourists through the exploitation of natural resources, to one in which the tourist satisfaction and fulfilment are achieved through the individual contributing and learning about natural and cultural environments. The positive outcome of such a shift is that tourists, host communities and the environment itself receive long-term benefits which outweigh the satisfaction resulting from the transient exchange of tourism. This can only be achieved through the careful management of ecotourism: a management approach which considers the social exchange of the experience as dynamic and which leads to a common social value being formed for the natural environment. Such an emphasis promotes a positive social value for ecotourism settings. Ultimately, this may translate into an environmental consciousness which can alter ecotourist behaviour and create more aware consumers who consider environmental impact as a primary factor in the choice of travel destinations.

Chapter 7

Developing the Self Through the Volunteer Tourism Experience

In moving towards the construction of social analysis that will provide a better understanding of alternative tourism experiences, this book has focused on the sociological investigation of what was termed a volunteer tourism experience and how the tourists themselves construct this.

As the volunteer tourism experience is socially constructed, the experience only takes on meaning through social interaction with others. The volunteer, as a tourist, goes on a trip, which involves taking on roles outside those in everyday life and interacting with others. These roles produce acts that are perceived and interpreted by 'significant others' (which can include tour group or host community members, their own community and elements of the site) and may redefine the individuals (the volunteer or the community members) as a result of each other's acts.

Complemented by insights from actual volunteer tourists and the SERR case study, this chapter will explore how the experience contributes to the personal development of participants. Mindful that the further developments in this area may enable a move towards providing us with a sounder basis to establishing tourism in developing and developed countries at both the individual and community level, an approach towards developing a volunteer tourism theory is then proposed.

Framing the Experience

According to Wright Mills (1959), the particular mode of thought and imagination that the sociologist employs in making sense of a social phenomenon is the ability to posit a link between individual biography and history, and the tracing of this link to contemporary social practices and lived experience (Kellehear, 1996). A prerequisite of this mode of thought and imagination must necessarily be in the process of social research in involving an interaction between researchers and people (Furze *et al.*, 1996, p. 48). This book has attempted an exploration of the social phenomenon of alternative tourism and linked, in a 'personal' way, the participants' experience, the researcher's experience and the community's reactions to such experience. It is not, however, within the scope of this book to place interactionist theory in the contemporary debate surrounding developing countries' communities as 'other' (see Spivak and Harasym, 1990) in a comprehensive way, as the limitations of interactionist theory and its evolution in relation to the ideas surrounding indigenous, ethnic and global communities are still to be explored theoretically. However, this book has examined the alternative tourist experience of the 'participant' (particularly as an ecotourist experience) within a process that enables an investigation of the 'social self' (see Kellehear, 1996) in an exchange with the destination environment (participant, participant group, site (SERR)–host community and natural environment).

The social interaction between participant on a particular project site with representatives of the community, group and natural environment forms an exchange of influence that creates a social value of the site for the alternative tourist. This influence can effect a change in self and identity. As such, the behaviour and values of the alternative tourist have been impacted upon, and they come away from the experience with a changed value for the social and physical environments visited. This experience may also have engendered changes within the field of interaction, such as in representatives of the host community.[25]

A caveat is necessary here: the SERR case study used in this book is representative of a specific type of alternative tourism experience, which, although falling generally within the context of ecotourism and volunteerism, should not, however, be used as a predicative model to enable development of general research for tourism. However, the research approach utilized for this study has demonstrated that there exist fundamental differentiating and processual elements that need to

---

[25] It is beyond the scope of this book to examine in detail the relationship of the individual community members, but the community's general attitudes are used to contextualize the SERR experience, providing for the understanding and development of a sociological response as to what an alternative tourist experience is.

be considered in examining alternative tourism experiences. In this way, analysis of ecotourism as a form of alternative tourism needs to move beyond a sole interactionist perspective in incorporating other components, such as community studies,[26] which allow longitudinal reviews of both host communities and place of origin communities. The approach used here has been able to provide information on the microsocial interaction that occurred on the site of the SERR in providing the baseline information for establishing the interactions that occurred on-site.

There is a recognition of the need to enable a multidisciplinary approach that provides frameworks for the multiplicity of information needed to study alternative tourism experiences. An extension of the techniques found within interactionism in the exploration of wider parameters may enable a research approach that would establish methods for helping to determine the attitudes and values held by community members and change within a destination community contributing to, amongst other things, the development of a framework that includes sociocultural carrying capacity in relation to addressing questions regarding sustainability of tourism experiences.

However, to understand the personal development of volunteer tourists, a definition or framing of the concept and related ideas in the words of volunteer tourists is required, illustrated in the verbatim quotes that have been reproduced in this chapter. To begin:

> Carrying gravel with our group was memorable. Everyone hated doing it, but then it became a real bonding thing, because it was so hard and everyone had to do it. By the time we got to Santa Elena, we were like a family. Probably as a group, the thing I really enjoyed was comfortability with each other. There were no divisions within the group, which I have since heard occurred in other groups, where people hung out solely with their friends and they didn't talk much to other people. As 12 people, we were all together and it didn't matter who you were near, or who you were working with that day, there was some sort of sense of comradeship and friendship. Memorable experiences really were just everyday. The laughter and the fun we had working beside people all day, coming back of an evening and relaxing with them and winding down, it was still the same feeling, but probably more so with laughter, sitting up late, playing guitars and talking. There were no TVs, no interruptions, no telephones, just sitting around and chatting. It was especially good being an Australian. There were only two of us there, myself and Katie. There were quite a few Canadians and unfortunately we didn't have any Guyanese, also

[26] A range of models exists that can be used to undertake research on the relationship between alternative tourism and host communities or the place of origin communities, using a community studies approach (see Wild, 1984). The interrelationships between the social value (constructed by communities and tourists), the tourism system and its parts, and the interaction of these at the regional, national and perhaps international level, would be a useful starting point for much of the research into alternative tourism.

> there were Costa Ricans, so you learn so much. I have a great interest in people, so I learnt so much about people generally and these people specifically. What Canadians are like and what the influences on their life are, what they think about things generally. I think I learnt a lot from the group with different cultures. People's humaneness stands out a lot more when you have to fight for it more through your own culture. You are so used to the everyday, whereas little things stand out a lot more. I think it was a really good sharing experience for a lot of us, working and relaxing together. I think there were a lot of memorable moments, like painting tops of tables with caricatures of the whole group, painting plastic to brighten up the camp, playing jokes on each other, working in the rain, but generally the whole thing of being with them.
>
> (Mic, SERR participant)

Personal Development in Volunteer Tourism Experiences

In Darby's (1994) study, the definition of personal development as provided by the volunteer participants themselves revolved around the concepts of developing confidence while developing an awareness to relate to other people and environments. Terms such as developing self-identity, self-esteem and self-actualization, raising awareness and changing behaviour were applied, with personal development also being considered a learning process that relates to an individual's attitude to move forward and continually challenge, take risks or strive to better themselves.

These definitions are comparable with those of Kuh *et al.* (1988), relating to the development of 'attitudes, skills and values' for the benefit of individuals and their community. The definitions also draw parallels with Schreyer and Driver's (1989, p. 389) definition of benefits of leisure, stating 'it is a desirable state of change; it is a specified improvement in condition or state of an individual, or group of individuals'. Viewing personal development as a learning process and encouraging people continually to challenge themselves is also compatible with the concept of experiential learning and personal development (Kolb, 1984).

Based on these understandings of the concept of personal development, the personal development that volunteer tourists experience has been grouped into four main categories: (i) personal awareness and learning; (ii) interpersonal awareness and learning; (iii) confidence; and (iv) self-contentment. It is recognized, however, that the clusters are obviously interrelated in many ways as personal, or interpersonal awareness and learning, can result in increased confidence, which can also lead to greater self-contentment.

Personal awareness and learning

This cluster relates to a wider awareness of self from an affective perspective, as well as beliefs, values, abilities and limitations. It also incorporates awareness and learning in more general areas of culture and development, at times related to professional development. While there may not be direct learning of new skills, an affirmation of current personal abilities may occur.

> I think the biggest impact was the way that the experience affected me. I think my tolerance level and my acceptance levels aren't as black and white any more. It doesn't necessarily have to be about environmental things, just generally. You may not agree with the way someone lives or someone else's value system, but you've got no right to sit there and judge it, or try and change it unless you really see some benefit in re-educating people to another way of thinking. It doesn't matter that they have a totally different system to the way we do things, just enjoy the differences.
>
> (Amy, SERR participant)

Participants have recounted such things as an awareness of self, a heightened awareness of their beliefs and abilities, an awareness of accepting responsibility, stronger determination and the development of new skills. Additionally, aspects of personal awareness and learning have been attributed somewhat to the experience of cultural exchange, cultural awareness and cross-cultural comparisons through interaction with host communities. Furthermore, an awareness and learning about a developing country and development issues are also prominent in volunteer tourist experiences.

> Santa Elena for me was probably one of the most worthwhile projects. I think it embellished the real spirit of ecotourism and sustainable development. It allowed a community to get completely involved. It was one of the projects that really did have a lot of community support. Santa Elena was run, to a degree, by good people that really knew what they were doing. That was one project that I could take with me a positive view. In light of doing something in the future, that's in my nature from the experience I got, learning from the leaders and from the community itself. So for me I could take away heaps of positive thoughts about Santa Elena and how to run projects, and how to get the community involved.
>
> (Jen, SERR participant)

The emphasis on personal awareness and learning as a motivation for volunteers is supported by many other studies (Donovan, 1977; Clark, 1978; Rohs, 1986; Beighbeder, 1991; Tihanyi, 1991). As Clark (1978) indicated with the selection of volunteer participants, the balance of motivation between the 'self' and altruism is important in a volunteer. While not always ready to recognize this personal learning as a primary aspect of their experience, it is for many the reason that they remain involved (Whitmore, 1988).

Based on this, the identification of personal development related to personal awareness/learning is to be expected, and is synonymous with the term personal development itself. Volunteer tourism participants tend to show a greater sense of personal awareness, including beliefs/values, abilities/limitations, than of specific skills or knowledge. When relating this learning to a specific stage of the experience, however, the skills that they possessed or had learnt while on project were the reason for their confidence.

> It puts you in such a radically different environment. Over the years, you've got used to the environment and it doesn't change much, like what car you drive, what clothes you wear, etc. You get there, and that all shrinks in because there is none of that there, it's just you, and no-one really gives a stuff what car you have back home. So it really shrinks your sense of self. You've got to get down to yourself and it's not all these other consumer things which we tend to take for granted. Then when you then step back into this society, your sense-of-self, or your identity has shrunk a fair bit. You're not as attached to those things that were slowly growing over you like a parasite. So when you come back, you just naturally adjust yourself with all the attachments that you used to have. So I think it does make quite a large difference. I work sometimes and I don't work others, but I'm not too worried about the money I make. I may have been before I went there, but now I'm more likely to do what I think, rather than think about what my attachments are, or think that I need more money for my car, or to buy clothes or CDs. It just shrinks you down until you're just you.
>
> (Mic, SERR participant)

The impact of cultural exchange was a powerful experience which generated a range of learning and awareness. This corresponds with other studies (American Field Service, 1986; Stitsworth, 1987; and Operation Raleigh USA, 1989) which indicate the impact of cultural exchange on increased interest in welfare of others, self-confidence and well-being, and international awareness. It can even impact on other touristic activities:

> Over January/February I went to Thailand and Nepal. Particularly in Thailand, I didn't really relate to the experience at all, because we were tourists coming in, looking and going again. I just couldn't really get into that, because of my experience in Santa Elena and Costa Rica, we were part of the community, we were giving something back to the community. In Thailand, I almost felt like a thief in a way. I was taking and not giving anything back. And the same in Nepal, I wasn't giving anything back. I wasn't taking the time to get to know the people. Costa Rica was the first time I had been overseas and I think that has really laid the groundwork for me in what I want when I travel, because I didn't see myself as a tourist when I was in Santa Elena, I was living. A tourist is someone

who just comes and goes without giving anything. But I felt in Costa Rica and in Santa Elena, at the time it felt like we were really doing something that was benefiting the community, and I think that's an experience you can get by doing that sort of thing. Next time I travel I will take time to find out about the culture. I found I really made assumptions about the people in Thailand that I had no right to make. I always came across people who were trying to rip you off.

(Sue, SERR participant)

Professional learning arises either when a direct correlation between a participant's area of knowledge and their experience occurs, or the participant is considering work in the community development or international development fields. Learning about developing country issues is part of the reality of the experience – they simply cannot be escaped. This is comparable with Stitsworth's (1987) findings highlighting students' new-found awareness of developing nations and the issues that they face.

The change in ourselves and our identity, I think it is a really long-term process. I think it is just one experience, it is a pretty big peak I guess, it leads you slowly but gradually off to a different path.

(Mic, SERR participant)

Interpersonal awareness and learning

As far as working in a group, I realized my strengths and weaknesses in a group . . . overall I think the group, in fact, was very beneficial. I keep in contact now with a lot of people that I didn't know.

(Ros, SERR participant)

This area relates to an awareness of other people and, through this, an appreciation of effective communication. Interestingly, a large part of the experience and learning results from interaction within the group of volunteer tourists. While frustrations can and do occur, from this and other aspects of the experience, participants often identify an increased awareness and appreciation of other people. This awareness results in a variety of learning and behavioural changes, such as being less self-centred, more thoughtful and more open. Additionally, the development of effective interpersonal communication within and outside the group, especially given the often challenging nature of projects, can be observed.

Learning from a group situation is identified in Whitmore's (1988) study of experiential learning which related to community volunteer involvement. The group aspect has also been highlighted in other studies which relate to overseas youth volunteer programmes (Stitsworth, 1987; Operation Raleigh USA, 1989) and provide a reflective and supportive base for their learning.

> By the time we got to Santa Elena, everyone had basically got used to everyone and knew their different traits and personalities. So everyone was pretty well adjusted, which was good because we knew how to handle each other. I learnt how to live in a very close proximity to other people. I started to feel really close to other people even though they were from different countries.
>
> (Pen, SERR participant)

Also, much can be learnt through adversity and difficulties that arise amongst the group as personal conflicts force participants to confront issues. Studies of challenging group-shared experiences in the outdoors through adventure recreation have long indicated the value of learning in the areas of interpersonal skills, sociability, friendship and companionship (Csikszentmihalyi, 1975; Richards, 1977; Abbott, 1989; Ewert, 1989).

> Yes, I've never had so much mud around me before. It was so green. The rainforest was so green. In Santa Elena there were green trees with green trunks, there were plants all over the trunks of the trees. So it was totally encompassing when you had the mist, the rain, the trees, the green and the mud ground, it could get very oppressive sometimes. One morning we went out into the freezing cold and we were in the middle of the mud which was really thick and revolting. We got back to camp for lunch, stripped off and got into some dry clothes and ate. Then everyone crashed because they were so cold and exhausted. We then had to get up at 2 or 3 in the afternoon and go back out. None of us had dry clothes, so we put on the wet clothes again which were freezing. Going back out into the rain and mud, we were wondering what the hell were we doing here. But then you would have other days that were just amazing.
>
> (Kim, SERR participant)

Confidence

A firmer belief in one's self, abilities and skills characterizes this cluster. Participants benefit from an increased confidence in their own ability, confidence in organizing themselves and, a greater self-assurance and determination. As a SERR participant reflects:

> I had no preconceived ideas about what I was getting myself into, what I wanted out of it or where I was going to land. Because I didn't have any preconceived ideas, the experience I went through was amazing, the community, the language, their way of life and how simple it was, and I had never seen a cloudforest. The other thing would be my imagination, I guess necessity *is* the mother of invention. That is something you forget in a society like ours. It is so easy to just buy something from the shop or get someone in to fix things and whatever else. We made a tent, a kitchen and shelves and we did it all ourselves. Everything we did, we pulled it out of nowhere and created it. Even their houses, they

> had old batteries as steps into the house which isn't such a bad thing. So the imagination and creative side of people all of a sudden kicked into gear. That is something I have come back with, knowing that I can fix things myself.
>
> (Sue, SERR participant)

The development of self-confidence is generally synonymous with any programme in which learning or awareness has taken place for individuals. The majority of studies identified across volunteering, experiential learning and service/exchange programmes have all identified self-confidence with a positive (and sometimes 'negative') learning experience (Clark, 1978; American Field Service, 1986; Whitmore, 1988; Ewert, 1989; Operation Raleigh USA, 1989; Tihanyi, 1991; Little, 1993).

> Personally I think it gives you motivation because you have had a hands-on practical experience that has generally been pretty successful. It gives you confidence and self-esteem.
>
> (Mic, SERR participant)

Self-confidence is referred to as 'confidence in one's ability to accomplish a goal or task' (Klint, 1990, p. 164). Terms such as self-concept (how we define ourselves), self-esteem (satisfaction and confidence in ourselves) and self-efficacy (the strength of our belief in being able to accomplish a task) are all interlinked and relate to confidence (Ewert, 1989; Klint, 1990). Based on motivational theory, it is these terms, amongst others, that have been the basis of the development of psychological tools to 'measure' benefits.

Self-contentment

This relates to a sense of confidence, manifesting in a stronger sense of self. It is reflected in an individual's perceptions of themselves, as well as the way they perceive how other people view them. This can be characterized by being more relaxed, more emotionally comfortable and enhanced individually.

> Having confidence in yourself and who you are . . . and just not worrying about the future too much. When you're out on project and don't have those everyday stresses that you've grown up with all your life . . . you sort of get to know yourself as who you are.
>
> (Solomon Islands participant, in Darby, 1994, p. 102)

Stitsworth (1987) identified from participants' involvement on 4-H programmes in Africa, 'a sense of peace'. In some cases, self-contentment was associated with cultural exchange and a realization of 'reality', comparing the 'richness' of the Solomon culture and way of life, with their own. A greater value and appreciation of friends and family in Australia was a response to this awareness.

Breaking away from previous social groups and perceptions gives participants a chance to review their 'self', their relationship to other people, and their goals and aspirations for the future. This new view, as well as greater self-confidence, appeared to generate a feeling of self-contentment. Whether this new 'sense of peace' (Stitsworth, 1987) is associated with a new awareness and appreciation of what they have in relation to others, confidence in themselves or just breaking away from their context and recreating themselves is worthy of further study.

Evidently, a variety of personal development concepts are part of the volunteer tourism experience. Notably, this development can be associated with various stages throughout an individual project. For example, interpersonal awareness and communication is an inherent part of the actual experience, whereas the greater sense of self may not be truly realized until reflection after the project:

> I didn't get a lot from it at the time in terms of development, but you do when you take a step back from it and start synthesizing through your experience when you come home. There is just so much to take in at the time and there is so much happening, and then a couple of months down the track you start thinking through your experience and you realise what you did get from your experience.
>
> (Amy, SERR participant)

While defining these categories individually aids an understanding of participant personal development, it is recognized that the categories are very much interrelated. Personal awareness of humility could help in interpersonal relationships, resulting in a greater sense of confidence, and thus self-contentment. Indeed, connections and parallels can be drawn between the areas of personal development that have been identified. For example, confidence and self-contentment usually stem from a complex mix of experiences and learnings about the individual, from the cultural experience and from interpersonal awareness/learning.

Reflecting on the case study, the SERR participants navigated a new social world of Costa Rica and the Santa Elena community. It is in this sense that the participant's self-identity is defined and expressed by her/his place identity; a complex pattern of beliefs, values, feelings, expectations and preferences relevant to the nature of the physical world (Proshansky, 1978, p. 161). The participant's experience takes place in this unfamiliar exterior world (the SERR site) and, as such, new information is presented and must be dealt with. Sometimes the navigational tools are insufficient to cope with the new situation. It is at these times that environmental stress and alienation are experienced, and the individual must become reflexive, reconsidering and/or changing certain aspects of self, as they are now experienced as outmoded or insufficient in addressing the new situation.

The participant's values, ideas, beliefs, desires and motives change as they go through life, thus the self is in continual development. The recognition of the social construction of individual qualities does not disregard the fact that people can and do change (Vance, 1992). Individual qualities, no longer appropriate for new situations that the individual finds themselves within or new situations they desire to be within, can and do change. The intimate objective gaze of the participant at self ultimately enables and facilitates personal development.

Conceptualizing the Development of Self

The differential elements of the volunteer tourism experience – ecotourism, volunteerism and serious leisure – have placed the experience in stark contrast to that of mass tourism. These elements have been explored subsequently through an interactionist paradigm located in leisure theory in examining the experience of participants on the SERR project.

> I think 'tourists' has also turned into a very negative word, it is used in a negative sense, like 'that person is a tourist and that one's not'. There were visitors at the reserve who came for a short time, but they played by the local rules, they weren't noisy or throwing cigarette butts around, they had a bit of respect for the place. They might not have been there very long, but they were still getting something out of it. I think the reason that 'tourist' gets its bad name is because they seem to walk around in a little bubble within this other culture and it's all bouncing off. They're acting and walking around as though they still haven't left anywhere. But some people come for a much shorter time, and they would walk through the reserve once, but they would do it in a way that you can see that they're interacting with it. I think some tourists only interact with each other, like the other members of the tour party and that's it. It doesn't go out into the environment or the community, it just stays between them. It's like they're coming in and feeding the animals and memories and taking them home to share with people back home, not to provide sharing between themselves and the community, which they can both remember. They're coming and taking and then going back home, like a competition.
>
> (Mic, SERR participant)

Ittleson *et al.* (1974, p. 5) maintain that the individual is not a passive product of their environment but interacts with their environment and is in turn influenced by it. Interactionism suggests that the individual is an active, thinking unit who is able to construct a meaningful existence and a sense of self from the social milieu in which she/he lives:

> The individual expresses himself [*sic*] as such, not directly, but only indirectly, from the particular standpoints of other individual members of the same social group or from the generalised standpoint of the social group as a whole.
>
> (Mead, 1934, p. 138)

Meanings are formed by the individual and the process that takes place within the context of the social groups that surround them. The experience takes form from the meaning which the participants place on their own acts and the acts of others, and it is the act of interpretation that gives interaction its symbolic character. In this way, the self is an 'ontological structure which manifests itself in social space' (Wilson, 1980, p. 145). As outlined above, the self and actions made by the self are socially mediated and constructed. The meanings of the SERR are largely derived from social interaction (with representatives of the community, other group members and, to a degree, other tourists). All qualities of the self that establish identity (e.g. desire, reason, emotion, motives, values and beliefs) and which affect the participants' behaviour in space are socially constructed; the self is not static. Continually open to new possibilities, change and growth are possible through a complex learning process (Wilson, 1980, p. 140).

It is noted that the SERR participants studied came from a developed nation. As such, the sociological analysis of contemporary social systems founded on post-industrial production and focusing on urban dwelling lifestyles and the attendant processes of self-construction through the work and production ethics of those countries (see Bell, 1978; Berman, 1983; Campbell, 1987) is relevant to the discussion of the experience and its effect on the participants' sense of self and identity. The participants come from a country where value or social value (as understood in relation to Weber's analysis of instrumental reason and the protestant work ethic) is formed around discipline, control, work, 'clock time', deferred gratification and calculative rationality (see Bell, 1978; Berman, 1983; Campbell, 1987). In such a society, based on principles of commodification and consumption, a hedonistic valuation edict determines individual and social values in relation to personal identity, with the concomitant encouragement of the pursuit of identity through self-expression, leisure, consumer goods and pleasure (Moorhouse, 1983; Campbell, 1987).

The participants' experiences could then be said to fall within the tension created by their desire to choose an experience that can satisfy the values surrounding these areas. Feminist analyses have critiqued the excessive emphasis on the productive sphere and the work ethic as the basis of identity construction. This analysis suggests that identity can actually depend more heavily on the non-productive sphere of consumption and leisure as a source of some autonomy and sense of individual identity (Wearing, 1990) while also satisfying an altruistic need that may be seen in relation to the work ethic.

Feminist analysis has done much to rewrite the notion of identity itself. J. Butler (1990), in a radical re-writing of the perennial sociological debate on agency and structure, questions the binary opposition of the two concepts claiming there is no 'I' which expresses an inner identity. Drawing on de Beauvoir (1973, p. 301), Butler maintains that subjectivity is a process of 'becoming' through repeated performative acts, and in this respect she suggests that gender is itself a cultural inscription written on sexed bodies through a continual process of repeated acts which are culturally discursively constructed. Similarly, in the relationship between the participant, group member and representatives of the host community, power relations inherent in their respective social structures construct and position the host community member as being the 'other' in a discursive relationship synecdochically aligned to the positioning of the 'female other' in the patriarchal capitalist society of which most participants are residing members.

However, if identity is not a unified concept and identities are constructed through the dynamic social exchange between individuals and groups, then possibilities exist for the reorientation of this 'other' through the interaction between the alternative tourist and significant elements of the site, whereby ecotourism enables the incorporation and transformation of values and identity of the alternative tourist. Subversion (or at least challenging or critical re-appraisal) of the developing/developed dichotomy may then occur through this social exchange. Braidotti's (1993) claim that post-structuralism allows the idea of living transformations to be examined, taken together with Butler's attempts to deconstruct a fixed notion of identity, contributes to the underlying structure of the idea of a dynamic social exchange creating a change in identity of the alternative tourist. This idea is investigated in this book by examining the values of the alternative tourist and the social value they hold for the protected area. In post-structuralist thought, the subject (alternative tourist, host community member and protected area) is not a rational whole but a changing contradictory site (see Doxey, 1975; Butler, 1980 with regard to tourist host communities, or Cohen, 1988; Kenny, 1994; Kellehear, 1996, for community change in general), thus making possible, through social exchange, the formation of new identities based around the alternative tourist experience that may change the hierarchies of causation and initiate political action, similar to the feminist post-structuralist project that recognizes: 'the essence of femininity . . . as a historical construct that needs to be worked' (Braidotti, 1993, p. 9). This opens up the way for new identities to be constructed through on-going lived experiences (supporting the idea of the alternative tourism experience) which challenge and go beyond dominant capitalist cultural practices.

The tourist experience in this way can assist the alternative tourist and their group members in a mutual process of 'becoming' (see Irigaray, 1974; Braidotti, 1993). Through the alternative tourist's desire in this case to experience the natural world and the host community member's desire to gain an economically sustainable lifestyle, the social exchange, as a lived experience, may then allow alternative subjectivities that move beyond the traditionally acceptable, recognizing both commonality and diversity between alternative tourist and group member and thus creating the social value necessary for the sustainability and preservation of the protected area which is essential to the idea of an alternative tourism experience such as ecotourism.

> This person will eventually acquire a consciousness and knowledge of the natural environment together with its cultural aspects, that will convert him (*sic*) into somebody keenly involved in conservation issues.
> (Ceballos-Lascurain, personal communication, 1987)

The experience, if it engenders a critical period of identity formation, may be seen as a site, or topos, where identities are tried out and developed, thus contributing to the acquisition of an environmental consciousness. By providing an alternative to the traditional tourism options currently available which promote and actively construct dominant stereotypes (such as the overseas 'resort' holiday, entailing only a cursory encounter with divergent cultures and lifestyles while promoting the utility value of the environment), individuals may be able to challenge and resist orthodox representations and utilize an avenue that provides the possibility of exploring alternative identities and lifestyles whilst investigating a new and profound relationship with natural ecosystems.

In providing an in-depth analysis and exploration of the elements and themes that relate to the alternative tourism experience, two primary outcomes have been identified:

1. The experience and its process as a learning experience cause the tourist to come away from the experience with an increased value for the social and physical environments of the destination area, and this environment is the source of information that will inform their recollections of the experience.
2. The ecotourist is receiving and processing information through a social exchange (group, representatives of the community and nature) within the context of the site visited which has a significant influence on the experience.

The relationship between ecotourist and environment is two-way. Not only does the environment influence the alternative tourists' perception and behaviour, but the behaviours influence the environment. In modelling the alternative tourist–environment interaction, it is found that the alternative tourist, with their developed country value system, has formed beliefs of the destination around images from the media, brochures and perceptions and attitudes developed from these images, then makes a decision to visit the area, takes the trip and interacts with the significant 'others' (in what may be considered a new area of interaction through the social reality of the society/country/ environment visited). This experience and its meanings then become a part of the identity and self of the alternative tourist.

Interactionism would inform us that the alternative tourist develops a value system from their interaction with those in their own country. They see images of the natural environment and affiliated cultures (which are perceived as the 'other') and decide to visit. They thus leave the environment of the developed country and, as outlined previously, travel to the environment of a developing country where they vary their daily behaviour, are influenced by significant others, and thus a different social reality is encountered through first-hand experience. The primary area of interaction was located in/with the SERR site, with the 'significant others' (from the participants' perspective) being the ecotour group, the SERR itself and specific groups and individuals within the Santa Elena community, which have all been identified through the focus provided for by the first research question posed. Contemporaneously, it is the 'generalized others', such as the Santa Elena community, tourism industry, conservation groups, government, YCI and Costa Rica, that give the research its broad social context. The identification of the function of these differential elements within the research process allows for the investigation of the relational intersection between the particular concepts. For instance, in detailing social context, the concern is with the significant 'others', the relationship between them and how they influence the potential environmental information available to the alternative tourist and thus the tourist experience.

Hamilton-Smith's model (in Mercer, 1994) suggests that a process of social exchange will occur. This interaction has a location in time/ space, is affected by the physical–aesthetic characteristics of the setting and involves behaviour and actions, significant personal–social relationships and social constrictions. These produce a dynamic social exchange that creates for the alternative tourist and their groups shared meanings of the SERR site (a social value).

Representatives of the host country are an integral part of this experience, as some are group members, others work on site with them and others socialize with them. It is suggested that the sociological framework developed here of the alternative tourism experience has:

- synthesized previous research into a coherent whole and established the idea of an alternative tourism experience with emphasis being placed upon interaction of the tourist and his/her environmental context (the SERR project site);

- produced a conceptual schema of the tourism experience as an interaction/exchange embodying the components of the site and identifying significant elements of the alternative tourism experience; and
- clarified the nature of the alternative tourism experience and some of its components.

Thus, the framework produced to contextualize the experience illustrates that the participant traverses through a process (social exchange as outlined by interactionist theory and conceptualized by Hamilton-Smith's model) that affects the participant to the extent that they incorporate what might have been the 'other' (natural environments, representatives of host community and country and other group members) into their own self and identity (as is represented by the ecotourists, social valuing of the protected area involved, other group members and the representatives of the associated host community).

The Selves of Volunteer Tourism

A comprehensive analysis of how the volunteer tourism experience can contribute to the personal development of participants, and subsequently an approach towards developing a volunteer tourism theory, enables us to move towards a sounder basis for establishing tourism in developing and developed countries at both the individual and community level.

The growth of tourism as a leisure-related social phenomenon and an economic enterprise was dramatic during the last half of the 20th century. The profusion of touristic experiences that have resulted during the last 20 years have generated a variety of means of theorizing, analysing and marketing tourism. This chapter has attempted to demonstrate that the volunteer can *become* rather than just *be*. This means that the predominant male, western writing on tourism is re-examined and recontextualized in the light of current sociological conceptualizations to include views from the 'other'. The potential of volunteer tourism for changes in self and identity through cultural diversity is then able to be discussed.

This approach is person centred, rather than those focused on economics, marketing or management. Nevertheless, it has been demonstrated that the usefulness of such a people-orientated perspective for volunteer tourism could be of interest to all aspects of the tourism industry. At the same time, the threads of an interactive, person-centred approach are being woven together to emphasize the importance of interactions – personal, communal and cultural – in the tourist enterprise and to position the selves and identities of tourists and hosts at the ethical centre.

Chapter 8

The Impacts on Communities: Moving Beyond the Passing Gaze

In this chapter, the growing convergence of aims between local communities and the tourism sector will be examined. While there is a clear recognition at a community level of the threat that tourism can pose to community well-being, communities also perceive that tourism – if developed and managed carefully – can assist in efforts to maintain and enhance their environments (Wearing, 1998). At the same time, the tourism sector is reaching the understanding that there is a need to ensure that host communities can be sustainably involved in the tourism sector. This in turn means not only presenting the natural environment and community heritage, but also providing demonstrable support to the maintenance of that heritage.

This book has pursued the avenue that volunteer tourism can offer alternative approaches that move beyond the ideas inherent to mass tourism – the latter often being viewed as a threat to environmental and cultural degradation. There are a wide range of actions individuals can take at a local level to manage and protect their natural and cultural resources, activities that have the potential to help reverse, arrest or prevent environmental decline caused by tourism, industrialization or other developments. When such actions are undertaken, they stem primarily from a concern for livelihood, with people's desire to maintain …nprove levels of living which, in many local communities, depend …tent on the ability to make productive use of community …ces. This chapter is thus concerned with what has …vn as 'sustainable tourism development' and how …n fits into that auspice.

It is the goal of this chapter to contribute to a better understanding of how people can participate in the development of tourism as an aid to better management of their environment, both in situations where they are motivated, encouraged and supported by outside actors such as the state or international organizations, and in situations where they can formulate their travel plans and conduct their activities in spite of the neglect, resistance or even active opposition to external market forces. The main premise underlying the selection of this focus is that volunteer tourism is at the forefront of sustainable environmental management for tourism and, where necessary, environmental rehabilitation is most likely where active local-level support exists (Horwich *et al.*, 1993; Pimbert and Pretty, 1995; Christ, 1998; Drumm, 1998) and can be enhanced by organizations and individuals interested in volunteer tourism. It is clear that managing resources sustainably on the local level is essential for achieving the global goal of sustainable development and, although more macro-level activities are also important, it is the combined impact of the small-scale activities – either constructive or destructive – undertaken by vast numbers of individuals which will determine the fate of many community resources and ecosystems.

Emphasis is placed on the diversity of ways in which people act in the tourism sector to influence the utilization of their resource base, thus employing a broader definition of the term 'participation' than is currently used in the tourism literature. Much earlier use of this term discussed participation primarily in the context of commercial tourism opportunities, with a focus on more efficient management styles being created and promoted by agencies wishing to increase the success rates of their tourism venture. As this book presents and is shown here, people participate in tourism in a variety of ways which do not always involve the mainstream industry agencies. The development of rules and structures by a society to ensure that resources are not over-exploited by any individuals or groups, for instance, is a kind of participation which forms the basis of many communities. In addition, people often organize volunteer tourism ventures to provide economically viable alternatives to the resource management priorities of external agencies such as government. Such social mobilization is an especially important form of participation in tourism. It is not claimed, however, that to establish volunteer local-level participation in tourism – which may be called, more specifically, 'community-based tourism' – is sufficient by itself to prevent or reverse environmental degradation in situations where national policies or global-level ecological changes create major destructive forces. Rather, it is widely acknowledged that effective local-level participation is a necessary component of sustainable tourism development.

Although the importance of people's participation for sustainable tourism development recently has become increasingly acknowledged, there is as yet insufficient analysis of the multiple dimensions that such participation involves – particularly in the area of volunteer tourism. Specifically, the emphasis in much of the literature on sustainable development and participation has not been on people's initiatives as keys to finding *solutions* for environmental problems; rather it has been on people's *lack* of participation as an *obstacle* to the solution (by outsiders) of environmental problems. In other words, there has been much more attention paid to ways in which local people can be persuaded to provide the necessary support for tourism projects designed outside the community than to ways in which grassroots initiatives, stemming from indigenous environmental concerns, can inform the development of more successful tourism projects – or can supplement or even replace the project approach. Of course, local people cannot and do not always provide solutions to their environmental problems, but the argument in this book is that the potential of community-based tourism has been unduly neglected, and that a wider recognition of the ways in which people act to protect their environments can only advance the search for sustainable tourism development. This development will enhance the opportunities offered by agencies that can provide volunteer tourist experiences; thus volunteer tourism becomes one avenue that communities can explore in building sustainable projects.

There is a broad democratic premise that, whatever the level of decision making, ordinary people can be trusted to solve their own problems if they are given the chance. No policy or programme is likely to succeed unless ordinary people are given this opportunity. The specific area of training and education for volunteer tourism is examined because of its positive connotations for the environment and for local people. Volunteer tourism, then, suggests a symbolic or mutual relationship where the tourist is not given central priority but becomes an equal part of the system. This is not apparent in much of the tourism that occurs in the world today, nor does it appear likely to occur without the empowerment of host communities. Further, the tendency to ignore or exploit local culture in order to enhance tourist experience has seen conflict arise. In the main, tourists have been conditioned to accept a structured experience often packaged by large operators with little understanding of the local natural and cultural resources. The framework created relegates the local people and their natural and cultural resources to a mere stage show. This ignores the opportunity for cultural exchange, and forgoes understanding of the rich natural and cultural heritage that can be part of the tourist experience. Overcoming this problem takes us back to the underlying problems inherent to development issues, which is moving to acknowledge that organizations can be involved in the tourism system that have other motives outside the predominance of profit motives.

While mainstream tourism organizations are often defined as private companies or enterprises whose existence is focused on profit motives, in reality a range of organizations can operate with a focus on achieving both tourism and conservation, social justice and/or research outcomes. They can offer a range of experiences aimed at developing the tourists' valuing of the need for those outcomes. Volunteer tourism suggests that definitions of tourism organizations need to be expansive enough to include organizations such as One World Travel, whose focus is beyond normal profit motives. This differs from the mainstream, for-profit tour operators, whose customers fit into Fussell's suggestion that 'the tourist is that which has been discovered by entrepreneurship and prepared for him by the arts of mass publicity' (Graham, 1991, p. 99); in other words, the commodified tourist (Wearing and Wearing, 1998).

Resisting the Impact of Global Capital in Developing Countries

Developing countries are in an unequal relationship with the industrialized world, as the structure of their economies are based historically upon 'imperial' domination over trading links and governance (Lea, 1988, 1993). Unfortunately, some elements of mass tourism effectively perpetuate this inequality through multinational companies of advanced capitalist countries retaining the economic power and resources to invest in and control the tourism industries of developing nations. In many cases, a developing country's engagement with tourism serves simply to confirm its dependent, subordinate position in relation to the advanced capitalist societies – illustrative of a form of neo-colonialism.

The economic patterns of consumption in developing countries have enabled modern tourism to be used as a vehicle for packaging their cultures as 'commodities of difference', filling a commercially created need in the mass consciousness. The ability of the developed nations to dominate market forces through the tourism industry is changing the shape of developing nations' communities. Crandell (1987, p. 374) maintains that indigenous cultures that have changed little for centuries are threatened by the powerful influences of western culture that often accompany the arrival of mass tourism in the developing world.

A failure by operators to change their 'developed world' operating philosophies and behaviours has resulted not only in the on-going degradation of already over-developed destinations in developing countries, but also a move by the promoters of mass tourism to the comparative pristine environments found in many developing nations.

These areas, in many cases free from the restraints, laws and regulations upheld in many developed nations, are then easily exploited for consumption by developed nations.

Unfortunately, in many countries, such as Costa Rica, Guatemala, Belize, Thailand, Indonesia, the Philippines, Malaysia and those in the South Pacific, much of what initially was so attractive to the visitor and inhabitant has already been adversely affected. Mass tourist promoters, utilizing their economic and political resources, have begun (largely unopposed) to imprint their modes of behaviour and control on the indigenous peoples' culture and protected areas. This form of tourism initially establishes footholds in developing countries by promising increased prosperity for the government and the host communities. Such results are seldom achieved. Culture is thus packaged, priced and sold like 'fast food and room service, as the tourism industry inexorably extends its grasp' (Greenwood, 1989, p. 179).

Can host communities resist the potential dangers and threat of commercial and cultural exploitation by commodified global tourism? Unfortunately, the domination of local industries and host communities by global tourism organizations continues. To date, few of the rare organized resistances to foreign-owned, often multinational organizations dominating all aspects of tourist trade have been effective. The consequences of this are obvious: Ascher (1985) and Lea (1988, 1993) suggest that much of the income and perceived benefits generated by mass tourism 'leak out' to the large, multinational companies in developed countries. This occurs through a corporate-controlled industry that is both vertically and horizontally integrated. One multinational corporation owns an airline, the tour buses, the hotel and recreational facilities. Profits in this case are mostly repatriated back to the home country (Trask, 1991). Though real global profits are difficult to gauge given the lack of comparative earnings data, it is generally accepted that only a minor percentage of tourist expenditure remains in the country.

Profits to local communities are reduced further through the importation of specialized goods and services that cater specifically to the needs of the tourists. Key management positions are often held by outside management companies, reducing the career opportunities for local people and the control they have of their resources. Even so, international tourism developments require high capital investment, and expensive, often imported infrastructure that would necessitate heavy borrowing for developing nations to finance (Hong, 1985).

While there is some evidence of local resistance to these global stakeholders – responses to forms of mass tourism have been seen in the limited formation of local lobby groups – there are numerous examples of ways in which developers have used their power bases very effectively. For example, in Costa Rica, foreign investors in tourist hotels can enjoy tax exemption, import all building materials and equipment duty free and also have been beneficiaries of aid money to help establish businesses. This is one example of a developing nation's government aiding powerful corporations while siphoning and diverting precious resources that could have been used to improve the quality of life of the local people (Hong, 1985).

Corporations promoting inappropriate development in developing countries for tourism often have little regard for the ways in which their practices impact upon local communities. There is little doubt that, at least in outcome if not by direct intention, the marketing strategy of such companies is to commodify cultures so as to better serve their profit margins.

The impact of global capital on tourism also has far reaching effects in the cultural sphere, particularly at the level of individual consciousness. Tourist preconceptions of their travel destinations are constructed from a series of interchanges with significant others, much of which is based on information found in the travel brochures used to sell tourism products. These groups portray messages of 'difference' appropriate to the socially acceptable values shared and internalized by the society for which they are constructed. 'Their Western-centred discourses, their wide-eyed cameras, construct the rest of the World as there for us' (Fiske *et al.*, 1987, p. 21). Urry asserts (1990, p. 1), '. . . the consumption of cultural difference is socially organised and systematised.' Thus what is portrayed as seemingly natural is in fact historically constructed through a complex system of social interaction.

The challenge for host communities, international activists and governments is how to control and regulate the multi- and transnational corporations to govern ethical practice and set standards for tourist operators. Indeed, 'controlling' tourism is a challenge faced by both industry and government agencies. The development of strategic plans and control mechanisms is only as effective as the will to implement them, and a free market system in a diverse and highly unregulated industry such as tourism will probably continue to defy most efforts to limit its expansion. In Australia, for example, effective regulation only occurs through integrated programmes that incorporate federal, state and local legislation and policy (McKercher, 1991, p. 69).

What responsibility do tour operators have for self-regulation? Many operators and ecotourists may have to accept the need to monitor and control their impacts on host communities and environments. The tourist experience may restrict access, for example, to interacting too closely with native fauna as the impacts are considered too high. One answer is to develop codes of ethics and industry standards with which the industry complies so that the international market is aware of environmental constraints and thus changes the free nature of the experience. Weiler and Johnson (1991, p. 125), for example, have advocated the development of a code of ethics for tourists. This would encompass appropriate social, cultural and environmentally responsible behaviour and so may impose on the ideas of freedom for the individual ecotourist while providing more freedom for the host community and environment through reducing impacts. Still, codes are of only limited effectiveness, often due to a lack of implementation enforcement mechanisms.

The Challenge of Community Involvement

It has been noted that tourism in developing countries, and to some degree in developed nations, is often owned and managed by people and companies physically external to the land areas and communities in which the operations occur. This generally results in high economic leakage, little local control over operations and relatively few local people being employed in the industry in that area. One of the main reasons for this is a lack of skills and little recognition of decision-making structures on behalf of local communities. It is proposed that one of the ways in which this can be overcome is through the implementation of volunteer tourism projects.

For example, local communities and indigenous people can acquire the necessary skills via education through volunteer programmes. However, it must be recognized that these efforts may be viewed as being external to their cultural landscape as the skills are imported through the volunteer tourists. Thus, in acknowledging this, there is a need to examine the most appropriate learning strategies and approaches to education and training that can have successful outcomes for the community and the volunteer. This could also allow for the local people to educate tourists in both cultural and environmental aspects of the local area – a fundamental goal of volunteer tourism.

Many of the concerns raised about tourism by local communities can be addressed by volunteer tourism. The concerns and conflicts expressed by representatives of host communities generally fall into a number of interrelated categories:

1. The first is the lack of opportunities for involvement in decision making relating to tourism.
2. The second arises from what these communities regard as inadequate responses from governments when administrative or legislative mechanisms have been established to involve them in such decision making.
3. The third relates to the lack of financial, social and vocational benefits flowing to these communities from projects that commercially exploit what they regard as their resources.

4. The fourth relates to the need to establish better tools for evaluating sociocultural impacts, and thus giving this precedence over the environmental impacts on the natural environments which are often of more interest to outside investors and conservation groups.

These concerns embrace a wide range of issues relating to the management of community resources. This area is large and diverse, and the main emphasis here will be with regard to the dynamic social exchange between the tourist and the host community. If the social structure and context of the community is not sustained, then the tourist experience can be compromised.

In response to these concerns listed above, communities interested in establishing sustainable forms of community-based tourism can incorporate volunteer tourism principles and programmes. Qualifiedly, evidence from the case study in this book indicates that initiatives from volunteer tourism can have significant effects – both positive and negative – upon the natural and cultural resources of a local community. However, volunteer tourism is ideally suited for the development of sustainable, community-based tourism as the principles of volunteer tourism incorporate the facilitation of community ownership and control, both of tourism and of the associated resource management. Communities that desire a more equal relationship with the tourist and the industry can also, through volunteer tourism, facilitate a cross-cultural flow of information and thus promote the development of the cross-cultural understanding.

The natural and cultural resources that attract visitors are often treated with a 'selling' mentality, distinct from a sense of ownership and stewardship. Local communities are not powerless but, in response to what has happened in the past, these communities must have a role in determining their future involvement in tourism. A number of writers support these arguments from a social and cultural viewpoint. Mathieson and Wall (1982, p. 135), for example, maintain that sociocultural impacts are the 'outcome of particular kinds of social relationships that occur between tourists and hosts as a result of their coming into contact'. De Kadt (1979) suggests that the tourist–host encounters occur in three main contexts: purchasing from the host, side by side interaction and where the two parties come face to face with the objective of exchanging information or ideas. Williams (1990, p. 84) suggests that ecotourism is a 'two-way and equal communication between hosts and guests'.

In order for communities to become aware of the place and role volunteer tourism can have in community-based projects, it is important to make them aware of the differing needs of the various operators in the tourism industry and the tourism system. This can be achieved with training and education of local communities (with the assistance of volunteer tourism projects) as well as empowerment of indigenous systems in larger planning structures. Different stakeholders, such as governments, private enterprise, local communities and organizations, conservation non-governmental organizations (NGOs) and international institutions, all need to be able to see the potential for the linking of this sector of tourism with local communities. If communities can reach an understanding of where they fit within the broader framework of the tourism and conservation sectors, there is a better chance of well-designed volunteer tourism programmes. This would give communities the opportunity to control where they fit in the tourism industry and enable a fostering of host communities' values while providing education for volunteer tourists.

Community-based tourism and volunteering has caught the imagination of many NGOs and local communities, governments, international organizations and the tourism industry. There is a current worldwide debate concerning how community-based tourism projects should be undertaken (Wearing, 1998). This is generating more and more interest in the potential of community-based tourism in developing countries. For while community-based tourism is being seen increasingly as a way to promote sustainable tourism, it is also seen as being able to provide valuable economic benefits. Volunteer programmes and community-based tourism offer new paths towards sustainable development and new ways of conducting tourism activities.

A wide range of institutions and organizations do, and will continue to, play an important role in the development of the community-based tourism industry. The types of organizations vary considerably, and a number provide international support and sponsorship for the implementation of research projects and community development. These organizations facilitate this process through provision of necessary resources that may not otherwise be available. The international scope of these organizations can provide invaluable assistance in terms of their accumulated knowledge and experience.

The tourism industry may be able to embrace the concept of volunteer tourism and community-based tourism as other NGOs and developing governments have. The ideas of self-sufficiency are now growing, and local communities now face the dilemma of how their small-scale effort can develop without being commodified and dominated by wider market forces (Wearing and Wearing, 1998).

The Quest for Sustainability

An element essential to the context of the community-based, volunteer tourism experience is sustainability. Community involvement is inherent to the concept of sustainability, and the concept of volunteer tourism (within the context of community-based tourism), in attempts to provide a resource base for the future, also echoes the tenets of the sustainability paradigm. However, for volunteer tourism to succeed, it has to be sustainable for both the *social* and natural environments of the area visited. It should not become another form of tourism based mainly on economic development but rather a mixing of elements with community and the natural environment as key elements, while allowing the volunteer to contribute, develop self, and possibly even contribute further to influencing their home communities positively when they return.

It has been demonstrated in earlier chapters that volunteer tourism can cause a change in individuals that will see a higher value accrued to indigenous communities and their values in the tourism industry. While value in the past has been seen to be gained from 'tourist gaze', it would now be generated largely from the interactions with the community itself. Many developing countries require sustainable developments in order to ensure that the needs of the present communities are met without compromising the needs of future ones (World Commission on Environment and Development, 1987, p. 8), and this may be achieved with a shift to this way of valuing. Indeed, volunteer tourism can offer some answers in response to the ideals and goals of sustainable development. Volunteer tourism seeks to capitalize on the increase in tourism to different cultures in search of authenticity and return the benefits of this to the host community. Volunteer tourism is premised on the idea that it can only be sustainable if the natural and cultural assets it is reliant on survive and prosper.

Volunteer tourism is represented as the means by which tourism can become an 'environmentally friendly' industry. There are well-documented examples of tourist destinations becoming polluted, degraded and congested by mass tourism. One of the features of these impacts is the high sociocultural impact on host communities (Field, 1986, p. 6; Bates, 1991, p. 4; Sofield, 1991, p. 56; Burchett, 1992, p. 5; Lee and Snepenger, 1992, p. 368; Weiler and Hall, 1992, p. 117; Lea, 1993). Certainly many host communities feel that the tourism industry has a poor track record, and often it disregards their legitimate interests and rights. It is the local communities that bear the sociocultural impacts of mass tourism: disruption to established activity patterns, anti-social behaviour, crime and overcrowding caused by tourism developments, even an impact on local lifestyles and quality of life. To provide sustainability, local communities need more control, because if the ecological and cultural impacts and perceived social impacts are seen as imposed it may lead to diminished community and political support for the industry, particularly at local levels.

The sustainability of the volunteer tourism experience lies partially with host communities. Nonetheless, questions need to be raised about how such sustainability will be achieved. It has been found that as little as 20% of expenditure from tourism in the 'Third World' may remain in these host communities (Community Aid Abroad, 1991). This siphoning of profits by large foreign ownership in tourism and lack of government recognition of the impacts of tourism on minority cultures within their jurisdiction means that there is a need to question current tourism patterns and trends. As far back as 1980, the World Council of Churches decided that alternative ways of travel were needed in order to return tourism to the people so that the experience of travel could enrich all. This was seen as allowing economic benefits to be shared more fully, and allowing the people concerned to participate more fully in decision making (Wearing and Young, 1992).

Empirical Explorations of Commodification in Volunteer Tourism

The following is a brief evaluation using ethical, ecological and decommodified criteria of three Australian-based travel organizations, with Youth Challenge International included as a contrast (see Table 8.1 for a summary). This evaluation enables some discussion of the elements that might be essential in a travel organization that is seeking to take a volunteer, ecotourism approach. In Australia, companies that operate under the auspices of volunteer tourism vary considerably and provide a range of opportunities. It is maintained that Australians are looking to the shorter-stay trips in developing Asian countries (Larbalestier, 1990), organized through an agent providing a package tour. The range of tourism products available to Australian consumers is diverse, and these few operators are perceived to fall into the volunteer tourism segment of the market and are discussed here to give some organizational context to the fledgling Australian industry.

A brief exploration of the cultural representation of travel brochures of the three companies gives initial evidence to the cultural imperialism and neo-colonial attitudes of several of these operators. These representations indicate more general trends in the industry in combining neo-colonial displays of the product with the quest to make profits. In the majority of cases, the travel literature does not portray marginalized peoples as they might represent themselves (Silver, 1993, p. 305); the host communities have little or no ability to influence its construction. The symbolic colonization of host community cultures through the global tourist gaze underlies the insidious nature of commodifying processes and their impact on local cultures and economies. The nexus between the commodifying of volunteer tourism and

Table 8.1. Comparing travel organizations (adapted from Wearing and Wearing, 1999).

Issues	World Expeditions	Adventure World	One World Travel	Youth Challenge
Type of tour	Adventure tour to remote destinations internationally	Adventure to remote destinations internationally	Travel wise group tours internationally	Working with local communities internationally
Theme	'Discovering the difference of our world'	'. . . see Aboriginal tribes living off the land'	Understand culture and respect for host community	Working in and with local communities
Pre-departure programme	Video information and trip notes	Limited if any	Interviews all travellers and holds education sessions	9 months, week-end selection programme, language and cultural programme
Environmental experience	Consumption of the environment	Consumption of the environment	Ensures interaction with the environment	Ensures interaction with the environment, stay in it
Interpreta-tion/education	Limited visitation to site controlled by tour operator	Images rather than education	Extensive use of protected area agencies to assist	Extensive, developed in conjunction with local people
Conservation ethic	No guarantee local communities receive a return for involvement	Non-apparent in any literature or operational method	Underlies all operations and is guaranteed	Underlies all operations and is guaranteed
Cultural/ heritage	Staged authenticity (MacCannell, 1976) using 'traditional costumes'	Subservience of local communities, use of inappropriate gender and racial images	Respectful and spends time to ensure not a fleeting gaze	Live with the community and work with them
Operations	Tends to use own staff and resources rather than local	Tends not to use any local staff or resources; all packaged	Employs all local staff, accommodation and resources	Employs all local resources, staff and accommodation
Transport means	Local transport and airlines	Tend to pick cheapest and generally outside owned	Local and stays within ethical considerations	Local and stays within ethical considerations

continued

Table 8.1. *Continued.*

Issues	World Expeditions	Adventure World	One World Travel	Youth Challenge
Accommodation	Guarantees all needs met and stay at places like the Holiday Inn	Generally five star at Holiday Inn	Local where possible	Local with communities, often in community homes
Marketing	Glossy, magazine-style brochures using emotive language	Glossy, magazine-style brochures using emotive language	Brochure printed on 100% recycled paper	Brochure printed on 100% recycled paper
Contribution to local community	Limited and relies on goodwill	Nearly non-existent	Extensive	Work with the local community on projects they establish

global processes can potentially be broken down, and a different set of relationships established.

'World Expeditions': the market denying nature and traditional community

World Expeditions does not really fall within the general criteria that are mentioned earlier in the chapter for a volunteer tourism organization. Its approach is one of traditional marketing that uses emotive language that presents images of indigenous people in 'traditional' costumes, frequently interacting delightedly with white tourists. These images are not balanced with representation of the issues and concerns facing the host communities, and the unequal relationship between the developed and developing countries is ignored. Still, the symbols combine to create an image of authenticity, packaged for tourist consumption of the authentic. MacCannell would see this symbolic representation as 'staged authenticity': 'What is taken to be real might, in fact, be a show that is based on the structure of reality' (MacCannell, 1976, p. 95).

World Expeditions appears not to support its commitment to local community leaders, particularly when the tour leaders photographed and described in the brochures are from developed countries. The images presented are of comfortable, up-market outdoor equipment, with the local host community members serving as an outside element reinforcing the idea of them as 'other'. All this contributes merely to extend a developed nation lifestyle to these areas. The staff from the developed country generally are responsible for the day-to-day living arrangements such as preparation of all meals from a combination of local and imported products, thereby further restricting the opportunity of this falling within the idea of a volunteer tourism experience.

A transnational company registered in the USA is used for accommodation (Hong, 1985) and it features developed country food, luxury accommodation and entertainment. The accommodation on the treks is in cabins, owned and controlled by Malaysian protected area authorities, as well as in a traditional 'longhouse' with the indigenous community, the *Iban*. This part of the experience is only one night, and as such the opportunity to provide a dynamic exchange of culture between hosts and guest is minimal. This stay is also under the control of an agent from outside the host community. World Expeditions maintains that it uses local transport resources if available in the area, and that it recommends flying by Malaysian Airlines. It is faced with a dilemma, however, as this airline is boycotted by a number of environmental organizations, including Community Aid Abroad, as it is owned and controlled by the Malaysian government that supports logging in the Sarawak rainforests.

World Expeditions also offers an orientation programme that includes meetings, audio-visual information and written information. It is questionable whether this gives the 'tourist customer' deeper cultural sensitivity as the information provided gives an idea of the culture, customs, religion and appropriate behaviour. A further dimension to the western gaze of World Expeditions is embedded in their management culture and practice. There is a centralized management structure where tours and leaders are answerable to the senior management in the traditional hierarchy of mass tourism organizations. Payments are distributed by the Malaysian operators without guidelines, indicating little concern for the benefits that the Iban communities receive.

'Adventure World': market colonization of local communities

The next company, Adventure World, provides a range of tours for groups both in Australia and in the rest of South East Asia. Modes of imperialist representation are immediately evident in the glossy brochures provided to tourists informing them in text and photographs of the exotic and safe – yet possibly dangerous – tour locations. Its brochure for one trip to Malaysia displays the neo-colonialist discourse and subsequent inferiorizing of host populations that cast the guest's role as dominant over that of the host community. The information provided gives the impression of the host community as inferior, less powerful and a commodity. The population is presented to create images of these roles, with women presented as 'beautiful', 'native' and 'girls' providing grounds for gender and racial inequalities and contributing to the idea of women's subservience and reinforcing many of the dominant patriarchal attitudes that prevail in the developed countries from which tourists originate.

The natural environment is also used to attract the tourist: the brochure promotes Sarawak's 'lush green forest' (Adventure World 1992 brochure, p. 6). The brochure also suggests that it is offering an opportunity to change environmental policy and practices by producing information about what is really happening with the depletion of Malaysian rainforests, i.e. the extensive logging which currently is occurring. The accommodation advertised in this brochure utilizes the same transnational hotel chain mentioned earlier. Of note is that a number of foreign-owned hotels in the Asian region, including the chain used, have been accused of using local women as objects to attract guests (Hong, 1985, p. 68). Women from the local areas are dressed in uniforms that are sexually provocative, relating not to the local culture but rather to images of that culture held by males in developed countries. A range of other problems included food not conforming to local religious custom and a lack of provision of appropriate staff facilities such as prayer rooms for Muslim staff (Hong, 1985, p. 68).

Adventure World appears to fall well short of any guidelines that would define its tours as volunteer tourism. The operator provides marketing material that gives evidence to a 'staged authenticity' for tourist consumption, with images of host communities dressed in traditional costumes and described as 'natives, the former headhunters of Borneo!'. Furthermore, it is clear that these communities have no control over the images presented. Hong (1985, p. 99) finds that tourists have been known to ask male elders of a longhouse to take off shirts and trousers they are wearing and to dress themselves in loin cloth in order to photograph exposed tattoos on their backs, hands and legs.

Armstrong *et al.* (1992) suggest 'the commercialisation of local culture in the Adventure World travel brochure is creating an arena for "staged authenticity" whereby what is shown to tourists is not the institutional back stage . . . rather a staged back region'. One tour with Adventure World consists of 3 days in the Sarawak region; one day in Kuching, one day in the National Park and one afternoon with the local community. The filtered and distorted perceptions of the gazing tourist are engaged in a commodified experience rather than the cultural and natural environments that are visited. Another of their tours involves an overnight visit to a 'longhouse'. As mentioned earlier, one prerequisite for a company to commodify is that it provides all aspects of the tour product and infrastructure. Such is the case with this tour; the tour package is all-inclusive, and profits for the local host communities are therefore minimal.

Adventure World does not offer any orientation or any appropriate advice regarding tourist behaviour. Although representative of the bulk of accredited products being offered to the Australian consumer, Adventure World's tour to Sarawak, as marketed in its brochure, failed to meet any of the criteria for responsibility (Armstrong *et al.*, 1992).

'One World Travel': guest–host dialogues beyond colonization

One World Travel offers a different perspective from that of the purely commercial ends and neo-colonialism of World Expedition and Adventure World. One World Travel is owned and operated by Community Aid Abroad (CAA), an organization that re-directs all profits from its trading back into host communities. The aim of this process is to give host communities a higher degree of autonomy so that they are able to direct their resources and dictate exactly what occurs. CAA operates as a normal travel agency but offers a range of special 'Travel Wise' tours. Its guiding principles relate to cultural understanding, respect and sensitivity for the host community, and 'treading softly' on the physical environment (Community Aid Abroad, 1991).

The brochure presents just a photograph of people in the area. One World Travel advises that it avoids using Malaysian Airlines due to the Malaysian government's involvement in the logging of Sarawak rainforests. One World does, however, utilize foreign-owned hotels in Kuala Lumpur in order to take advantage of international airline deals. Although this reduces direct economic benefits to Malaysia, any profits made by One World Travel are returned back to the local community through non-government social organizations.

CAA researches such study tours to ensure that host communities get direct benefit, that local guides and tour operators are used and that profits are distributed equitably. Local food is consumed, local transport is utilized, and cultural and survival issues are presented realistically. One World Travel interviews all potential travellers to ensure they have an understanding of the factors and difficulties facing the host community, and an orientation session is scheduled. Such survival and cultural issues are fully discussed in the interviews.

When visiting parks, accommodation is provided by the National Parks services, and tour notes are in-depth and more field-related than glossy brochures. The tour package also includes briefings from representatives of NGOS operating in the areas visited. Armstrong *et al.* (1992) found that One World Travel raises issues of direct relevance to the host community. In its Thailand brochure, the impacts of modernization on a remote hill tribe are discussed; in another brochure, the impact of new agricultural practice on a traditional farming community is detailed (Community Aid Abroad, 1992).

In Sarawak, One World Travel allows 4 days to visit the Penan and Kelabit tribal people, emphasizing the opportunity for 'learning their culture and survival issues'. Visits to logging areas are also scheduled in order to assess 'the damage'. Accommodation is in locally owned and controlled hotels and hostels, and all tours are facilitated by indigenous leaders. Time is allocated for reflection on the tour: one day is set aside to 'discuss experiences and any follow up you may wish to institute' (Armstrong *et al.*, 1992).

These three examples of ecotour operators available in Australia provide some qualitative evidence for a continuum of such organizations along the spectrum from commodified to decommodified ecotourist activity. Of the three, One World Travel stands out as unique in the sensitivity of marketing content and strategy to the cultures and environments that the tourist will enter. As illustrated by Table 8.1, Youth Challenge International provides the model volunteer tourist experience. For the longer-term sustainability of the industry, the commercial and largely for-profit organizations involved in Australian-based ecotours would do well to emulate the standards set by One World Travel for a much deeper and richer approach to the tourist experience. Unfortunately, market principles and criteria seem to hold most sway in for-profit organizations.

The IUCN (World Conservation Union) IVth World Congress on National Parks and Protected Areas made several recommendations regarding the relationship between tourism, indigenous communities and protected area management. The key recommendations focus on cooperation between local communities and the tourist industry that in effect emphasize a less commodity- or market-driven approach. Writers (such as Young, 1973; Hong, 1985; Lea, 1988, 1993; Smith, 1989; Urry, 1990) and global organizations concerned with the impact of modern tourism (Contours, Community Aid Abroad and ECTWT) believe that organizations can operate beyond the economic limitations of the mindset of the industry. But does volunteer tourism fall outside the forms of tourism proposed above or is it just another product of profit motivated tourism organizations and so considered as commodified tourism?

Commodification places work and leisure in direct opposition, whereby leisure and hence tourism are seen as an arena to satisfy these respective needs. As an industry and a leisure activity, tourism revolves around the production and consumption of cultural difference (Hawkins, 1991) and so the thirst for 'nature' and other 'cultures' is endless as it attempts to commodify them by capturing their essence. Yet it can never totally succeed because it is really an experience that provides only a fleeting gaze. While this book has suggested we can move beyond the experience level, what occurs at a policy level is unavoidably linked to that experience.

Natural Resource Conservation Through Volunteer Tourism

> With the recognition that conservation often fails to achieve its goals when local people are unsupportive, or are not meaningful partners, the question of local participation is now firmly on international conservation and sustainable development agendas.
>
> (Furze *et al.*, 1996, p. 3)

It is no secret that nature requires government intervention in order to survive in a free market economy. Just as societies regulate to protect those disadvantaged in society by the inequity of the system through state intervention, the same principles and policies need to be applied to nature. Natural heritage resources are disadvantaged by the anthropocentric nature of the free market system and western society; what is not valued by the commercial interests of humans has no value at all in the system. Volunteer tourism has, however, brought that value to nature. But how do we now formulate mechanisms, models, principles or policies to enable this value to be recognized in the market place?

The invention of the term 'volunteer tourism' itself is the result of an increased recognition of, and reaction to, 'the negative impacts being caused by mass tourism . . . . and recognition of the importance of conserving natural environmental quality' (Orams, 1995, p. 3). The underlying ideology of volunteer tourism represents a transition in society from an anthropocentric view, where the world is interpreted in terms of people and their values, to an ecocentric view, where the world fosters the symbiotic relationship between humans and nature.

There are already signs that tourism operators are using terms such as ecotourism as a label to market conventional ventures. This point has been made by a leading Australian conservationist who has accused two Australian State governments of being 'ecowolves in tourism sheep's clothing' (Collins, 1994). One of the activities that prompted this accusation was the Tasmanian government's decision to bulldoze a road into the heart of the Tarkine wilderness area '. . . to enable more tourists to visit the region' (Collins, 1994, p. 8). Attempts to commodify some of Australia's pristine wilderness receive regular press attention. One recent example is an alleged attempt by a developer to bribe New South Wales State government politicians to turn an old colliery in the Blue Mountains into a $15 million wildlife tourist development. The local community lobbied for this site, and the government eventually agreed to declare the area part of the Greater Blue Mountains National Park (*Sydney Morning Herald*, 2 March 1999). This type of activity raises questions for volunteer tourism – what practices it uses and what funding support it should negotiate.

A cultural and ethical framework that promotes host self-determination in the industry is central to the volunteer tourism experience. This means operators who are willing to be slow in developing a product that will then allow input from host communities, and aim to have a minimalistic impact by staying within the social and physical carrying capacities of an area, would fall more closely within a framework of operations for volunteer tourism. These types of organizations need to see their operations as a two-way interactive process between host and guest whereby the natural resource amenities, the local community and the visitor benefit from the experience (Lee and Snepenger, 1992, p. 368).

Therefore, it is necessary that volunteer tourism operators generally maintain an approach that meets certain criteria. These criteria align themselves with those found in the ecotourism literature (see Wearing and Wearing, 1999; Wearing and Neil, 2000). To illustrate, some of the following might be useful as core criteria.

- Generally, tourism products should be culturally and environmentally sensitive.
- The product should be portrayed in promotional material that provides a realistic image of the destination area.
- Ensure benefits of the sale of the product go directly to the host community.
- Organizations that control tourism at a larger scale should share the benefits of tourism with the host community, with opportunities for participation, employment and career paths for the local community.
- The visitor could also be provided with educational/orientation information providing culturally specific guidelines.
- Ethical concerns about the impact of the product mean that operators need to provide the opportunity for the guest's interaction with the host community.
- The most appropriate basis for this interaction is to base it on equality and respect for the rights and the wishes of the local population.

Despite the success of some initiatives, as well as the obvious advantages for the tourism industry to develop sustainable practices, the main priority of tourism organizations is to make a profit and therefore unavoidably to provide a commodified experience. As suggested throughout this book, there is no guarantee that profit-driven firms will act according to any ethical principles if profit may be lost. This also suggests that if an evaluation of the implementation of ethical practices by a firm leads to the conclusion that the practices were not economically viable, then they would cease to continue. Volunteer tourism operators, however, are able to operate beyond these parameters through the use of wider volunteer frameworks that can incorporate ethical and sustainable practices.

Beyond the Passing Gaze

Based on the above analysis, it can be concluded that although there has been some progress towards sustainable tourism through the initiatives of industry, government and associations, the majority of effort by the tourism industry has been focused towards self-interest rather than a true conservation ethic. Figgis (1993, p. 8), for example, goes so far as to state that 'essentially ecotourism's been a smokescreen for "business as usual" with no real change in on-ground behaviour'.

Kennedy states (1993, p. 4) that: '[T]he fundamental philosophical changes that need to take place are the development of a true conservation ethic within the travel industry, and the use of ecological principles in all management'. This involves a move away from tourism-centred planning – where needs, demands and pressure lead to major modification and adaptation by local communities to accommodate tourism – towards ethical-centred planning, where host community needs and requirements lead to need modification, demand adaptation and pressure education of the tourist industry, operators and tourists.

Volunteer tourism can incorporate the need for a greater emphasis on behavioural aspects of the visitor and resident. To accommodate the reciprocal effects of interactions on the community and its tourists, operators need to ensure local participation and input into tourism developments, incorporating resources that enhance the local culture and build on the skills and resources of the community. These changes in themselves will move the industry towards more ethical practices, beyond the colonialist attitudes of mass tourism and its associated experiences, helping to embed these tourists more richly in the local cultures and gain an understanding of host values and traditions.

Where developments already exist, volunteer tourism projects by their nature utilize local resources and thus can reduce the importation of specialized goods and services. Career opportunities within the tourism industry can be extended to the local community through the importing of skills through volunteers and the use of these volunteers to train residents. Local tourism developments can begin to correspond to local cultural development: 'The sustainable tourism approach advocates building on cultural strengths and marketing the local culture as attractive for what it is' (Gilmore and Dunstan, 1989, p. 2). Furthermore, the development can become sustainable; combining social thinking, encompassing an innovative, progressive approach, incorporating a new social responsiveness for cultural and environmental preservation and a long-term planning strategy.

Additionally, within the volunteer tourism approach is the firm acknowledgement that local economies are the main beneficiaries of such tourism. Global or external organizations may have a role to play in facilitating and, in select cases, making a commercial gain. Sound ethical and cultural tourist practice does not necessarily mean that the economic value of tourism is forgotten, as the success of Aboriginal-based and, in New Zealand, Maori-based tourism testifies. Beyond the advantages that can be gained from adopting sustainable practices (Harris, 1997), host communities need to remain aware of the domination and commodifying impetus of markets and their global protagonists in order to ensure that such advantage is gained in the use of volunteers as a means towards sustainable development.

Chapter 9

Volunteer Tourism: Moving on from the Empty Meeting Ground

This book has explored the notion of an alternative tourism experience – volunteer tourism – attempting not to reduce ideas as MacCannell (1992, p. 6) suggests to a dialogic model of impossible realities related to dialectal materialism, but to make it more concrete and more grounded in human interactions. In this chapter, volunteer tourism is presented as a means of examining the empty meeting ground that MacCannell (1992) proposes. He sees that 'the one path that still leads in the direction of scholarly objectivity, detachment, and neutrality is exactly the one originally thought to lead away from these classic virtues. That is, an openly autobiographical style in which the subjective position of the author, especially on political matters, is presented in a clear and straightforward fashion. At least this enables the reader to review his or her own position to make adjustments necessary for dialogue' (1992, p. 10). This book has proposed that alternative forms of tourism experience can exist apart from the realm of the mass tourism experiences as proposed by other tourism authors (MacCannell, 1976, 1992; Urry, 1990; Rojek, 1993), and in doing so it has provided a model of tourist behaviour that gives perspective to the tourist experience. In order to capture the individual tourist's construction of her/his experience, the meanings given and the remembrance of the tourist space, qualitative methods have been used to allow for greater variety of response as well as being able to explore the impacts on the self.

If it is recognized that the alternative tourist experience is based on interactions that people have with elements of the space visited, then this can be invaluable for understanding and therefore providing sustainable tourist experiences. Documentation of the real value of the tourist experience to the tourist could suggest that the industry is not compelled to create and promote artificial environments. A focus on the on-site interactions and the importance of them to the tourist will lead to the consideration and development of strategies around these ideas as opposed to repeatedly attempting to create authentic objects to gaze at or places to escape to (see MacCannell, 1976, 1992; Urry, 1990; Rojek, 1993). This can enable another look at how the industry structures tourism and may provide directions for policy in the future.

The Self and Community

Tourism is often seen as providing an attractive alternative to other forms of economic development because of its potential for growth, employment generation, protection of natural and cultural assets and support for activities and facilities which make local areas more interesting and rewarding places to live (see Mieczkowski, 1995). During the 1970s and 1980s, integrated rural development projects were used to raise rural living standards in developing countries, focusing primarily on irrigation, roads and social services. The World Bank (1992, p. 86), however, found that the results were often disappointing, with low success rates, because of overemphasis on appraisals on outcomes, a tendency to select large and complex projects, and overly optimistic projections of project outcomes. Development of tourism infrastructure for providing tourism experiences in the 1990s may have suffered the same fate.

In relation to this problem, the focus in this book has been on the microsocial analysis of the tourist experience, provisionally assessing its contribution to an understanding and, hence, development, of the issues relating to this area. By drawing on the concepts of interactionist theories, the research approach utilized here attempted to give added dimensions to the ideas that surround the notion of a tourism experience. In previous chapters, the relationship between identity/value and the tourist experience has been examined. Now, we will tentatively place this relationship within its macrosocial context; specifically with respect to the dynamic nexus of self and community. The agenda for research in this area is that people and their ideas must become fundamental to the process, and for this to occur there is a need for the development of theoretical approaches that are enabling for people such as the host community member and alternative tourist.

It is obvious that ecologically sustainable development is essential for the long-term profitability of the tourism industry. In order to ensure that tourism does not exceed its sustainable base, an understanding of the elements of the experience are essential. Thus the need for theoretical approaches that provide for the microsocial construction of the experience of the self (both tourist and community member) allows for a change in emphasis from the currently accepted paradigms that were assessed negatively by the World Bank.

An understanding of the self and community interactions on site and its contribution to the tourist experience may enable a move away from approaches to tourism planning and management based simply on maximizing volume, especially since volume is not necessarily the most important factor determining the impact and acceptability of tourism development. Large developments may have relatively small impacts on local environments and communities if they are well designed and well implemented. Conversely, relatively small developments may have a high level of impact on both the natural and social environment if they lack a sensitive approach to design and implementation.

> Whatever the overall economic situation, the long-term solutions to the fundamental problems of development ultimately lie in local communities, especially the rural communities, where most of the world's population still live. These changes have been so great as to precipitate the breakdown of the social geographic units which are basic to people's lives.
>
> (MacPherson in Jayasuriya and Lee, 1994, p. 193)

A general framework and provisional conceptual map for future research in utilizing an understanding of self and identity, facilitated in the alternative tourism experience, as a catalyst for developing research agendas could well enable the development of a management and decision-making framework for tourism. The tourist has been conceptualized in mass tourism theory as an agent only in so far as they see the objects presented for their gaze in the tourist place (Pfohl, 1992). Whether that image actually corresponds to the image presented in the tourist brochure or whether the object of his/her gaze is authentic/unauthentic, historical/modern or romantic/collective becomes somewhat subordinated to the particularity of the perceptor of the 'gaze'. It can be argued that the 'reality' of the tourist experience relies on the interaction that the tourist has within the tourist space (for instance the SERR site); that is, the tourist destination and the meaning that the tourist gives to this interaction. Each individual meaning will be constructed according to the tourist's own cultural and social background, the purpose of the visit, the companions, preconceived and observed values of the host culture, the marketing images of the destination and, above all, the relationships of power between visitor and host cultures and within the host culture. If the space is perceived as one in which interactions occur and the self is enlarged or expanded, challenged, renewed or reinforced, the tourist experience becomes an on-going process which extends beyond the time and place boundaries of the tourist visit.

Such a recognition necessitates the exploration of theoretical models that can link interactionist research on the social self to models that are more encompassing of the self and community. Existing methods in the area of community or social development and community studies (see Furze *et al.*, 1996) are able to provide analysis of community responses to tourism which, allied with a theoretical analysis of the relationship to self, enable a substantial advancement in the theoretical understanding of alternative tourism experiences.

Exploring alternative methods for an understanding of the process of construction of self and community may provide a means of addressing some of the problems that have arisen in developing nations from existing forms of tourism growth. Conventional tourism brings with it many of the same problems we have found in the exploitation of developing nations in the past. It is often driven, owned and controlled by the developed nations, with a high return to these nations. Packaged tours are offered and the only use of local people is through the use of their resources at a minimum or no cost to the operator. Where local people are used as guides, they are paid minimal salaries, in contrast to the profits made by the investors and owners – defended on the pretext that if these operators did not come, there would be no money injected into the community at all. The SERR project demonstrates that different modes of tourism experience and development are available.

> In this dominant 'market' paradigm the good life is obtained by the buying of commodities, the environment is fragmented; its holistic properties are ignored; and the costs of environmental disruption are externalised.
>
> (Gudynas in Encel and Encel, 1991, p. 140)

Research agendas based around theoretical approaches linking self and community enable better models for alternative tourism experiences to be established. Crocker (in Encel and Encel, 1991, p. 150) maintains that participatory eco-development is one such means of achieving results, being made up as it is of cooperative, self-management (autogestion), co-management (cogestion) and solidarity (solidarism) movements. It has been largely recognized that existing economic models have created problems in developing nations, often benefiting only the developed nations who end up controlling the economy.[27] Similarly, allied models contribute to the ideas behind Croker's participatory eco-development model (satisfaction of human needs, democratic, self-determination, respect for nature) in negotiating conflicts of moral principles while providing a real opportunity for personal development based around the ideas of self and community, as suggested in this book.

In the last decade, western economists, politicians and business representatives have advocated 'letting markets set the agenda'. In the case of tourism, this translates as tourists selecting their preferred option from a range of possibilities. If developed countries within the context of a market economy are responsible for determining the range of options available within alternative tourism, then the agenda becomes an expression of their desire and motives. The commodification of tourism introduces some doubt as to the ability of alternative tourism to continue in a sustainable manner. However, providing local communities with more control over the development process is the first step in this regard. To support this process, there is a need to locate the area of alternative tourism within frameworks that are both inside and outside those of the tourism industry (inherently based as it is within the context of profit/loss). Otherwise profit is likely to dominate and thus subordinate the reorientation that alternative tourism can initiate. The identification of the differential elements of alternative tourism, as seen with respect to the SERR project, situate tourism experience around a series of significantly divergent value systems – altruism, sustainability and ecological preservation for example. This has led to the examination of the areas of community or social development and community studies.

The exponential rate of global expansion of the tourism industry during the last decade has seen an increasing domination by multinational corporations. Sociological perspectives have reflected the dominant theoretical concerns of the discipline, assuming initially that developing countries' predominantly male views of the phenomenon were universal. However, gradual acknowledgement has been given to microsocial differences such as class, race, ethnicity, age and gender.

The linking of alternative tourism experiences analysis between self and identity and self and community establishes a fundamental underpinning for alternative tourism experiences with the recognition that communities represent a central relationship between individuals and groups (see Menzies, 1989). Alternative tourism experiences occur in an interactive process and, as Menzies (1989) suggests, the content of these processes is subordinated (although not precluding content) but focuses chiefly on the interactive processes. Initially utilizing interactionism's evolution as a theoretical paradigm in providing explanations of social meaning and spatial experiences (Wilson, 1980,

[27] The World Bank has recognized the inadequacies of existing economic models in reports such as 'The World Bank and the Environment' (World Bank, 1992), which notes policy review as essential, supporting the United Nations Conference on Environment and Development's blueprint for environmental action – Agenda 21 – which notes that unregulated economic growth can have profound and sometimes irreversible effects on the environment (World Bank, 1992, p. 8).

p. 145) through the interaction of the individual with their social world, the research design utilized for this study can now move towards incorporating the analysis of the self and community.

MacPherson (in Jayasuriya and Lee, 1994, p. 202) suggests that although a local project may be small, it is socially complex: a health centre, for example, may only serve a small area but may encompass a wide range of beliefs and practices; similarly, a school may only serve a few hundred children but its impact on the local culture may be profound. These ideas are fundamentally relevant to alternative forms of tourism, such as the SERR project. Research surrounding the evolution of self through the process and context of community can provide the potential for alternative forms of tourism to build upon an approach that is able to accommodate new concepts while recognizing the complexity of the actual experiences. Such a process facilitates analysis premised on the cross-cultural interchange between the tourist and community member (the individual interactions that occurred on the SERR site are transferred through further social interaction between community members and the tourist with family members and other social milieux). In thematizing self and community, the focus on people, their culture and the nature of the interaction between them allows the idea of 'social value', relating to space and place,[28] to emerge. This facilitates the transfer of the microsocial explanations of the elements of the on-site experience (analysed through the social valuing of the alternative tourist and the attendant impacts on self and identity) into a more expansionary context. This could include the impact that the social value an individual community member or alternative tourist might have on the wider community, which may, in fact, lead to more general social change and allow a more effective cooperative management mechanism to be established. Tourism operators and protected area agencies may come to terms with each other's interpretation and view any given situation through a shared sense of social value.

Thus, there is a recognition that ideas surrounding the self and community are able to devolve into approaches that can be applied to conservation management.

> [C]ultural learnings influence the perception of other people. Developing crosscultural understanding involves perceiving members of other cultural groups positively. By understanding the basic principles of person perception, and the natural effects of one's own cultural experience and learnings on perceiving other people, unproductive explanations of crosscultural misunderstandings as prejudice or even just differences may be replaced with productive methods of avoiding misunderstandings and stimulating positive perceptions of other people. How we perceive

---

[28] See Simmel (1965), MacCannell (1976, 1992), Harvey (1985), Urry (1990), Rojek (1993), Grosz (1995) and Watson and Gibson (1995).

other people affects how we behave towards them and how they, in turn, behave towards us.

(Robinson, 1988, p. 49)

Alternative tourism forms, such as the SERR project, are based essentially on community support (both the tourist's home community and the host community), with representatives of the host community being involved in all aspects of management of the resource, with the community itself being the primary focus in tourism of this kind. Effective conservation of natural and cultural heritage (these may in fact be one and the same) within the framework of alternative tourism may require education of both the tourist and the host communities. If tourists are to change their attitudes and behaviour towards the environment, local communities and their cultures, then they must develop a cross-cultural understanding and appreciation. Similarly, if local communities are to manage alternative tourism ventures, then they must understand not only the tourists' cultural background, but also how to preserve the integrity of their own lifestyles and environment from the effects of tourism. Recognition of the relationship to community-based approaches allows these ideas to be examined in the more general community at a macrosocial level.

The flexibility of community-based approaches is an important feature: 'The process of informal theorising (in community studies[29]) is crucial because it is necessary to constantly reinterpret the accumulating new findings until they appear "strategically relevant" to some central problems of the discipline' (Wild, 1981, p. 49). For example, when applied to the involvement of Aboriginal communities and individuals in the joint management of national parks, this process is driven by observations from the community and the researcher which are then incorporated into the broader joint management theory.

In this way, alternative tourism experiences can be placed in the context of the wider body of theory. It would seem that all parties in the area of alternative tourism management processes are still in their preliminary stages. This may be able to be used to reinforce or enhance present understanding, contributing to the process while also benefiting from it. An added appeal of this approach is that the theoreticians are also the practitioners of the theory, i.e. the reserve workers and

---

[29] 'Method-type community studies use a locality as a source of data in order to test ideas generated in the wider body of sociological theory' (Wild, 1984, p. 3). Community study models enable the analysis of competition over economic resources, political power and prestige, with contenders defining themselves, or defining others, in terms of particular status characteristics. The notion of community as a process that changes through time would also be a particularly useful aspect of this approach (Wild, 1984, p. 4). Allied to the idea of social value and linked to ideas of change in tourism (see Butler, 1980, 1991; Doxey, 1976), adaptations of this model may provide useful frameworks in the future.

community members. Thus theory mirrors practice more closely and evolves more readily.

Leisure, in Kelly's (1987) terms, emphasizes the 'existential' openness of activity, i.e. acts engaged in primarily for the experience. The focus is on the element of becoming through the real experience of leisure. Such experiences need, of course, to be seen in the context of the underlying power structures such as the relationship of the tourist to the community. Nevertheless, as Kelly points out, there remains much value in analysing leisure in terms that combine action and structure with a focus on identity in the situation of the social world: 'It includes discourse as well as action, culture as well as structure, and imposed as well as individually constructed meanings' (Kelly, 1994, p. 94). Following Heywood (1991), it is suggested that interactionist theories have value for understanding how individuals experience tourism in interaction with the people and symbols encountered in the tourist space. The places of tourism thus provide individuals with profound centres of meanings and symbols endowed with cultural significance which are in some ways different from their own environments (Brown, 1992, p. 64). As Pearce (1990, p. 32) observes: 'Meeting new people, making friends and expanding one's view of the world through these contacts is a little publicised but important social impact'.

Concomitantly, it is fundamental that we rethink the way social theory has been conceptualized and has been practised in relation to social change. Modernist social theory, of which sociology is a prime example, has been imbued with the biases of the Enlightenment in privileging and valorizing an essentialized male rational actor as a foundational paradigm for humanity as a whole. As a consequence, it has produced narratives and practices that are not in the interest of the host community, especially those who have been dominated and oppressed. In order to live up to its potential as a vehicle for the improvement of social conditions, sociological analysis needs to include the values of the people involved in its researching and theorizing activities (Spivak and Harasym, 1990).

Simmel (1936) argued that in complex industrial societies, the very variety of groups to which one may belong produces a unique pattern of group affiliations for each person, thus contributing to individuality. In earlier societies, one's web of group affiliations tended to be concentric, reinforcing the values and assigned status of that society (Deleuze and Guattari, 1992). In contemporary society, however, they do not necessarily overlap, providing opportunities for individual identity construction. Contact with different cultures (communities) through tourism experience can also add to the variety open to one in terms of identity construction. In Mead's conception of self (1934)[30] the 'me' which is socially constructed through contact with 'significant others', 'significant reference groups' and the 'generalized other' is open through tourism to both growth and constraint. This contact with alternative cultures, as seen in the SERR experience, affects the experiential sense of 'me'. In addition, the self is an 'I' which selectively synthesizes the societal input into the 'me'. Presumably this cumulative 'I' can be enlarged by interaction in tourist space. The 'me' and the 'I' which make up the self must be changed in some way by the interactions and symbols experienced in the tourist space. It is this self which is taken home with the tourist. Tourism is thus a process in which both agency and societal structures play a part. It is a process which extends beyond the visit to a specific tourist destination.

For research to provide an understanding of the self and community in this way, there is a need for the construction of frameworks that enable the inclusion of the influence of host communities and their members. One author who has attempted to go beyond previous sociological analyses to open out the possibilities through tourism of widening culturally constructed identities, including gender, is MacCannell. He also emphasizes the need for a sociology of interaction in conjunction with elements of deconstruction in order to 'gain access to the realm of contingency and determinism, and especially resistance to and struggles against [cultural] determinism' (MacCannell, 1992, p. 3). MacCannell sees the movement of peoples both to and from the western world, through tourism, as an opportunity to form hybrid cultures which will be a precondition for inventiveness in creating subjectivities which resist cultural constraints. He claims that the neo-nomads of tourism in the post-modern era cross cultural boundaries, not as invaders, but as imaginative travellers who benefit from displaced self-understanding and the freedom to go beyond the limits that frontiers present.

However, the power differentials between western tourists and the dominant discourses of their culture and those of the host culture may in fact mean that the tourist merely imposes his/her ideas and values on to the host culture and thus comes away more confirmed than ever in gender, race, age and/or ethnic rigidities, i.e. the self may be confirmed in its pre-tourist subjectivities. Nevertheless, the possibilities for growth and enhancement of identity do inhere in the experience itself and must be conceptualized in the construction of further research. In this way, areas such as participatory research[31] (see Conchelos, 1983; Couto, 1987; Anyanwu, 1988; Maclure, 1990; Park, 1992) may offer the

---

[30] Jagtenberg and Mckie (1997, p. 134) suggest that Mead's insights on the 'I', the 'me' and the 'self ' are still a useful starting point for theory in an ever complicating social world. They maintain that the increased mediation of the self and its broader ecological identifications does not negate the fundamentally social nature of self that interactionism identifies, but the meanings of self, society and social may be more ambiguous, comprising the multiplicity of discourses that provide for multiple horizons of meaning and the possibility of more heterogeneous processes of identity formation.

potential to initiate a paradigm shift in the social sciences approaches used to examine tourism, primarily due to its exploration of an expanded conception of knowledge and its re-orientation of the relationship between the researcher and the researched and between theory and practice (Park, 1992).

Tourism research, in encompassing such approaches, may be able to provide stronger links to the ideas of self and community, thus enabling identification of alternative approaches.[32] A major study of some 400 grassroots programmes worldwide, in looking at successful approaches to rural development, provided strong evidence for participating effectiveness in promoting equitable, self-reliant development (Burbidge, 1988). In MacCannell's terms, the face to face interactions of tourists and hosts may provide some space for individuals to challenge the way culturally specific discourses construct the 'I' and 'you' of their culture in opposition to the 'he' of 'other' inferiorized ethnic cultures (MacCannell, 1992, p. 125). Thus these approaches open up new ways of understanding and constructing tourism experiences.

If it is recognized that the alternative tourist experience is based on interactions that people have with elements of the space visited, then this may be invaluable for understanding, and therefore providing, sustainable tourist experiences. Documentation of the real value of the tourist experience to the tourist could suggest that the industry may not be compelled to create an environment artificially and to promise this as an image, focusing instead on the on-site interactions and their importance to the tourist, thus initiating the development of strategies around these ideas rather than attempting to create authentic objects to gaze or places to escape to (see MacCannell, 1976, 1992; Urry, 1990; Rojek, 1993).

If forms of alternative tourism experiences such as SERR are to be understood within the complexities of the exchanges that occur, there

---

[31] PAR (Participatory Action Research; see Johnson, 1994) is always an emergent process that works effectively to link participation, social action and knowledge generation (Greenwood *et al.*, 1993) and thus has direct links with grounded theory. Conchelos (1993) has demonstrated this by the development and application of a method which combined content analysis with the generation of a grounded theory. This offers the area of alternative tourism sound practice while also letting it explore new theoretical applications. Participatory research is seen as a cooperative inquiry by both the researcher and the people who constitute the object of study. Central features of participatory research include joint identification of the problem studied, analysis of the best way to study the problem and incorporation of results in future solution (Ramphele, 1990). This makes PAR ideally suited to resolving community conflicts arising from cross-cultural misunderstandings and misconceptions between tourist, alternative tourist and community member.

[32] An example is the basic classical model of action research applied to social problems which comprises five key elements: a change in orientation toward democratic, humanistic values; context-bound, real-world inquiry; systematic data collection over time; collaboration with participants in the research process; and diffusion of knowledge (Elden and Chisholm, 1993).

is a need for a focus on questions that introduce theories which push thinking beyond previous explanations of tourism. By examining the SERR as a tourist destination, a site and as a space in which dynamic social interactions occur, rather than as a static and bounded place, research can link tourist experiences to possibilities for extending the self beyond the limitations of culturally specific discourses. This expands and modifies the concept of the universalizing gaze, suggesting that the alternative tourist in this specific context is interacting in a creative way with the tourist space so that the self is involved. An asymmetrical perspective focusing on the one-way action of the tourist upon the host culture gives way to a more symmetrical approach which recognizes the two-way interaction between tourist and host and includes the subjective experiences of both.

Towards a Sociology of Volunteer Tourism Experiences

Principally, the conceptualization of alternative tourism experiences beyond the influences of a simple polarization of subject/object – which largely rely on pre-coded categories to elicit information concerning the functional, physical and measurable attributes of the destination, as well as the psychological abstract impressions formed by the tourist (see Echtner and Ritchie, 1991) – encompasses the individual tourist's construction of her/his experience, the meanings given and the remembrance of the tourist space, placing qualitative methods as essential through their inherent allowance of a greater variety of response as the ability to tap into the impacts on the self (see Denzin and Lincoln, 1994). Secondly, if it is recognized that the tourist experience is based on the interactions that people have, then the members of the destination (or host community) become a valuable component in determining the 'identity' of the destination through exploring the value that they have for particular places, events and traditions endemic to their lifestyle and environment. Their input into the social value of the space is invaluable for understanding and therefore for providing sustainable tourist experiences. This has significance for the industry by recognizing that there is no necessary compulsion to create an environment artificially which is then promoted to potential tourists as an image. Documentation of the real value of the tourist experience to the visitor would enable the elements that make it up to be provided for in the destination space.

Thirdly, previous research into the sustainability of tourism based predominantly on image suggests that '[t]he outcome for many cities drawn on by the urban "tourist mirage" . . . will be to exacerbate rather than to arrest civic decline' (Rowe and Stevenson, 1994, p. 191). Future research could well examine the social and economic impact for the host community, as well as for the tourist, of tourist ventures which take into account both host and tourist experiences as an on-going process which impacts on self-conceptions.

Instead, ‘cannibalistic’ tourism continues apace; a tourism that imposes, neither indirectly or directly, neither motivated nor non-motivated, the hegemonic values of predominantly western industrialized countries. Such cultural ‘cannibalism’ serves to homogenize and reinforce the endemic cultural constraints of the dominant culture. In this model, there is little room for self-development through tourism, because the economic power of tourist marketeers has enabled the commodification of interpretations of the ‘other’ culture through images which are at least one remove from the people themselves. Tourists are encouraged to be voyeurs who glimpse aspects of the other culture often dressed up to conform to the image which has been presented in glossy advertising brochures. Tourist destinations become places for viewing the ‘other’ rather than as spaces for interaction with them.

Instead, this book has concerned itself with the voice of the ‘other(s)’ in the tourist enterprise: social value, interactions with and between the host community, and the self that evolves through the volunteer tourist experience, indeed the *nature*, in its most inclusive sense, of the experience itself. If the social value(s) of a particular site – that has and is in process, both through historical aggregation and through contemporary practices of meaning making – is able to be engendered within the interaction with the tourist, there is more likelihood of a genuine exchange with both the space and its people. Such an experience includes the other’s view as well as one’s own, which facilitates a mutual process of learning and personal growth. Where local communities have been involved in the planning, preparation, management and implementation of tourist enterprises – evidenced in the Santa Elena experience – exclusion and inferiorization of the ‘other’ can give way to dialogue in which there is a sharing and exchange of cultural meaning. The power balance between tourist and hosts can be destabilized, cultural hegemony can be challenged and tourist spaces constructed for genuine exchange which will benefit all the selves involved.

References

Abbott, C. (1989) The wilderness experience as personal development – why it works and how to enhance it; lessons from a drug rehabilitation program. In Hayllar, B. (ed.) *Sixth National Outdoor Education Conference Proceedings*. University of Technology, Sydney.

Adventure World (1992) *Brochure*. Produced for Adventure World, Sydney.

Allen, L.R. (1991) Benefits of leisure services to community satisfaction. In: Driver, B.L., Brown, J. and Peterson, L. (eds) *Benefits of Leisure*. Venture, State College, Pennsylvania, pp. 60–65.

Allen, N.J. and Rushton, J.P. (1983) Personality characteristics of community health volunteers: a review. *Journal of Voluntary Action Research* 12, 36–49.

Altman, J.C. (1987) *The Economic Impact of Tourism on the Warmun (Turkey Creek) Community, East Kimberley*. East Kimberley Impact Assessment Project: Working Paper No. 19. CRES, ANU, AIAS, UWA, ASSA, Canberra.

American Field Service Research Department (1986) *The AFS Impact Study: Final Report*. American Field Service, Washington, DC.

Anyanwu, C.N. (1988) The technique of participatory research in community development. *Community Development Journal* 23, 11–15.

Armstrong, P., Hannah, J., Mulguiny, C. and Trass, M. (1992) (unpublished) Responsible tourism: responsible tourism is a sustainable alternative to current mainstream tourism practices. University of Technology, Sydney.

Ascher, F. (1985) *Tourism, Transnational Corporations and Cultural Identity*. UNESCO, France.

Australian Bureau of Statistics (1986) *Volunteering in NSW*. Australian Government Publishing Service, Canberra.

Australian Volunteers Abroad (1989) *Australian Volunteers Abroad: 25 Years Working for the World*. Australian Government Publishing Service, Canberra.

Bates, B. (1991) Ecotourism – a case study of the lodges in Papua New Guinea. Paper presented at the *PATA 40th Annual Conference*. Nusa Indah Convention Centre, Bali, Indonesia, 10–13 April.

Bates, B. and Witter, D. (1992) Cultural tourism at Mutawintji – and beyond. In: Birckhead, J., de Lacy, T. and Smith, L. (eds) *Aboriginal Involvement in Parks and Protected Areas.* Australian Institute of Aboriginal and Torres Strait Islander Studies Report Series. Aboriginal Studies Press, Canberra, pp.

Beighbeder, Y. (1991) *The Role and Status of International Humanitarian Volunteers and Organisations.* Martinus Nijhoff, London.

Bell, D. (1978) *The Cultural Contradictions of Capitalism.* Harper Torchbooks for Basic Books, New York.

Bella, L. (1989) Women and leisure: beyond androcentrism. In: Jackson, E.L. and Burton, T.L. (eds) *Understanding Leisure and Recreation: Mapping the Past, Charting the Future.* Venture Publishing, State College, Pennsylvania, pp. 43–50.

Bennett, D. (1988) Wrapping up postmodernism: the subject of consumption versus the subject of cognition. In: Jackson, E.L. and Burton, T.L. (eds) *Postmodern Conditions.* Centre for General and Comparative Literature, Monash University, Victoria, pp. 115–122.

Berger, P. and Luckmann, T. (1981) *The Social Construction of Reality.* Penguin, London.

Berman, M. (1983) *All That is Solid Melts into Air.* Verso, London.

Bilsen, F. (1987) Integrated tourism in Senegal: an alternative. *Tourism Recreation Research* 13, 19–23.

Bishop, J. and Hogett, P. (1986) *Organising Around Enthusiasms – Mutual Aid in Leisure.* Comedia, London.

Blangy, S. and Epler-Wood, M. (1992) *Developing and Implementing Ecotourism Guidelines for Wild Lands and Neighbouring Communities.* The Ecotourism Society, Vermont.

Blumer, H. (1969) *Symbolic Interactionism: Perspective and Method.* Prentice-Hall, Englewood Cliffs, New Jersey.

Boer, B. (1993) Ecotourism and sustainable development: the international and national legal framework. In: *Proceedings of 'Law Asia 93' Asia on the Leap – The Role of Law.* Colombo, Sri Lanka, 12–16 September, pp. 121–127.

Boo, E. (1990) *Ecotourism: the Potentials and Pitfalls.* World Wide Fund for Nature, Washington, DC.

Braidotti, R. (1993) Embodiment, sexual difference, and the nomadic subject. *Hypatia* 8, 1–3.

Bramwell, B. and Rawding, L. (1996) Tourism marketing images of industrial cities. *Annals of Tourism Research* 23, 201–221.

Brightbill, C.K. (1960) *The Challenge of Leisure.* Prentice-Hall, Englewood Cliffs, New Jersey.

Britten, S and Clarke, W.C. (eds) (1987) *Tourism in Small Developing Countries.* University of the South Pacific, Suva.

Britton, R.A. (1977) Making tourism more supportive of small state development: the case of St-Vincent. *Annals of Tourism Research* 6, 269–278.

Brown, G. (1992) Tourism and symbolic consumption. In: Johnson, P. and Thomas, B. (eds) *Choice and Demand in Tourism.* Mansel, London, pp. 102–107.

BTCV (2001) *BTCV Position Statement on Biodiversity*, 2/1/01, www.btcv.org.

Burbidge, J. (ed.) (1988) *Approaches that Work in Rural Development: Emerging Trends, Participatory Methods and Local Initiatives.* IERD series, Vol. 3. K.G. Saur, Munich.

Burchett, C. (1992) A new direction in travel: Aboriginal tourism in Australia's Northern Territory. Paper presented at the *Northern Territory Tourist Commission Environmental Conference.* Expo 1992, April.

Burden, J. and Kiewa, J. (1992) Adventurous women. *Refractory Girl* 42, 29–33.

Burkart, A.J. and Medlik, S. (1974) *Tourism: Past, Present and Future.* Heinemann, London.

Butler, J. (1990) *Gender Trouble: Feminism and the Subversion of Identity.* Routledge, New York.

Butler, J.R. (1992) Ecotourism: its changing face and evolving philosophy. Paper presented at the *International Union for Conservation of Nature and Natural Resources (IUCN), IVth World Congress on National Parks and Protected Areas.* Caracas, Venezuela, 10–12 February.

Butler, R.W. (1980) The concept of a tourism area cycle of evolution: implications for management of resources. *Canadian Geographer* 24, 5–12.

Butler, R.W. (1990) Alternative tourism: pious hope or Trojan horse? *Journal of Travel Research* 3, 40–45.

Butler, R.W. (1991) Tourism, environment and sustainable development. *Environmental Conservation* 18, 201–209.

Buttimer, A. (1980) Home, reach and the sense of place. In: Buttimer, A. and Seamon, D. (eds) *The Human Experience of Space and Place.* Croom Helm, London, pp. 70–77.

Campbell, C. (1983) Romanticism and the consumer: intimations of a Weber-style thesis. *Sociological Analysis* 44, 279–296.

Campbell, C. (1987) *The Romantic Ethic and the Spirit of Modern Consumerism.* Blackwell, Oxford.

Carlson, J.S. (1991) *Study Abroad: the Experience of American Undergraduates in Western Europe and the United States.* Council of International Educational Exchange, New York.

Carpenter, E. (1973) *Oh! What a Blow that Phantom Gave Me!* Holt, Rinehart and Winston, New York.

Cater, E. (1987) Tourism in the least developed countries. *Annals of Tourism Research* 14, 202–206.

Cater, E. and Lowman, G. (eds) (1994) *Ecotourism a Sustainable Option?* John Wiley & Sons, Chichester, UK.

Ceballos-Lascurain, H. (1990) Tourism, ecotourism and protected areas. Paper presented at the 34th Working Session of the Commission of National Parks and Protected Areas. Perth, Australia, 26–27 November.

Chan, J. (1993) World Wide Fund for Nature research report: evaluating methods used for assessing the limits of ecotourism. Tourism Studies Project, University of Technology, Sydney.

Chapman, R. (1982) *In the Eye of the Wind: the Story of Operation Drake.* Hamilton, London.

Chavalier, C. (1993) Letter to the Editor *The London Times* 3.

Chenitz, W.C. and Swanson, J.M. (1986) *From Practice to Grounded Theory.* Addison-Wesley, Sydney.

Chickering, A.W. (1969) *Education and Identity.* Jossey-Bass, San Francisco.

Christ, C. (1998) Taking ecotourism to the next level: a look at private sector involvement in with local communities. In: Lindberg, K., Wood, M.E. and Engeldrum, D. (eds) *Ecotourism: a Guide for Planners and Managers*, Vol. 2. The Ecotourism Society, North Bennington, Vermont, pp. 183–202.

Clark, J. and Critcher, C. (1985) *The Devil Makes Work: Leisure in Capitalist Britain*. MacMillan, London.

Clark, K. (1978) *The Two-way Street – a Survey of Volunteer Service Abroad*. New Zealand Council for Educational Research, Wellington.

Clarke, J., Hall, S., Jefferson, T. and Roberts, B. (1975) Subcultures, cultures and class. In: Hall, S. and Jefferson, T. (eds) *Resistance Through Rituals*. Hutchinson, London, pp. 32–35.

Clarke, R. and Stankey, G. (1979) *The Recreation Opportunity Spectrum: a Framework for Planning, Management and Research*. General Technical Report, Pacific North-West Forest and Range Experiment Station, US Department of Agriculture, Seattle.

Clawson, M. and Knetsch, J.L. (1966) *Economics of Outdoor Recreation*. Johns Hopkins Press, Baltimore, Maryland.

Cohen, C.B. (1995) Marketing paradise, making nation. *Annals of Tourism Research* 22, 404–421.

Cohen, E. (1972) Towards a sociology of international tourism. *Social Research* 39, 164–182.

Cohen, E. (1987) Alternative tourism – a critique. *Tourism Recreation Research* 12, 13–18.

Cohen, E. (1988) Authenticity and commoditization in tourism. *Annals of Tourism Research* 15, 371–386.

Cohen, E. (1995) Contemporary tourism – trends and challenges: sustainable authenticity or contrived post-modernity? In: Butler, R.W. and Pearce, D. (eds) *Change in Tourism: People, Places and Processes*. Routledge, London, pp. 65–72.

Cohen, S. and Taylor, L. (1976) *Escape Attempts*. Penguin, Harmondsworth.

Collins, C. (1994) State's ecowolves in tourism sheep's clothing: Brown. *The Australian* 8 November, 8.

Colton, C.W. (1987) Leisure, recreation, tourism: a symbolic interactionism view. *Annals of Tourism Research* 14, 345–360.

Community Aid Abroad (1991) *Travel Wise Sarawak*. One World Travel, Melbourne.

Community Aid Abroad (1992) *Thailand Study Tour Notes*. One World Travel, Melbourne.

Conchelos, G. (1983) Participatory research: development of a political–economic framework. PhD Thesis, Ontario Institute for Studies in Education, Ontario.

Couto, R.A. (1987) Participatory research: methodology and critique. *Clinical Sociology Review* 5, 83–90.

Cox, J. (1985) The resort concept: the good, the bad and the ugly. Keynote paper presented to National Conference on Tourism and Resort Development. Kuring-gai College of Advanced Education, Sydney, 4–11 November.

Craib, I. (1998) *Experiencing Identity*. Sage, London.

Craig, G.J. (1983) *Human Development*, 3rd edn. Prentice-Hall, Sydney.

Craik, J, (1986) *Resorting to Tourism: Cultural Policies for Tourist Development in Australia*, ACS, Sydney.

Crandell, L. (1987) The social impact of tourism on developing regions and its management. In: Ritchie, J. and Goeldner, C.R. (eds) *Travel, Tourism and Hospitality Research*. John Wiley & Sons, New York.

Crick, M. (1991) Tourists, locals and anthropologists: quizzical reflections on 'otherness' in tourist encounters and in tourism research. *Australian Cultural History* 10, 6–18.

Crompton, J.L. (1979) Motivations for pleasure vacations. *Annals of Tourism Research* 3, 408–424.

Cronin, L. (1990) A strategy for tourism and sustainable developments. *World Leisure and Recreation Journal* 2, 12–18.

Csikszentmihalyi, M. (1975) *Beyond Boredom and Anxiety*. Jossey-Bass, San Francisco.

Cunneen, C., Findlay, M., Lynch, R., and Tupper, V. (1989) *Dynamics of Collective Conflict: the Riots at the Bathurst 'Bike Races*. The Law Book Company, Sydney.

Curry, S. and Morvaridi, B. (1992) Sustainable tourism: illustrations from Kenya, Nepal and Jamaica. In: Cooper, C.P. and Lockwood, A. (eds) *Progress in Tourism, Recreation and Hospitality Management*, Vol. 4. Belhaven, London, pp. 16–21.

Dann, G. (1995) A socio-linguistic approach towards changing tourist imagery. In: Butler, R. and Pearce, D. (eds) *Change in Tourism: People, Places, Processes*. Routledge, London, pp. 55–62.

Darby, M. (1994) International development and youth challenge: Personal development through a volunteer experience. MA (Leisure Studies) Thesis, School of Leisure and Tourism Studies, University of Technology, Sydney.

de Beauvoir, S. (1973) *The Second Sex* (transl. Parshley, E.M.). Vintage, New York.

de Carlo, L. and McConchie, J. (1980) Women and volunteering: perceptions, motivations and effects. *Volunteer Administration* 13, 27.

de Kadt, E. (ed.) (1979) *Tourism – Passport to Development? Perspectives on the Social and Cultural Effects of Tourism in Developing Countries*. Oxford University Press, New York.

de La Court, T. (1990) *Beyond Brundtland: Green Development in the 1990s*. New Horizons Press, New York.

Deleuze, G. and Guattari, F. (1992) *A Thousand Plateaus* (transl. Massumi, B.). The Athlone Press, London.

Denzin, N.K. (1977) *Childhood Socialisation*. Jossey-Bass, San Francisco.

Denzin, N.K. (1989a) *The Research Act: a Theoretical Introduction to Sociological*. Sage, Thousand Oaks, California.

Denzin, N.K. (1989b) *Interpretive Interactionism*. Sage, Thousand Oaks, California.

Denzin, N.K. (1992) *Symbolic Interactionism and Cultural Studies*. Blackwell, Oxford.

Denzin, N.K. (1994) The art and politics of interpretation. In: Denzin, N.K. and Lincoln, Y.S. (eds) *Handbook of Qualitative Research*. Sage, Thousand Oaks, California, pp. 154–155.

Denzin, N.K. and Lincoln, Y.S. (eds) (1994) *Handbook of Qualitative Research.* Sage, Thousand Oaks, California.

Dernoi, L.A. (1981) Alternative tourism: towards a new style in north–south relations. *International Journal of Tourism Management* 2, 253–264.

Dernoi, L.A. (1988) Alternative or community based tourism. In: D'Amore, L. and Jafari, J. (eds) *Tourism – a Vital Force for Peace.* L. D'Amore, Montreal, pp. 91–95.

Dewey, J. (1960) *How we Think: a Restatement of the Relation of Reflective Thinking to the Educative Process* (revised edn Heath, D.C.). Lexington, Massachusetts.

Dickson, A. (1976) *A Chance to Serve.* Dennis Dobson, London.

Dilley, R.S. (1986) Tourist brochures and tourist images. *Canadian Geographer* 30, 59–65.

Donovan, F. (1977) *Voluntary Organisations – a Case Study.* Preston Institute of Technology Press, Bundoora, Victoria.

Dowden, R. (1992) Eco-missionaries preach the new gospel in Africa. *Independent* June 3.

Doxey, G.V. (1975) A causation theory of visitor–resident irritants, methodology, and research inferences. *The Impact of Tourism, Sixth Annual Conference Proceedings of the Travel Research Association.* San Diego, pp. 195–198.

Doxey, G.V. (1976) When enough's enough: the natives are restless in Old Nigeria. *Heritage Canada* 2, 26–27.

Driver, B.L., Brown, P.J. and Peterson, G.L. (1991) Research on leisure benefits. In: Driver, B.L., Brown, P.J. and Peterson, G.L. (eds) *Benefits of Leisure.* Venture, State College, Pennsylvania, pp. 5–11.

Driver, B.L., Dustin, D., Baltic, T., Elsner, G. and Peterson, G.L. (1996) *Nature and the Human Spirit: Toward an Expanded Land Management Ethic.* Venture, State College, Pennsylvania.

Drumm, A. (1998) New approaches to community based ecotourism management. In: Lindberg, K., Wood, M.E. and Engeldrum, D. (eds) *Ecotourism: a Guide for Planners and Managers*, Vol. 2. The Ecotourism Society, North Bennington, Vermont, pp. 197–213.

Dunning, J.H. and McQueen, H. (1983) The eclectic theory of the multinational enterprise and the international hotel industry. In: Rugman, A.M. (ed.) *New Theories of the Multinational Enterprise.* Helm, London, pp. 43–47.

Durst, P. and Ingram, C. (1988) Nature-orientated tourism promotion by developing countries. *Tourism Management* 26, 39–43.

Eagles, P.F.J., Ballantine, J.L. and Fennell, D.A. (1992) Marketing to the ecotourist: Case studies from Kenya and Costa Rica. Paper presented at *International Union for Conservation of Nature and Natural Resources (IUCN) IVth World Congress on National Parks and Protected Areas.* Caracas, Venezuela, 10–12 February.

Echtner, C.M. and Ritchie, J.R. (1991) The meaning and measurement of destination image. *Journal of Tourism Studies* 2, 2–12.

Eckersley, R. (1992) *Environmentalism and Political Theory.* University College London Press, London.

Ecologically Sustainable Development Working Groups (ESDWG) (1991) *Final Report – Tourism.* Australian Government Publishing Service, Canberra.

Ecotourism Society (1992) *Membership Brochure.* The Ecotourism Society, Washington, DC.

Elden, M. and Chisholm, R. (1993) Emerging varieties of action research: introduction to the special issue. *Human Relations* 46, 121–142.

Encel, J.R. and Encel, J.C. (1991) *Ethics of Environmental Development: Global Challenge and International Response.* University of Arizona Press, Tucson.

Erikson, E.H. (1971) *Identity, Youth and Crisis.* Faber and Faber, London.

Ewert, A.W. (1987) Research in experiential education. *Journal for Experiential Education* 10, 4–7.

Ewert, A.W. (1989) *Outdoor Adventure Pursuits: Foundations, Models and Theories.* Publishing Horizons, Columbus, Ohio.

Farrell, B.H. and Runyan, D. (1991) Ecology and tourism. *Annals of Tourism Research* 19, 752–770.

Field, D.R. (1986) Community and natural resource development: another look at tourism. Paper presented to the 18th World IUFRO World Congress. Ljubljana, Yugoslavia, April.

Figgis, P. (1993) Ecotourism: special interest or major direction? *Habitat Australia* 21, 8–11.

Fiske, L., Hodge, J. and Turner, L. (1987) *Myths of Oz.* Allen and Unwin, Australia.

Fly, J. (1986) (unpublished) Nature, outdoor recreation and tourism: the basis for regional population growth in northern lower Michigan. PhD thesis, University of Michigan, Michigan.

Ford, P. and Blanchard, J. (1985) *Leadership and Administration of Outdoor Pursuits.* Venture, State College, Pennsylvania.

Foucault, M. (1978) *The History of Sexuality,* Vol. 1. Penguin, Harmondsworth, UK.

Foucault, M. (1981) *The History of Sexuality,* Vol. 1, 2nd edn. Penguin, Harmondsworth, UK.

Foucault, M. (1983) The subject and power. In: Dreyfus, H. and Rabinow, G. (eds) *Michael Foucault: Beyond Structuralism and Hermeneutics.* Chicago University Press, Chicago, pp. 141–144.

Fox, W. (1990) *Towards a Transpersonal Ecology.* Shambhala, Boston.

Frank, D. (1992) Volunteers . . . a force to be reckoned with! *Australian Journal of Leisure and Recreation* 2, 33–39.

Frisby, D. (1989) Simmel and leisure. In: Rojek, C. (ed.) *Leisure for Leisure.* Macmillan, London, pp. 70–73.

Furze, B., De Lacy, T. and Birkhead, J. (1996) *Culture, Conservation, and Biodiversity: the Social Dimension of Linking Local Level Development.* John Wiley & Sons, Sydney.

Fussell, P. (1982) *Abroad: British Literary Travelling Between the Wars.* Oxford University Press, New York.

Gartner, W. (1993) Image formation process. *Journal of Travel and Tourism Marketing* 2, 191–215.

Gillette, A. (1968) *One Million Volunteers.* Pelican, Ringwood, Victoria.

Gilmore, L. and Dunstan, G. (1989) (Unpub.) *Sustainable Tourism.* Position statement for sustainable tourism. East Brunswick, Victoria.

Glaser, B.G. and Strauss, A.L. (1967) *The Discovery of Grounded Theory: Strategies for Qualitative Research.* Aldine, New York.

Glasser, R. (1976) Leisure policy, identity and work. In: Haworth, J. and Smith, M.A. (eds) *Work and Leisure.* Princeton Book Co., New Jersey, pp. 62–70.

Godkin, M.A. (1980) Identity and place: clinical applications based on notions of rootedness and uprootedness. In: Buttimer, A. and Seamon, D. (eds) *The Human Experience of Space and Place.* Croom Helm, London, pp. 14–19.

Goffman, E. (1974) *Frame Analysis: an Essay on the Organisation of Experience.* Harvard University Press, Cambridge, Massachusetts.

Gold, S.M. (1973) *Urban Recreation Planning.* Lea-Febiger, Philadelphia.

Gonsalves, P.S. (1984) Tourism in India: an overview and from leisure to learning: a strategy for India. In: Holden, P. (ed.) *Alternative Tourism: Report on the Workshop on Alternative Tourism with a Focus on Asia.* Ecumenical Coalition on Third World Tourism, Bangkok.

Graburn, N.H.H. (1995) The past in the present in Japan: nostalgia and neo-traditionalism in contemporary Japanese domestic tourism. In: Butler, R.W. and Pearce, D. (eds) *Change in Tourism: People, Places and Processes.* Routledge, London.

Graham, S. (1991) *Handle with Care: a Guide to Responsible Travel in Developing Countries.* Novel Press, Chicago.

Greenwood, D.J. (1989) Culture by the pound: an anthropological perspective on tourism as cultural commoditization. In: Smith, V.L. (ed.) *Hosts and Guests: the Anthropology of Tourism.* University of Pennsylvania Press, Philadelphia, pp. 48–53.

Greenwood, D.J., Whyte, W.F. and Harkavy, I. (1993) Participatory action research as a process and as a goal. *Human Relations* 46, 175–192.

Grosz, E. (1995) Women, *chora*, dwelling. In: Watson, S. and Gibson, K. (eds) *Postmodern Cities and Spaces.* Blackwell, Oxford, pp. 27–31.

Hall, C.M. (1995) *Introduction to Tourism in Australia: Impacts, Planning and Development*, 2nd edn. Longman Chesire, Melbourne.

Hall, C.M. and McArthur, S. (1991) Commercial white water rafting in Australia. *Leisure Options* 1, 15–21.

Hamilton-Smith, E. (1990) Directions for recreation benefit measurement in Australia: some preliminary thoughts. In: Hamilton-Smith, E. (ed.) *Papers on Recreation Benefit Measurement.* Phillip Institute of Technology, Melbourne, Victoria, pp. 61–66.

Hamilton-Smith, E. (1992) Work, leisure and optimal experience. *Leisure Studies* 11, 243–256.

Hamilton-Smith, E. (1994) Outdoor recreation and social benefits. In: Mercer, D. (ed.) *New Viewpoints in Australian Outdoor Recreation Research and Planning.* Hepper Marriot, Melbourne.

Hansel, B. (1993) *Exchange Student Survival Kit.* Intercultural Press Inc., Maine.

Hardin, G. (1968) Tragedy of the commons. *Science* 162, 1243–1248.

Hare, B. (1991) Ecologically sustainable development. *Habitat Australia* April, 10–12.

Harris, R. (1997) Sustainable tourism development in natural areas in Australia: Industry responses and associated issues. In: *Australia and New Zealand Association of Leisure Studies (ANZALS) 3rd conference proceedings, University of Newcastle, July*, pp. 71–78.

Hartig, T., Mang, M. and Evans, G.W. (1991) Restorative effects of natural environment experiences. *Environment Behaviour* 23, 3–27.
Harvey, D. (1985) *Consciousness and the Urban Experience.* Basil Blackwell, Oxford.
Hattie, J. (1992) *Self-Concept.* Lawrence Erlbaum Associates, London.
Hawkins, G. (1991) *Responding to Local Cultures*, Community Arts Network Western Australia, Perth.
Hazelworth, M.S. and Wilson, B.E. (1990) The effects of an outdoor adventure camp experience on self concept. *Journal of Environmental Education* 21, 33–37.
Heimstra, N.W. and McFarling, L.H. (1974) *Environmental Psychology.* Brooks/Cole, Monterey, California.
Henderson, K.A. (1981) Motivations and perceptions of volunteerism as a leisure activity. *Journal of Leisure Research* 13, 260–274.
Henderson, K.A. (1984) Volunteerism as leisure. *Journal of Voluntary Action Research* 13, 55–63.
Henderson, K.A. (1991) *Dimensions of Choice: a Qualitative Approach to Recreation, Parks and Leisure Research.* Venture, State College, Pennsylvania.
Hewitt, J.P. (1979) *Self and Society: a Symbolic Interactionist Social Psychology.* Allyn and Bacon Inc., Boston, Massachusetts.
Heywood, J.L. (1991) *Social Order in Forest Recreation Settings.* Ohio State University, Columbus.
Hill, S. (2001) *Options for School Leavers 2001.* Sydney Morning Herald Supplement, Sydney.
Holden, P. (ed.) (1984) *Alternative Tourism: Report on the Workshop on Alternative Tourism with a Focus on Asia.* Ecumenical Coalition on Third World Tourism, Bangkok.
Hong, E. (1985) See the world while it lasts. In: *The Social and Environmental Impact of Tourism with Special Reference to Malaysia.* Consumers Association of Penang, Malaysia, pp. 80–85.
Horwich, R.H., Murry D., Saqui, E., Lyon, J. and Godfrey, D. (1993) Ecotourism and community development: a view from Belize. In: Lindberg, K. and Hawkins, D. (eds) *Ecotourism: a Guide for Planners and Managers.* The Ecotourism Society, North Bennington, Vermont, pp. 152–158.
Independent Sector (1990) *Giving and Volunteering in the United States.* Independent Sector, Washington, DC.
Ingham, R. (1987) Psychological contributions to the study of leisure. *Leisure Studies* 6, 1–14.
Ingram, D. and Durst. P. (1989) Nature-oriented tour operators: travel to developing countries. *Journal of Travel Research* Autumn, 11–15.
International Ecotourism Society (TIES) (2001) Ecotourism Statistical Fact Sheet, 16.1.01. www.ecotourism.org.
Irigaray, L. (1974) *Speculum of the Other Woman* (transl. Gill, G.C.). Cornell University Press, Ithaca, New York.
Irigaray, L. (1986) The sex which is not one (transl. Reeder, C.). In: Marks, E. and de Courtivron, I. (eds) *New French Feminisms.* Harvester, Sussex, pp. 99–106.
Iso-Ahola, S.E. (1984) Social psychological foundations of leisure and resultant implications for leisure counselling. In: Dowd, E.T. and Charles, C. (eds)

Leisure counselling: Concepts and Applications. Thomas, Springfield, Illinois, pp. 102–108.

Iso-Ahola, S. (1989) Motivation for leisure. In: Jackson, E. and Burton, T. (eds) *Understanding Leisure and Recreation: Mapping the Past, Charting the Future.* Venture, State College, Pennsylvania, pp. 247–280.

Iso-Ahola, S.E. (1994) Leisure, lifestyle and health. In: Compton, J. and Iso-Ahola, S.E. (eds) *Leisure and Mental Health.* Family Development Resources, USA, pp. 71–77.

Ittelsen, W.H., Proshansky, H.M. and Rivilin, L.G. (1974) *An Introduction to Environmental Psychology.* Holt, Rinehart and Winston, New York.

Jackson, E. and Burton, T. (eds) (1989) *Understanding Leisure and Recreation: Mapping the Past, Charting the Future.* Venture, State College, Pennsylvania.

Jagtenberg, T. and Mckie, D. (1997) *Eco-impacts and the Greening of Postmodernity: New Maps for Communication Studies, Cultural Studies, and Sociology.* Sage, Thousand Oaks, California.

Jayasuriya, L. and Lee, M. (eds) (1994) *Social Dimensions of Development.* Paradigm, Curtin University, Western Australia.

Jenner, P. and Smith, C. (1991) *The Tourism Industry and the Environment.* Condor, The Economist Intelligence Unit Special Report No. 2453, London.

Johnson, H. (1992) *Review of Youth Challenge International.* CIDA, Toronto.

Johnson, S. (1994) *Participatory Research: a Selected Annotated Bibliography.* NPASIA Bibliography Series 11. A joint publication of the International Development Research Centre (Canada) and the Norman Paterson School of International Affairs, Carleton University, Ottawa.

Jones, A. (1987) Green tourism. *Tourism Management* 26, 354–356.

Kaplan, M. (1975) *Leisure: Theory and Policy.* Thomas, Springfield, Illinois.

Kaplan, R. and Kaplan, S. (1989) *The Experience of Nature: a Psychological Perspective.* Cambridge University Press, Cambridge.

Kaplan, S. and Talbot, J.F. (1983) Psychological benefits of a wilderness experience. In: Altman, I. and Wohlill, J.F. (eds) *Human Behaviour and Environment: Advances in Theory and Research*, Vol. 6, *Behaviour and the Natural Environment.* Plenum Press, New York, pp. 87–93.

Karen, C.S. (1990) Personal development and the pursuit of higher education. Paper presented at Annual Meeting of American Educational Research Association. Boston, 16–20 April.

Kauffmann, N.L. and Kuh, G.D. (1984) The impact of study abroad on personal development of college students. Paper presented at the *American Educational Research Association.* New Orleans, 4–7 April.

Kellehear, A. (1996) Social self, global culture: a personal introduction to sociological ideas. In: Kellehear, A. (ed.) *Social Self, Global Culture: an Introduction to Sociological Ideas.* Oxford University Press, Melbourne, pp. 115–121.

Kelly, J.R. (1982) *Leisure.* Prentice-Hall, Illinois.

Kelly, J. (1983) *Leisure Identities and Interactions.* Allen and Unwin, London.

Kelly, J. (1987) *Freedom to Be: a New Sociology of Leisure.* Macmillan, New York.

Kelly, J.R. (1991) Leisure environments and actions: change and conflict. Keynote address to the World Leisure and Recreation Association, World

Congress, Leisure and Tourism: Social and Environmental Change, Sydney, 16–19 July.

Kelly, J. (1994) The symbolic interaction metaphor and leisure: critical challenges. *Leisure Studies* 13, 81–96.

Kelly, J.R. (1996) *Leisure.* Allyn and Bacon, Massachusetts.

Kenny, S. (1994) *Developing Communities for the Future: Community Development in Australia.* Thomas Nelson, Australia.

Kerr, J. (1991) Making dollars and sense out of ecotourism/nature tourism. In: Weiler, B. (ed.) *Ecotourism Incorporating the Global Classroom.* Bureau of Tourism Research, Canberra, pp. 57–61.

Kleiber, D., Larsen, R. and Csikszentmihalyi, M. (1986) The experience of leisure in adolescence. *Journal of Leisure Research* 3, 169–176.

Klint, K.A. (1990) New directions for inquiry into self-concept and adventure experiences. In: Miles, J.C. and Priest, S. (eds) *Adventure Education.* Venture, State College, Pennsylvania, pp. 43–48.

Kolb, D.A. (1984) *Experiential Learning.* Prentice-Hall, Englewood Cliffs, New Jersey.

Kottler, J.A. (1997) *Travel That Can Change Your Life: How to Create a Transformative Experience.* Jossey-Bass Publishers, San Francisco.

Kozlowski, J. (1985) Threshold approach to environmental planning. *Ekistics* 311, 146–153.

Krippendorf, J. (1982) Towards new tourism politics. *Tourism Management* 3, 135–148.

Krippendorf, J. (1987) *The Holiday Makers.* Heinemann, London.

Kuh, G.D., Krehbiel, L.E. and MacKay, K. (1988) *Personal Development and the College Student Experience: a Review of the Literature.* New Jersey Department of Higher Education, New Jersey.

Kutay, K. (1990) Ecotourism: travel's new wave. *Vis a Vis* July, 4–80.

Larbalestier, M. (1990) Segmentation study of potential Australian holiday travellers to the Pacific-Asia area: a PATA co-operative study. Paper presented to the *Pacific Asia Travel Association, 39th Annual Conference.* Vancouver, Canada.

Lea, J.P. (1988) *Tourism and Development in the Third World.* Routledge, London.

Lea, J.P. (1993) Tourism development ethics in the third world. *Annals of Tourism Research* 20, 701–715.

Lea, J.P. (1995) Tourism and the delivery of positive development. *Contours* 17, 4–10.

Lee, D. and Snepenger, D. (1992) An ecotourism assessment of Tortuguero, Costa Rica. *Journal of Tourism Research* 7, 367–370.

Levi-Strauss, C. (1964) *Totemism.* Merlin Press, London.

Little, D.E. (1993) Motivations and constraints influencing women's participation in adventure recreation. M.A. thesis, Griffith University, Brisbane.

Lucas, R. and Stankey, G. (1988) *Shifting Trends in Wilderness Recreational Use.* United States Forest Service, Missoula, Montana.

Luks, A. and Payne, P. (1991) *The Healing Power of Doing Good.* Fawcett Columbine, New York.

MacCannell, D. (1976) *The Tourist: a New Theory of the Leisure Class.* Macmillan, London.

MacCannell, D. (1992) *Empty Meeting Grounds: the Tourist Papers.* Routledge, London.

Maclure, R. (1990) The challenge of participatory research and its implications for funding agencies. *International Journal of Sociology and Social Policy* 10, 1–21.

Mader, V. (1988) Tourism and environment. *Annals of Tourism Research* 15, 274–276.

Mannell, R.C. and Iso-Ahola, S.E. (1987) Psychological nature of leisure and tourism experience. *Annals of Tourism Research* 14, 314–331.

Manning, R.E. (1986) *Studies in Outdoor Recreation: a Review and Synthesis of the Social Science Literature in Outdoor Education.* Oregon State University Press, Corvallis, Oregon.

Mason, P. (1990) *Tourism: Environment and Development Perspective.* World Wide Fund for Nature, UK.

Mathieson, A. and Wall, G. (1982) *Tourism: Economic and Social Impacts.* Longman, London.

McCool, S.F., Stankey, G.H. and Clark, R.N. (1984) Choosing recreation settings: processes, findings and research directions. In: McCool, S.F., Stankey, G.H. and Clark, R.N. (eds) *Proceedings – Symposium of Recreation Choice Behaviour.* United States Department of Agriculture Forest Service, United States Forest Service, Missoula, Montana.

McIntyre, N. (1994) The concept of 'involvement' in recreation research. In: Mercer, D. (ed.) *New Viewpoints in Australian Outdoor Recreation Research and Planning.* Hepper Marriot, Melbourne.

McKercher, B. (1991) The unrecognised threat to tourism: can tourism survive sustainability? In: Weiler, B. (ed.) *Ecotourism Incorporating the Global Classroom.* Bureau of Tourism Research, Canberra.

McNeely, J.A. and Thorsell, J. (1989) *Jungles, Mountains and Islands: How Tourism can Help Conserve the Natural Heritage.* World Leisure and Recreation Association, Geneva.

McRae, K. (ed.) (1990) *Outdoor and Environmental Education.* Macmillan, Melbourne.

Mead, G.H. (1934, 1972) *Mind, Self, Society.* University of Chicago Press, Chicago.

Menzies, C. (1989) *Community Development.* Inner Sydney Regional Council for Social Development, Sydney.

Mercer, D.C. (1981) Trends in recreation participation. In: Mercer, D. (ed.) *Outdoor Recreation: Australian Perspectives.* Sorrett, Malvern, Victoria, pp. 52–59.

Mercer, D.C. (ed.) (1994) *New Viewpoints in Australian Outdoor Recreation Research and Planning.* Hepper, Marriot and Associates, Melbourne.

Mieczkowski, Z. (1995) *Environmental Issues of Tourism and Recreation.* University Press of America, New York.

Miranda, W. and Yerks, R. (1985) Women outdoors – who are they? *Parks and Recreation* 20, 48–51.

Mohanlall, P. (1992) Meet the jungle man. *The Open Road* April, pp. 58–61.

Moorhouse, H.F. (1983) American automobiles and worker's dreams. *Sociological Review* 31, 403–426.

Murphy, P. (1985) *Tourism: a Community Approach.* Methuen, London.

Murphy, P. (1988) Community driven tourism planning. *Tourism Management* 19, 96–104.
Neulinger, J. (1982) *To Leisure: an Introduction.* Allyn and Bacon, Boston.
Office of National Tourism (1996) *Projecting Success: Visitor Management Projects for Sustainable Tourism Growth.* Commonwealth Department of Industry, Science and Tourism, Canberra.
O'Hanlon, R. and Washbrook, D. (1992) After orientalism: culture, critism and politics in the third world. *Comparative Studies in Society and History* 34, 141–167.
O'Neill, M. (1991) Naturally attractive. *Pacific Monthly* 25 September.
Operation Raleigh USA (1989) *Operation Raleigh: Returned Venturer Program Evaluation.* Raleigh, North Carolina.
O'Reilly, A.M. (1986) Tourism carrying capacity: concept and issues. *Tourism Management* 7, 254–258.
Park, P. (1992) The discovery of participatory research as a new scientific paradigm: personal and intellectual accounts. *The American Sociologist* Winter, 29–42
Parker, S. (1992) Volunteering as serious leisure. *Journal of Applied Recreation Research* 17, 1–11.
Pearce, D. (1980) *Tourist in the South Pacific: the Contribution of Research to Development and Planning.* UNESCO Man and Biosphere Report no. 6. National Commission for UNESCO, Christchurch, New Zealand.
Pearce, D. (1989) *Tourist Development.* Longman, Hong Kong.
Pearce, L. (1982) *The Social Psychology of Tourist Behaviour.* Pergamon Press, Sydney.
Pearce, L. (1984) Tourist–guide interaction. *Annals of Tourism Research* 11, 129–146.
Pearce, P. (1988) *The Ulysses Factor: Evaluating Visitors in Tourist Settings.* Springer-Verlag, New York.
Pearce, P. (1990) Social impact of tourism. In: Griffin, T. (ed.) *The Social, Cultural and Environmental Impacts of Tourism.* NSW Tourism Commission, Sydney, pp. 12–15.
Pepper, D. (1984) *The Roots of Modern Environmentalism.* Croom Helm, Sydney.
Pettit, A.G.J. (1989) Towards realities: the outdoor educator as a developer of human potential. In: Hayllar, B. (ed.) *Sixth National Outdoor Education Conference Proceedings.* Centre for Leisure and Tourism Studies, University of Technology, Sydney, pp. 110–115.
Pfohl, S. (1992) *Death at the Parasite Café: Social Science (Fictions) and the Postmodern.* St Martins Press, New York.
Phillips, M. (1982) Motivation and expectation in successful voluntarism. *Journal of Voluntary Action Research* 11, 118–125.
Pigram, J.J. (1992) (unpublished) Human–nature relationships: leisure environments and natural settings. University of New England, Armidale.
Pimbert, M.P. and Pretty, J.N. (1995) *Parks, People and Professionals: Putting 'Participation' into Protected Area Management.* United Nations Research Institute for Social Development.
Pleumarom, A. (1990) Alternative tourism: a viable solution? *Contours* 4, 12–15.

Plog, S.C. (1991) *Leisure Travel: Making it a Growth Market . . . Again!* John Wiley & Sons, New York.

Proshansky, H.M. (1973) The environmental crisis in human dignity. *Journal of Social Issues* 29, 12–22.

Proshansky, H.M. (1978) The city and self-identity. *Environment and Behaviour* 10, 47–168.

Rachowiecki, R. (1991) *Costa Rica.* Lonely Planet Publications, Melbourne.

Ramphele, M. (1990) Participatory research: the myths and realities. *Social Dynamics* 16, 1–15.

Richards, G.E. (1977) *Some Educational Implications and Contributions of Outward Bound.* Australian Outward Bound Foundation, Sydney.

Richardson, J. (1991) The case for an ecotourism association. In: Weiler, B. (ed.) *Ecotourism Incorporating the Global Classroom.* Bureau of Tourism Research, Canberra, pp. 202–207.

Roberts, H. (ed.) (1981) *Doing Feminist Research.* Routledge and Kegan Paul, London.

Roberts, K. (1978) *Contemporary Society and the Growth of Leisure.* MacGibbon and Kee, London.

Robinson, G. (1988) *Crosscultural Understanding.* Prentice Hall, London.

Roggenbuck, J.W. and Lucas, R.C. (1987) *Wilderness Use and User Characteristics: a State of Knowledge Review.* United States Forest Service, Missoula, Montana.

Roggenbuck, J.W., Loomis, R.J. and Dagostino, J.V. (1991) The learning benefits in leisure. In: Driver, B.L., Brown, P.J. and Peterson, G.L. (eds) *Benefits of Leisure.* Venture, State College, Pennsylvania, pp. 195–214.

Rohs, F.R. (1986) Social background, personality, and attitudinal factors influencing the decision to volunteer and level of involvement among adult 4-H leaders. *Journal of Voluntary Action Research* 15, 85–99.

Rojek, C. (1993) *Ways of Escape: Modern Transformations in Leisure and Travel.* Macmillan, London.

Rojek, C. (1995) *Decentring Leisure: Rethinking Leisure Theory.* Sage, London.

Ross, G.F. (1994) *The Psychology of Tourism.* Hospitality Press, Melbourne.

Rovinski, Y. (1991) Private reserves, parks, and ecotourism in Costa Rica. In: Whelan, T. (ed.) *Nature Tourism: Managing for the Environment.* Island Press, Washington, DC.

Rowe, D. and Stevenson, D. (1994) Provincial paradise: urban tourism and city imaging outside the metropolis. *Australian and New Zealand Journal of Sociology* 30, 178–193.

Sachs, W. (1995) *The Development Dictionary.* Zed Books, London.

Saglio, C. (1979) Tourism for discovery: a project in Lower Casemance, Senegal. In: de Kadt, E. (ed.) *Tourism– Passport to Development? Perspectives on the Social and Cultural Effects of Tourism in Developing Countries.* Oxford University Press, New York.

Said, E.W. (1976) *Orientalism.* Penguin, Harmondsworth, UK.

Samdahl, D.M. (1988) A symbolic interactionist model of leisure: theory and empirical support. *Leisure Sciences* 10, 27–39.

Santosa, A. (1985) The swastika spins ever faster. *Contours* 6, 2–8.

Scherl, L.M. (1988) The wilderness experience: psychological and motivational considerations of a structured experience in a wilderness setting. PhD thesis, James Cook University of North Queensland, Townsville, Australia.

Scherl, L.M. (1994) Understanding outdoor recreation experiences: applications for environmental planning and policy. In: Mercer, D. (ed.) *New Viewpoints in Australian Outdoor Recreation Research and Planning.* Hepper Marriot, Melbourne.

Scheyer, R. and Driver, B.L. (1989) The benefits of leisure. In: Jackson, J. and Burton, E. (eds) *Understanding Leisure and Recreation: Mapping the Past, Charting the Future.* Venture, State College, Pennsylvania, pp. 385–420.

Shafer, E. and Mietz, J. (1969) Aesthetic and emotional experiences rate high with northeast wilderness hikers. *Environment and Behaviour* 1, 187–197.

Shaw, S.M. (1985a) The meaning of leisure in everyday life. *Leisure Sciences* 7, 1–24.

Shaw, S.M. (1985b) Gender and leisure: inequality in the distribution of leisure time. *Journal of Leisure Research* 17, 266–282.

Shelby, B. and Heberlein, T.A. (1986) *Carrying Capacities in Recreation Settings.* Oregon State University Press, Corvallis, Oregon.

Silver, I. (1993) Marketing authenticity in third world countries. *Annals of Tourism Research* 20, 302–318.

Simmel, G. (1936) *The Web of Group Affiliations* (transl. Bendix, R.). The Free Press, New York.

Simmel, G. (1965) *Essays on Sociology, Philosophy and Aesthetics*, 2nd edn. Harper and Rowe, New York.

Simmel, G. (1978) *The Philosophy of Money.* Routledge and Kegan Paul, London.

Smith, V.L. (ed.) (1989) *Hosts and Guests, the Anthropology of Tourism*, 2nd edn. University of Pennsylvania Press, Philadelphia.

Smith, V.L. and Eadington, W.R. (1992) *Tourism Alternatives.* University of Pennsylvania Press, Philadelphia.

Sofield, T.H.B. (1991) Sustainable ethnic tourism in the South Pacific: some principles. *Journal of Tourism Studies* 2, 56–72.

Sofield, T.H.B. and Birtles, R.A. (1996) Indigenous peoples' cultural opportunity spectrum for tourism. In: Butler, R. and Hinch, T. (eds) *Tourism and Indigenous Peoples.* International Business Press, London.

Spivak, G. and Harasym, S. (1990) *The Post-colonial Critic: Interviews, Strategies, Dialogues.* Routledge, New York.

Squire, S.J. (1994) The cultural values of literary tourism. *Annals of Tourism Research* 21, 103–120.

Srisang, K. (1991) Alternative to tourism. *Contours* 5, 8–10.

Stankey, G. and McCool, S. (eds) (1985) *Proceedings – Symposium on Recreation Choice Behaviour.* United States Forest Service general technical report INT-184. United States Department of Agriculture, Ogden, USA.

Stankey, G.H., Cole, D.N., Lucas, R.C., Peterson, M.E. and Frissell, S.S. (1985) *The Limites of Acceptable Change (LAC) System for Wilderness Planning.*

United States Forest Service general technical report INT-176. US Department of Agriculture, Ogden, USA.
Stanley, L. and Wise, S. (1984) *Breaking Out: Feminist Consciousness and Feminist Research.* Routledge and Kegan Paul, London.
Stear, L., Buckley, G. and Stankey, G. (1988) Constructing a meaningful concept of the tourism industry: some problems and implications for research and policy. In: Faulkner, B. and Fagence, M. (eds) *Frontiers in Australian Tourism: the Search for New Perspectives in Policy Development and Research.* Bureau of Tourism Research, Canberra, pp. 4–6.
Stebbins, R.A. (1982) Serious leisure: a conceptual statement. *Pacific Sociological Review* 25, 251–272.
Stebbins, R.A. (1992) *Amateurs, Professionals, and Serious Leisure.* McGill-Queen's University Press, Montreal.
Stitsworth, M. (1987) Third world development through youth exchange. Paper presented at the Annual Third World Conference. Chicago, 9–11 April.
Strauss, A. and Corbin, J. (1990) *Basics of Qualitative Research: Grounded Theory Procedures and Techniques.* Sage, Thousand Oaks, California.
Stryker, S. (1980) *Symbolic Interactionism: a Social Structural Version.* Benjamin/Cummings Publications, California.
Swanson, M.A. (1992) Ecotourism: embracing the new environmental paradigm. Paper presented at the *International Union for Conservation of Nature and Natural Resources (IUCN) IVth World Congress on National Parks and Protected Areas.* Caracas, Venezuela, 10–12 February.
Telisman-Kosuta, N. (1989) Tourism destination image. In: Witt, S.F. and Moutinho, L. (eds) *Tourism Marketing and Managing Handbook.* Prentice Hall, New York, pp. 112–114.
Terenzini, P.T. and Wright, T.M. (1987) Student's personal growth during the first two years of college. Paper presented at the *Annual Meeting of the Association for the Study of Higher Education.* February 14–17.
Thomas, M. (1971) *Work Camps and Volunteers.* PEP, London.
Tihanyi, P. (1991) *Volunteers, Why They Come and Why They Stay.* Centre for Voluntary Organisations, London School of Economics, London.
Tobias, D. (1989) Biological aspects of ecotourism – the Monteverde case: an examination of tourist pressures in Monteverde, Costa Rica. Masters thesis, Harvard University, USA.
Trask, H.K. (1991) The lovely hula hands: corporate tourism and the prostitution of Hawaiian culture. *Contours* 5, 18–24.
Travis, A.S. (1985) The consequences of growing ecological consciousness, and changing socio-cultural needs, on tourism policy. *Trends in Tourism Demand.* AIEST, Bregenz, September.
Turner, L. and Ash, J. (1975) *The Golden Hordes: International Tourism and the Pleasure Periphery.* Constable, London.
Ulrich, R.S., Dimberg, U. and Driver, B.L. (1991) Psychophysiological indicators of leisure benefits. In: Driver, B.L., Brown, P.J. and Peterson, G.L. (eds) *Benefits of Leisure.* Venture, State College, Pennsylvania, pp. 62–67.
Unger, L.S. (1984) The effect of situational variables on the subjective leisure experience. *Leisure Sciences* 6, 291–312.
United Nations Department of Economic and Social Affairs (1975) *Service by Youth.* United Nations, New York.

United States Peace Corps (1980) *A Survey of Former Peace Corps and VISTA Volunteers*. United States Peace Corps, Washington, DC.

United States Peace Corps (1989) *Final Report from the Returned Peace Corps Volunteer Pretest (RPCV) Survey*. United States Peace Corps, Washington, DC.

Urry, J. (1990) *The Tourist Gaze: Leisure and Travel in Contemporary Societies*. Sage, London.

Valentine, P.S. (1987) Towards an alternative view of tourism. *Magnus Taurus* 1, 16–18.

Valentine, P.S. (1991) Nature-based tourism: a review of prospects and problems. In: Miller, M.L. and Auyong, J. (eds) *Proceedings of the 1990 Congress on Coastal and Marine Tourism*. National Coastal Resources Research and Development Institute, Newport, Oregon.

Valentine, P.S. (1992) Nature based tourism. In: Weiler, B. and Hall, C.M. (eds) *Special Interest Tourism*. Belhaven Press, London, pp. 43–49.

Vance, C.S. (1992) Social construction theory: problems in the history of sexuality. In: *Knowing Women: Feminisms and Knowledge*. Polity, Cambridge.

van Raaij, W. and Francken, D. (1984) Vacation decisions, activities and satisfactions. *Annals of Tourism Research* 11, 101–112.

van Til, J. (1979) In search of volunteerism. *Volunteer Administration* 12, 8–20.

Vir Singh, T., Theuns, H.L. and Go, F.M. (eds) (1989) *Towards Appropriate Tourism: the Case of Developing Countries*. Peter Lang, Frankfurt.

Wallace, G. (1992) Real ecotourism: assisting protected area managers and getting benefits to local people. Paper presented at the *International Union for Conservation of Nature and Natural Resources, IVth World Congress on National Parks and Protected Areas*. Caracas, Venezuela, 10–12 February.

Watson, S. and Gibson, K. (eds) (1995) *Postmodern Cities and Spaces*. Blackwell, Oxford.

Wearing, B.M. (1990) Beyond the ideology of motherhood: leisure as resistance. *Australian and New Zealand Journal of Sociology* 26, 36–58.

Wearing, B.M. and Wearing, S.L. (1998) All in a days leisure: gender and the concept of leisure. *Leisure Studies* 7, 111–123.

Wearing, S.L. (1986) Outdoor recreation: a catalyst for change. *Recreation Australia* 9, 18–21.

Wearing, S.L. (1992) Ecotourism: the Santa Elena rainforest project. *The Environmentalist* 3, 125–135.

Wearing, S. (1998) The nature of ecotourism: the place of self, identity and communities as interacting elements of alternative tourism experiences. Unpublished PhD Thesis, School of Environmental and Information Sciences, Charles Sturt University, Albury, Australia.

Wearing, S.L. and Wearing, M. (1999) Decommodifying ecotourism: rethinking global–local interactions with host communities. *Loisir et Société* 22, 39–70.

Wearing, S. and Neil, J. (2000) Refiguring self and identity through volunteer tourism. *Society and Leisure* 23(2), 389–419.

Weaver, D. and Opperman, M. (2000) *Tourism Management*. John Wiley & Sons, Milton Keynes, UK.

Weiler, B. and Hall, C. (eds) (1992) *Special Interest Tourism*. Belhaven Press, London.

Weiler, B. and Johnson, T. (1991) Nature based tour operators. Are they environmentally friendly or are they faking it? In: Stanton, J. (ed.) *The Proceedings of the Benefits and Costs of Tourism: Proceedings of a National Tourism Research Conference*. Marie Resort, Nelson Bay, 3–4 October, University of Newcastle, Newcastle, pp. 115–126.

Weinmann, S. (1983) *Cultural Encounters of the Stimulating Kind: Personal Development Through Culture Shock*. Department of Humanities, Michigan Technological University, Michigan.

Welton, C.E. (1978) Natural freedom and wilderness survival. *Journal of Physical Education and Recreation* 4, 1–29.

Wheeler, B. (1992) Is progressive tourism appropriate? *Tourism Management* 13, 104–105.

Whelan, T. (ed.) (1991) *Nature Tourism – Managing for the Environment*. Island Press, Washington, DC.

Whitmore, E. (1988) Adult learning through participation in rural community groups. *Journal of Voluntary Action Research* 17, 53–69.

Wild, R.A. (1981) *Australian Community Studies and Beyond*. Allen and Unwin, Sydney.

Wild, R.A. (1984) *For Community Studies*. La Trobe University Sociology Papers No 4, Melbourne.

Williams, P. (1990) Ecotourism management challenges. In: *Fifth Annual Travel Review Conference Proceedings 1990: a Year of Transition*. Travel Review, Washington, DC.

Wilson, B.A. (1980) Social space and symbolic interaction. In: Buttimer, A. and Seamon, D. (eds) *The Human Experience of Space and Place*. Croom Helm, London, pp. 132–136.

Winslow, E.A. (1977) *A Survey of Returned Peace Corps Volunteers*. Office of Special Services, United States Peace Corps, Washington, DC.

Withey, L. (1997) *Grand Tours and Cook's Tours: a History of Leisure Travel, 1750 to 1915*. William Morrow and Company, New York.

Wolff, K. (1950) *The Sociology of George Simmel*. Free Press, New York.

The World Bank (1992) *The World Bank and the Environment*. The World Bank, Washington, DC.

World Commission on Environment and Development (WCED) (1987) *Our Common Future*, Australian edn. Oxford University Press, Melbourne.

World Tourism Organisation (WTO) (1999) *Tourism Highlights 1999*. WTO, Madrid.

World Travel and Tourism Council (WTTC) (1999) *World Travel and Tourism Council*, www.wttc.org.

World Wide Fund for Nature (WWF) (1992) *Beyond the Green Horizon: a Discussion Paper on Principles for Sustainable Tourism*. WWF (UK), UK.

Wright Mills, C. (1959) *The Sociological Imagination*. Oxford University Press, New York.

Young, G. (1992) The role of community participation in tourism planning. MSc thesis, Strathclyde University, UK.

Young, M. and Wearing, S. (1992) *WWF Draft Ecotourism Discussion Paper.* World Wide Fund for Nature, Australia and the University of Technology, Sydney.

Young, R.A. (1973) Towards an understanding of wilderness participation. *Leisure Science* 2, 5–16.

Yum, S.M. (1984) Case report on attempts at alternative tourism, Hong Kong. In: Holden, P. (ed.) *Alternative Tourism: Report on the Workshop on Alternative Tourism with a Focus on Asia.* Ecumenical Coalition on Third World Tourism, Bangkok.

Subject Index

Author Index